Creative Fidelity

Weighing and Interpreting Documents of the Magisterium

Francis A. Sullivan, S.J.

PAULIST PRESS
New York/Mahwah, N.J.

also by Francis A. Sullivan, S.J.
published by Paulist Press

MAGISTERIUM
THE CHURCH WE BELIEVE IN
SALVATION OUTSIDE THE CHURCH?

Library of Congress Cataloging-in-Publication Data

Sullivan, Francis Aloysius.
    Creative fidelity : weighing and interpreting documents of the magisterium
/ by Francis A. Sullivan.
        p.   cm.
    Includes bibliographical references and index.
    ISBN 0-8091-3644-9
    1. Catholic Church—Teaching office. 2. Theology—Methodology. I. Title.
BX1746.S798 1996   96-7
262'.8' 08822—dc20   CIP

Published by Paulist Press
997 Macarthur Boulevard
Mahwah, NJ 07430

Printed and bound in the
United States of America

Contents

Acknowledgements

The publisher gratefully acknowledges the use of the following material. Excerpts from "Instruction the the Ecclesial Vocation of the Theologian," by the Congregation for the Doctrine of the Faith. Copyright 1990 by Libreria Editrice Vaticana. Excerpts from "Declaration in defence of the Catholic doctrine on the Church against certain errors of the present day," by the Congregation for the Doctrine of the Faith. Copyright 1973 by Libreria Editrice Vaticana. Excerpts from "Il decreto tridentino sul peccato originale," by Zoltan Alszeghy and Maurizio Flick. In *Gregorianum* 52 (1971): 595–635. Excerpts from "Eucharistic Doctrine" and "Eucharistic Doctrine, Elucidation." In the *Final Report* of the Anglican–Roman Catholic International Commission. Copyright 1982 by CTS/SPCK. Excerpts from *The Letters and Diaries of John Henry Newman*, edited by C.S. Dessain et al., vols. 1–31. Copyright 1961–1984 by Oxford University Press. Reprinted by permission of Oxford University Press. Excerpts from *The Documents of Vatican II*, Walter M. Abbot, S.J., gen. ed. Reprinted with permission of America Press, Inc., 106 West 56th Street, New York, NY 10019. Copyright 1966. All Rights Reserved. Citations of official Church documents from Neuner, Josef, S.J., and Dupuis, Jacques, S.J., eds., *The Christian Faith in the Doctrinal Documents of the Catholic Church*, 5th revised and enlarged edition (New York: Alba House and Bangalore: Theological Publications in India, 1990). Used with permission. Excerpts from *Theology and Church* by Walter Kasper. Copyright © 1989 by Walter Kasper. Translated by Margaret Kohl from the German *Theologie und Kirche* (Introduction and Parts II and III). Matthias-Grünewald-Verlag, Mainz, 1987. Used with permission of The Crossroad Publishing Company, New York, Claretian Communications, Philippines, and SCM Press, London. Excerpts from "Heresies in the Church Today?" in *Theological Investigations*, vol. XII (*Confrontation II*), by Karl Rahner; excerpts from "The Presence of Christ in the Sacrament of the Lord's Supper," in *Theological Investigations*, vol. IV (*More Recent Writings*), by Karl Rahner; and excerpts from "Dogmatic Reflection on the Knowledge and Self-consciousness of Christ," in *Theological Investigations*, vol. V (*Later Writings*), by Karl Rahner. Copyright 1975. Used with the permission of The Crossroad Publishing Company, New York. Published and copyright by Darton Longman and Todd Ltd. and used by permission of the publishers.

Abbreviations

AAS   *Acta Apostolicae Sedis*

ARCIC   Anglican-Roman Catholic International Commission

CDF   Congregation for the Doctrine of the Faith

CSEL   *Corpus scriptorum ecclesiasticorum latinorum*

DS   Denzinger-Schönmetzer, *Enchiridion Symbolorum Definitionum Declarationum*, ed. 36, Barcelona-Freiburg-Rome-New York: Herder, 1976.

LG   *Lumen gentium*

Mansi   *Sacrorum Conciliorum Nova Collectio*

ND   J. Neuner & J. Dupuis, ed., *The Christian Faith in the Documents of the Catholic Church*, 5th ed., Bangalore: Theological Publications in India, 1991.

NJBC   *New Jerome Biblical Commentary*

PBC   Pontifical Biblical Commission

PG   *Patrologiae cursus completus, series graeca*

PL   *Patrologiae cursus completus, series latina*

Sum th   St. Thomas Aquinas, *Summa Theologiae*

T   Norman P. Tanner, ed., *Decrees of the Ecumenical Councils*, 2 vols., London: Sheed & Ward; Washington: Georgetown University Press, 1990.

Th Inv   Karl Rahner, *Theological Investigations*, 1961-1992.

TS   *Theological Studies*

Foreword

Several years ago, while I was still teaching at the Gregorian University, the council of the faculty of theology decided that candidates for the licentiate needed a more systematic introduction to the use of the basic sources of theology. Among the courses that were introduced to meet this need was the one that I was asked to give, on the evaluation and interpretation of documents of the magisterium. I gave such a course in Rome before retiring from the Gregorian, and since then I have taught a similar course in the department of theology at Boston College. The present book has profited from the comments of students in both of these institutions.

It has profited even more from the comments of several good friends. I take this opportunity to express my gratitude to Teresa Clements, Michael A. Fahey, William H. FitzGerald, Gerald O'Collins and Christopher O'Donnell, who have read the book in manuscript and given me many helpful suggestions for its improvement.

I dedicate this book to all the Jesuits, both living and dead, with whom I shared life and work during my thirty-six years at the Gregorian University.

Francis A. Sullivan
Pentecost, 1995

1 ‖ Weighing and Interpreting Documents of the Magisterium
What Is It? Why Do It?

Magisterium

Magister in classical Latin meant "master," not only in the sense of "school-master" or teacher, but in the many senses in which a person can be a "master," e.g., of a ship, of servants, or of an art or trade. Hence the word *magisterium* in classical Latin meant the role and authority of one who was a master in any of the various applications of the term. In the vocabulary of the medieval schoolmen, magisterium generally meant the role and authority of the teacher. The traditional symbol of teaching authority was the chair, and St. Thomas speaks of two kinds of magisterium: that of the pastoral chair of the bishop, and that of the academic chair of the theologian.[1]

In modern Catholic usage, the term "magisterium" has come to be associated almost exclusively with the teaching role and authority of the hierarchy. An even more recent development is that "magisterium" is now often used to refer not to the teaching office as such, but to those who exercise it, namely, the pope and bishops. The Second Vatican Council several times describes their role as *magisterium authenticum*. Here the Latin *authenticum* does not mean "genuine," but "authoritative," as is clear, for instance, from the council's description of bishops as "authentic teachers, that is, teachers endowed with the authority of Christ, who preach to the people committed to them the faith they must believe and put into practice."[2]

Each bishop who is the pastor of a diocese has responsibility and authority regarding the teaching of Christian doctrine in his

1

diocese. He exercises this responsibility by his own teaching, whether orally or in pastoral letters, and by his promotion of sound teaching in the catechetical and educational institutions of his diocese. The bishops of a nation or region exercise their teaching function collectively in episcopal conferences or regional councils. More rarely, the entire episcopal college, together with its head, the pope, gathers in an ecumenical council to decide matters of greater moment for the life of the church. During the usually long intervals between ecumenical councils, the supreme teaching authority is exercised by the pope, who, as Vatican I defined, has the same infallibility in defining doctrine as do ecumenical councils. However, popes have very rarely exercised their authority to define doctrine; for the most part they use their "ordinary" teaching power, in such documents as encyclicals and apostolic letters. The Vatican Congregation for the Doctrine of the Faith also issues doctrinal statements which participate in the pope's teaching authority, but not in his infallibility.

Documents of the magisterium

A complete collection of the documents which have been issued by bishops, councils and popes in the exercise of their teaching office during the almost two thousand years of the life of the church would fill a library. Obviously, the student of theology will need to have at hand a manageable collection of the most significant of these documents. Until recently, the only such collection available was the *Enchiridion Symbolorum Definitionum Declarationum de Rebus Fidei et Morum*, the first edition of which was published by Heinrich Denzinger in 1854. An *Enchiridion* is a handbook; *Symbola* are creeds; *Definitiones* are the solemn and definitive pronouncements of ecumenical councils or popes speaking *ex cathedra*. The term *Declarationes* in the title includes all other documents of the magisterium which do not have the weight of a solemn definition. The usefulness of this handbook is shown by the fact that it has been revised and brought up to date by successive editors in no less than thirty-seven editions, the most recent of which is the work of Peter Hünermann.[3]

The volume begins with a collection of the creeds and professions of faith of the first five centuries. The "definitions" and "declarations" then follow in chronological order, without any separation between the two kinds of documents. In his introduction to the 34th edition, Adolf Schönmetzer said that it had been suggested that he use some editorial device to mark out the dogmatic definitions from everything else in the enchiridion; he wisely refused to take up the challenge, correctly leaving that task to theologians.[4] However, he did greatly improve the work, especially by the historical and critical introductions he provided for many of the texts.

This handbook, the only collection of its kind for over a century, was so widely used by both students and teachers of theology that it gave rise to the pejorative term: "Denzinger-theology." As Karl Rahner and others have used this term it meant doing theology as though theologians had no other task than to defend and comment on the doctrinal pronouncements of the magisterium.[5] It also meant citing texts from Denzinger with little regard for their historical context, or for their different degrees of doctrinal weight. However, Rahner's disdain for "Denzinger-theology" by no means implied disdain for the enchiridion as such; in fact, he thought it so important that he devoted a good deal of his own time between 1952 and 1957 to seeing the 28th, 29th and 30th editions through the press. As Yves Congar has pointed out, the way to avoid the stigma of doing "Denzinger-theology" is not by throwing this book out, but by using it correctly.[6]

While the use of Denzinger requires a good knowledge of Latin (or German, for the latest edition), students who must rely on an English translation now have a handbook comparable to Denzinger in the volume edited by J. Neuner and J. Dupuis entitled: *The Christian Faith in the Doctrinal Documents of the Catholic Church*.[7] In Neuner-Dupuis, these documents are arranged according to topics, so that one finds together, in chronological order, documents concerning "Revelation and Faith," "Tradition and Scripture," "The Triune God," "Man and the World," etc. In using Denzinger, whose documents are given simply in chronological order, one can locate the documents that pertain to specific topics by consulting the exhaustive index at the end of the volume.

Another important reference work, now available in English, is the two-volume collection of the decrees of all the ecumenical councils, edited with the original text on one side, and an English translation on the facing page. The edition of the original texts was done by a group of scholars led by Giuseppe Alberigo of Bologna, Italy; the English version was edited by Norman Tanner, who enlisted twenty-nine fellow Jesuits to do the translating.[8]

Evaluation of documents

By "evaluation" is meant the determination of the relative weight of authority that is attached to any particular exercise of teaching authority. In its *Instruction on the Ecclesial Vocation of the Theologian*, the Congregation for the Doctrine of the Faith said that theologians "must take into account the proper character of every exercise of the Magisterium, considering the extent to which its authority is engaged."[9] It further attributed to theologians the task "to assess accurately the authoritativeness of the interventions which becomes clear from the nature of the documents, the insistence with which a teaching is repeated, and the very way in which it is expressed."[10] One should, of course, add that another crucial factor in assessing the authoritativeness of ecclesial documents is the source from which the document was issued. This could be an ecumenical council, a pope speaking *ex cathedra*, a regional council, an episcopal synod, a pope writing an encyclical letter, a Roman congregation, an episcopal conference, or an individual bishop in his diocese. Each of these sources of magisterial documents will have its own specific weight of authority.

Interpretation of documents

This means applying the principles of the science of hermeneutics to the documents of the magisterium. No one now questions the necessity of applying such principles to the interpretation of holy scripture. It is only recently that the necessity of applying such principles also to the documents of the magisterium has become generally recognized, although much work remains to be done in their application. How the science of hermeneutics can be used in the interpretation of documents of the magisterium will be the subject matter of a later chapter. For now it will suffice to note the two major steps that must be taken: the first is to determine the meaning of the document in its historical context, and the second is to determine the contemporary meaning of that document, and to express that same meaning in concepts and language that will make it intelligible to people of faith today.

Why should a Catholic theologian know how to evaluate and interpret documents of the magisterium?

The answer is based on what it means to be a Catholic theologian. I will spell this out in four theses: 1) Theology is faith seeking understanding. 2) Theologians are persons who are committed to seeking a contemporary understanding of their faith. 3) A Catholic theologian does this from within the Catholic tradition. 4) It is impossible to engage seriously in the search for a contemporary understanding of the faith from within the Catholic tradition without knowing how to evaluate and interpret documents of the magisterium.

1. Theology is faith seeking understanding.

Almost nine centuries have passed since Anselm of Canterbury defined theology in three words as *fides quaerens intellectum* (faith seeking understanding). Each of these words deserves comment.

Fides
The first word of St. Anselm's definition means that theology starts with faith, presupposes it, and is required by it. Theology springs from faith insofar as faith asks itself about itself and seeks to understand itself; faith turns into theology to the extent that it asks endless questions and seeks without acknowledging limits. The faith that seeks understanding is necessarily the faith of the theologian himself or herself. In the case of the Catholic theologian, this faith will be Christian, ecclesial, and Catholic. It is Christian in that it accepts Christ as the definitive word of God for humanity. It is ecclesial in that it is a faith that we have not

found by ourselves, but that we have received from the church. Ecclesial faith trusts that the Holy Spirit has maintained the church in the truth of the gospel, and that therefore in sharing the faith of the church we can be sure that our personal faith is soundly based on the word of God. As Avery Dulles has pointed out, "To be a true theologian, one must dwell in spirit within the community of faith; one must participate in the Christian symbols and in their meaning for the community. This kind of participatory knowledge will make it possible to see the formulas in relation to the unexplicit meaning which they carry for those who share in the tradition."[11]

If our faith is Catholic, we engage in the science of theology from within the Catholic tradition. This means that we do theology as committed participants in the faith, life and worship of the Catholic Church. The *credo ecclesiam* of our baptismal profession means that we look upon the Catholic Church with the eyes of faith. We see the church as the fruit of Christ's definitive victory over the powers of evil, assured of the abiding presence of the Holy Spirit, the Spirit of truth that will lead it into all truth. Our *credo ecclesiam* means also that we believe that the episcopal and papal structure of the Catholic Church corresponds to God's design for his church. We believe that the authority with which bishops and popes lead and teach in the church comes to them ultimately from Christ, and that in the exercise of their office they enjoy a special assistance of the Holy Spirit, in virtue of which we believe that when they teach in a definitive way they will not lead the church into serious errors in its faith, and that even in their non-definitive teaching they provide generally reliable witness to the faith of the church.

To sum up: the faith that seeks understanding when we do theology is necessarily our own faith, and that means that we seek understanding of a faith that is Christian, ecclesial, and Catholic.

Quaerens

The "seeking" that is the essence of the science of theology is one that is *critical*, that is, aware of its presuppositions and of the requirements of its mental process as universally valid; *methodical*, that is, carried on in accordance with the norms set by its object, its character as reflection on faith, and its purpose; and *systematic*, that is, directed to a coherent understanding of the revealed contents in their mutual connections, their relation to the center of faith which is Christ, and their significance for man's salvation. It is also *endless*, since it can never exhaust the intelligibility of its object, which is divine mystery.

Intellectum

The understanding of faith which theology seeks is an understanding that is appropriate to the culture in which we live today. It is crucial for faith that it be appropriate to the mental and cultural level of the individual believer, and of the church as a believing people. The life of faith is in danger when a person's understanding of what he or she believes remains at a childish level, when that person's secular education is appropriate for a mature adult. Analogously, there is an understanding of the faith that is appropriate for each cultural age of society. For instance, theologians at the Council of Trent, in their understanding of the doctrine of original sin, took the story of the fall in chapter 3 of Genesis far more literally than it is appropriate for modern theologians to do.

2) A theologian is a person who is committed to seeking a contemporary understanding of his or her faith.

Seeking a contemporary understanding of the faith has been an important part of the life of the church in every age, because every age has posed its own challenges to the faith. This seeking a contemporary understanding of the faith began during the time when the books of the New Testament were being written. Each of the evangelists interpreted the message of the gospel in the light of the problems that his Christian community was facing, half a century or more after the events which are recorded in the gospels actually happened.

Theology today is aware that it encounters Christian revelation in a text (the New Testament) which is itself the result of a process of interpretation. This revelation has subsequently been constantly reinterpreted by the church over the centuries and has therefore been re-expressed in various historical and cultural contexts, because in each age it was necessary to seek and express a contemporary understanding of the faith, meaningful to the people of faith in that period and in that culture. An unending series of new challenges to the faith made it necessary again and again to seek a deeper understanding of the gospel message, so as to respond to the new challenge while at the same time faithfully maintaining the substance of the original message. In each generation it has been the task of theologians to seek a contemporary understanding of the faith, and to express it in concepts and terms that would make it intelligible and meaningful to the people of their time.

3. A Catholic theologian is a person who is committed to seeking a contemporary understanding of the faith from within the Catholic tradition.

This means, in the first place, that a Catholic theologian shares in the contemporary faith and life of the Catholic Church. David Tracy has described the goal of all systematic theology as "the reinterpretation of a religious tradition by committed and informed thinkers in that tradition."[12] He insists that only those who are fully committed to a religious tradition can grasp the meaning of that tradition in such a way as to be able to achieve a reliable reinterpretation of it. Catholic theologians, therefore, will be those who first strive to know and understand the Catholic tradition of faith, and then seek to translate their understanding of it into concepts and terms that will make it more meaningful and intelligible for the Catholic faithful today. This leads us to our fourth thesis:

4. It is impossible to be committed to the search for a contemporary understanding of the faith from within the Catholic tradition without knowing how to evaluate and interpret documents of the magisterium.

It is of course true that magisterial documents such as decrees of councils and doctrinal pronouncements of popes are not the only source in which one can find the Catholic tradition as it has been handed down from "generation to generation. Vatican II has made it clear that the "sacred deposit of the word of God has been committed to the church" (that is, to the whole people of God, faithful as well as pastors), and that "the church, in her teaching, life and worship, perpetuates and hands on to all generations all that she herself is, all that she believes."[13] It is the church as a whole, then, and not only its leaders and official teachers, that has perpetuated and handed on all that she is and all that she believes. The church has done this not only by teaching, but also by its life and worship and, above all, by its sacramental liturgy, in which it hands on the very reality of Christian life and faith to each succeeding generation. The handing on of the deposit of faith by teaching has been accomplished not only by councils and popes, but also by the fathers and doctors of the earlier centuries, by theologians in every age, and by many others who, without being professional theologians, have been led by the Spirit into profound insights into the meaning of the faith, and have shared their insights by their words and writings.

Where is this tradition to be found? The fruit of it is to be found in the faith and life of the contemporary church. But by the very nature of the case, our access to the tradition of the past centuries will be primarily through the medium of texts in which this tradition has been recorded in writing. The first and most important of these texts is, of course, the bible. But we also have precious witnesses to the faith of the early church in the baptismal creeds that have been preserved in writing. Liturgical documents record the way in which the church in every age practiced its sacred worship, and thus also manifested its faith. The writings of the fathers of the church, many of whom were also bishops, tell us how they interpreted the faith for the people of their own generation, and thus handed it on as a living faith, and not a dead letter. And, finally, we have the documents issued by popes and councils, in which they gave authoritative answers to the questions that each age posed to the faith of the church.

Now it is obvious that no one person, in one lifetime, could even read all these documents, let alone be competent to interpret them all. As Bernard Lonergan insists, method in theology has to involve functional specialties, and no one can expect to be master of them all.[14] However, there is a certain level of competence that every theologian worthy of the name can be rightly expected to achieve. Surely every Christian theologian must be familiar with the principles to be applied in the interpretation of sacred scripture. It is equally certain that Catholic theologians must be familiar with the principles for the evaluation and inter- pretation of the documents of the magisterium, since these docu- ments represent key moments in the development of the Catholic tradition of faith in which they stand and of which they seek a contemporary understanding. In order to interpret a tradition one must know that tradition, and one cannot expect to know the Catholic tradition without being able to interpret the official doc- uments in which that tradition has been authoritatively expressed.

Lest the fact that I have spent most of my life teaching in Rome might lead the reader to suspect that I am inclined to attribute more importance to the evaluation and interpretation of magis- terial documents than most other Catholic theologians would tend to do, I shall conclude this chapter by invoking the authori- ty of three of the most respected Catholic theologians of our cen- tury. I shall begin by quoting two passages from the writings of Karl Rahner on the subject with which we are dealing.

> It is as a member of the Church and in the light of faith that the theologian must work, in real possession of the object of faith and in real contact with it through grace...In the long run the correct- ness of our arguments and deductions from the propositions of faith can only proceed from the heart of a faith known by being lived...But this original faith can only be explicated when we attend to the binding formulations in which it has never failed to express itself, and necessarily in objective propositional form.[15]

> If theologians want to live in the Church with the theology they want to live with, then their theology must really be an ecclesial one, and it must have in principle an open and positive relation- ship to the ecclesial teaching office. Those days are certainly gone when theology could be a Denzinger theology in the neoscholas- tic style of the nineteenth century or the first half of the twentieth century. But that is a far cry from saying that the only way young theologians can make their theology relevant today is by being asi- nine enough to eschew all contact with the doctrinal decisions of the Church and by attempting to pursue theology without formal and continuing dialogue with the Church, its teaching office, and its theological history.[16]

Edward Schillebeeckx has expressed himself in similar terms on this topic, as in the following statement:

> Catholic theologians acknowledge that Christian theologizing is possible only in a community. Under the norms of "the faith of the Church," the Church community is the foundation of theological work. With Vatican II they emphasize the Christian community as the subject of all that faith tradition found both in the Scripture and in the Church's tradition. In the Christian community, the official magisterium has a distinct and irreplaceable function...The theologians have a specific function on behalf of the whole faith community, both people and leaders. The theologians accept the magisterium's authority in faith.[17]

I shall conclude with a quotation from Avery Dulles which sums up what we have been saying in this chapter:

> The task of theology is to conduct a methodic or systematic reflection on faith. As an ecclesial discipline, theology is done within the believing community. It endeavors to give a coherent systematization of Christian faith, guided by the symbols and past formulations, especially those which have normative value in the Church...Recognizing the Church as the community to which he owes his own faith, the Christian theologian will treat its traditional formulas with great reverence, for only through the expressions of the faith of past believers can anyone today become a Christian.[18]

2 | Evaluating the Level of Authority Exercised in Documents of the Magisterium

On October 11, 1992, Pope John Paul II promulgated the new *Catechism of the Catholic Church* with an apostolic constitution in which he declared this Catechism to be "a sure norm for teaching the faith" and "a sure and authentic reference text for teaching Catholic doctrine."[1] Subsequently, the question was raised as to the degree of dogmatic weight that should be attributed to the doctrines contained in this Catechism, especially in view of its promulgation by the pope. To this question Cardinal Joseph Ratzinger, authoritative spokesman for the Vatican on questions of doctrine, gave the following answer: "The individual doctrines that the Catechism affirms have no other authority than that which they already possess."[2] His answer points to the fact that while all the 2865 numbered paragraphs in the new Catechism affirm what can be generally described as "Catholic doctrine," there will be considerable difference among these doctrines as to their respective degree of authority. While the new Catechism does not add to their authority, neither does it indicate the level of authority attached to each of its doctrines. It is reasonable to expect that to each degree of authority exercised by the church's magisterium, there will correspond a level of response expected of the Catholic faithful. How are the faithful to know what kind of response they are supposed to give to any particular doctrine contained in the Catechism? Presumably it is the professional theologians who should know how to answer such questions for the ordinary faithful. In order to be able to do so, they have to be familiar with the criteria by which one can

12

determine the relative degree of authority attached to the various statements of the magisterium, and the corresponding level of response due to them. What I intend to do here is to describe the criteria that a theologian would use in performing this task.

I do not know any better way to do this than to comment on the new Formula for the Profession of Faith which now must be used by those who are obliged by canon law to make a profession of faith at the beginning of their term of office in some responsible position in the church.[3] The first and longest paragraph of this formula is the Nicene-Constantinopolitan Creed with which we profess our faith each Sunday. The new part of the formula, on which I shall offer my comments, is divided into three brief paragraphs. As the introductory note explains, this division is intended to show the distinction among three different kinds of truths, and the corresponding kinds of assent that are required when they are proposed, with varying degrees of authority, by the magisterium. I shall quote each of these brief paragraphs, and then ask three questions about each: 1) What kind of doctrines are involved here? 2) With what degree of authority are they taught? 3) What level of response is required?

The first of these paragraphs reads as follows:

"I also believe with firm faith all those things which are contained in the Word of God, whether written or handed down, and are proposed by the Church, whether by a solemn judgment or by its ordinary and universal magisterium, as divinely revealed and to be believed as such."

What kind of doctrines are involved here? Here it is a question of doctrines that have been revealed by God, and thus are part of the "deposit of faith" entrusted to the church. They are truths that are part of the word of God as this has been handed down both in scripture and in tradition. Not all such truths can be found explicitly in the Bible, but they must be such as the church has come to recognize as really, even if only implicitly, contained in the sacred deposit committed to her.

How are they taught? Following an important statement of the First Vatican Council,[4] the text here distinguishes between two different ways that such revealed truths can be proposed for our faith. By a "solemn judgment" is meant the extraordinary exercise of teaching authority, whether by an ecumenical council or by the pope speaking *ex cathedra*, whereby a doctrine is defined as a dogma of faith. This is a rather rare occurrence, and canon law prescribes that no doctrine is to be understood as having been so defined unless this is manifestly the case.[5] It should be noted that no such "solemn judgment" was pronounced by the Second Vatican Council, even in the two documents which it called "dogmatic constitutions."

The second way that revealed truths can be presented for our faith is by the exercise of the "ordinary universal magisterium." Vatican II explained this to mean the kind of teaching which the whole college of bishops, including the bishop of Rome, do when they are not gathered in ecumenical council.[6] The case that is envisioned here is one where it is evident that the pope and the Catholic bishops all over the world have been in agreement in teaching a particular doctrine as definitively to be held as a matter of Catholic faith, even though it has never been solemnly defined as such. As examples of such truths, one could think of several articles of the "Apostles' Creed" which have never been the specific object of a solemn definition, but which are undoubtedly dogmas of Catholic faith, such as the communion of saints, the resurrection of the body, and life everlasting.

What kind of assent is required? When a truth has been solemnly defined, or definitively proposed by the ordinary universal magisterium as part of revelation, the assent required is an act of faith. In the decree of Vatican I to which this paragraph of the profession of faith corresponds, this is described as "divine and Catholic faith."[7] It is called "divine faith" because it is a response to God's word, and thus a personal response to God who has spoken it. It is called "Catholic" faith, because, having been definitively taught by the supreme teaching authority as something divinely revealed, it is now an article of the normative faith of the Catholic Church.

The First Vatican Council defined, as a dogma of faith, that when popes and ecumenical councils define a doctrine as a dogma of faith, they teach infallibly in doing so.[8] The Second Vatican Council has further declared (though not solemnly defined) that the whole college of bishops together with the pope teach infallibly when, in the ordinary exercise of their magisterium, they concur in proposing a particular doctrine as definitively to be held.[9] When it is clear that a doctrine has been thus proposed as divinely revealed, an assent of firm faith is called for. The ultimate motive of this act of faith is not the infallibility of the church in proposing it, but the authority of God who has revealed it.

The second of the three new paragraphs in the Profession of Faith is as follows:

"I also firmly accept and hold all those things concerning doctrine about faith or morals which are definitively proposed by the same Church."

What kind of doctrines are involved here? An authoritative answer to this question has been given by the Congregation for the Doctrine of the Faith in its 1990 *Instruction on the Ecclesial Vocation of the Theologian.* No. 23 of this "Instruction" contains what is obviously a paraphrase of the paragraph of the formula on which we are now commenting. It reads: "When the Magisterium proposes 'in a definitive way' truths concerning faith and morals, which, even if not divinely revealed, are nevertheless strictly and intimately connected with Revelation, these must be firmly accepted and held." This makes it clear that the doctrines envisioned in this paragraph of the Profession of Faith are not really contained in the deposit of faith. On the other hand, they are so closely connected with some revealed truth that the church needs to be able to speak definitively and even infallibly about them in order to be able to defend or explain what is revealed. Such matters are commonly referred to as the "secondary object of infallibility."

While it is official Catholic doctrine (though not a dogma of faith) that the church's charism of infallibility extends to its definitive teaching about such a "secondary object,"[10] there is no official statement specifying in detail what is included in it, nor is there unanimity among Catholic theologians about the exact contents or limits of this object. One question that has been much discussed in recent years concerns the extent to which the natural moral law falls within the scope of the church's infallible teaching authority. It should be clear that those principles or specific norms of the natural law which are also contained in the deposit of revelation, by that fact belong to the primary object of infallibility. The Congregation for the Doctrine of the Faith has affirmed this in its *Instruction on the Ecclesial Vocation of the Theologian,* saying: "Revelation also contains moral teachings which *per se* could be known by natural reason...It is a doctrine of faith that these moral norms can be infallibly taught by the Magisterium."[11] The term "these moral norms" obviously refers only to such norms of the natural law as are also contained in revelation. It is generally agreed that there are other moral norms accessible to human reason which have not been formally revealed.[12] Since such norms would belong only to the secondary object of infallibility, it follows that they can be infallibly taught, only if they are so intimately connected with revealed truth as to be required for its defense or exposition.

How are such truths taught by the church?

This paragraph speaks of doctrines concerning faith or morals which are "definitively proposed" by the church. As we have seen above, a doctrine can be recognized as having been "definitively proposed" either by the fact that an ecumenical council or a pope has pronounced a "solemn judgment" about it, or by the fact that the whole college of bishops, together with the pope in their ordinary exercise of teaching authority, have consistently proposed the same point of doctrine as "definitively to be held." What this paragraph envisions, therefore, is a case where the doctrine that has been defined, or has been universally taught as definitively to be held, is not actually a revealed truth, but belongs rather to the "secondary object" of magisterium. In such a case, the church does not define or teach the doctrine as something revealed; rather, it proposes its teaching on this point as something that is certainly, and even infallibly, true.

What kind of assent is required?

The text of the paragraph we are considering answers our question with the words: "I firmly accept and hold." The significant point to be noted is that this formula does not use the words "I believe," or "hold with faith," which were used in the previous paragraph. What this paragraph of the Profession of Faith requires is a firm interior assent of the mind to the proposition as true, but not an act of "divine and Catholic faith." In this respect, the new Formula for the Profession of Faith was consistent with the other documents of the magisterium which, since Vatican I, had spoken of the response due to definitive teaching about matter not in itself revealed but connected with revelation.[13] Hence it came as a complete surprise to find the following statement in the recently published *Catechism of the Catholic Church*:

> 88 The Church's Magisterium exercises the authority it holds from Christ to the fullest extent when it defines dogmas, that is, when it proposes truths contained in divine Revelation or having a necessary connection with them, in a form obliging the Christian people to an irrevocable adherence of faith.

It is obvious that the phrase "or having a necessary connection with them" refers to what theologians call the "secondary object of infallibility." It is equally obvious that the catechism declares that the magisterium can define such unrevealed truths as "dogmas" and oblige the Christian people to give them "an irrevocable assent of faith."

Here the Catechism has espoused an opinion that has been held by a number of prominent Catholic theologians (among them, F. Marin-Sola, Charles Journet and Yves Congar) to the effect that the proper response to infallibly defined doctrine would be an act of divine faith, even though the matter in itself was not revealed.[14] However, this opinion has been strongly contested by a great many Catholic theologians, who insist that only divinely revealed truth can be defined as dogma calling for an assent of divine faith.[15]

One does not expect a document of the nature of the *Catechism of the Catholic Church* to take sides on an issue disputed among reputable Catholic theologians. The fact that it has done so is all the more surprising in view of the fact that the opinion espoused by the new Catechism on this question has no support, to my knowledge, in any previous document of the magisterium. Of the many official documents that have suggested or explicitly asserted that the magisterium can speak with infallibility about truths that are not revealed, none has described the product of such teaching as a dogma of faith, or has described the response due to it as an irrevocable assent of faith. Cardinal Ratzinger has said that the definitive Latin text of the Catechism "would be published only after the editions in the chief national languages and would take account of observations made in the first phase of the reception of the catechism."[16] I am hopeful that when this Latin text is published, it will not say that truths that are not revealed but only connected with revelation can be defined as dogmas calling for an irrevocable assent of faith.

The third and last of the brief paragraphs in the Profession of Faith is as follows:

"Furthermore, I adhere with religious submission of will and intellect to the doctrines which either the Roman Pontiff or the College of Bishops propose, when they exercise their authoritative teaching office, even though they do not intend to proclaim those doctrines by a definitive act."

What kind of doctrines are involved here? They are the kind of doctrines concerning which the pastors of the church "exercise their authoritative teaching office": namely, doctrines relating to faith and morals. The Second Vatican Council described bishops as "teachers endowed with the authority of Christ, who preach to the people committed to them the faith they must believe and put into practice."[17] "Matter of faith and morals" embraces whatever pertains to Christian belief and to a Christian way of life.

When the church asserts its claim to speak authoritatively on matters of faith and morals, the latter term includes not only the moral teaching of the gospel, but also the natural moral law. Vatican II expressed this in the following way: "The church is, by the will of Christ, the teacher of the truth. It is her duty to give utterance to, and authoritatively to teach, that truth which is Christ himself, and also to declare and confirm by her authority those principles of the moral order which have their origin in human nature itself."[18] In its *Instruction on the Ecclesial Vocation of the Theologian,* the Congregation for the Doctrine of the Faith has further spelled out the grounds for this: "By reason of the connection between the orders of creation and redemption and by reason of the necessity, in view of salvation, of knowing and observing the whole moral law, the competence of the magisterium also extends to that which concerns the natural law."[19] But one must distinguish between competence to speak with authority, and a claim to speak with infallibility. The latter, as we have seen, is limited to truths which are either revealed or are required for the defense or explanation of some revealed truth. The church does not claim to be able to speak with infallibility on all moral questions, regardless of their connection with divine revelation.

The exercise of such authoritative magisterium, especially since the publication of the encyclical *Rerum novarum* by Pope Leo XIII in 1891, shows that the church does not see its teaching authority in matters of morals as limited to questions of personal morality. It has regularly asserted its competence to pass judgment on the broader issues affecting the order of human society, insofar as these are moral problems, to be determined in accordance with the "principles of the moral order which have their origin in human nature itself."

How are these doctrines taught by the pope or bishops? The paragraph we are commenting on answers this question when it says: "When they exercise their authoritative teaching office, even though they do not intend to proclaim those doctrines by a definitive act." Here it is a question of what is called the "ordinary," "authentic," "non-definitive," "non-infallible," "non-irreformable" exercise of the teaching function by the pope or by the whole college of bishops together with him. It is to be noted that mention is made here only of those who have authority to teach the universal church; no mention is made of the teaching office which bishops exercise either individually in their own dioceses, or collectively in particular synods or in episcopal conferences. Hence, the formula refers only to doctrines which have been authoritatively promulgated by the supreme teaching authority for acceptance by the universal church. Such doctrines are found, for example, in the documents of the Second Vatican Council, which, on the one hand, nowhere expressed its intention to define a doctrine, but, on the other hand, described itself as exercising the supreme teaching authority in the church, and hence calling for the acceptance of its teaching by all the Catholic faithful.[20]

The pope exercises his universal teaching office, without intending to make definitive pronouncements, in his encyclicals, apostolic letters and exhortations, and other documents addressed to the whole Catholic Church. He can also exercise his teaching office by his explicit approval of doctrinal statements which are promulgated for the whole church by the Congregation for the Doctrine of the Faith. In its *Instruction on the Ecclesial Vocation of the Theologian*, this congregation declared: "The Roman pontiff fulfills his universal mission with the help of the various bodies of the Roman curia, and in particular with that of the Congregation for the Doctrine of the Faith. Consequently, the documents issued by this congregation expressly approved by the pope participate in the ordinary magisterium of the successor of Peter."[21] However, the pope does not use such documents to proclaim doctrine in a definitive way, nor would any statement issued by the congregation participate in papal infallibility. Indeed, even with papal approval, statements issued by the congregation would be less authoritative than those issued by the pope in his own name.

While the Profession of Faith speaks only of the exercise of magisterium by the pope or the whole college of bishops with him, the Code of Canon Law speaks of the teaching authority which bishops exercise "whether they teach individually, or in episcopal conferences, or gathered together in particular councils."[22] Bishops, the code goes on to say, "while not infallible in their teaching, are the authentic instructors and teachers of the faith for Christ's faithful entrusted to their care." Obviously, the authority of statements made by individual bishops, episcopal conferences, and national or regional councils will be less than that of statements issued by the pope or an ecumenical council for the universal church.

It is obvious, then, that, within the category of the non-definitive magisterium, different degrees of teaching authority will be exercised. Referring to this fact, the CDF "Instruction" says: "Here the theologian will need, first of all, to assess accurately the authoritativeness of the interventions which becomes clear from the nature of the documents, the insistence with which a teaching is repeated, and the very way in which it is expressed."[23] I would say that the very first question to be asked in assessing the authoritativeness of an intervention is: "Who is speaking?" Non-definitive magisterium can be exercised by an ecumenical council, by a pope, by the Congregation for the Doctrine of the Faith, by a regional council, by an episcopal conference, or by a local bishop. Each of these sources possesses a different level of teaching authority. The second question is: "To whom is this teaching addressed?" Obviously, it is only those addressed by a teaching who are obliged by its authority. There is an important application of this principle with regard to papal teaching. All

Catholics are obliged by the authority of the teaching which the pope addresses to the universal church in such documents as encyclicals. But the pope is also bishop of the diocese of Rome, and when his teaching is directed specifically to the clergy and faithful of his own diocese, only they are obliged by it. Similarly, the teaching which the pope gives to groups of people, either in Rome or in the course of his travels to other countries, even though it is published by the Vatican, does not have the authority of papal teaching addressed to the universal church.

A third question is: "What kind of document is issued?" The Second Vatican Council issued two "dogmatic constitutions," one "pastoral constitution," one "constitution," nine "decrees," and three "declarations." There is no doubt about the intention of the council to indicate different levels of authority by these different titles. Similarly, there are different kinds of papal documents with different levels of authoritativeness. One visible sign of this diversity is the kind of seal affixed to the document. The most authoritative documents are sealed with a lead seal (in Latin *bulla*) and on that account are called "bulls"; lesser documents are sealed with wax, and on others the papal seal is merely stamped in ink. Among the documents thus diversely sealed, the most authoritative are "apostolic constitutions," "apostolic letters," "encyclical letters," and "apostolic exhortations." Such documents are usually addressed to the universal church.

A fourth consideration, in assessing the authoritativeness of any non-definitive exercise of magisterium, is suggested by the CDF in its *Instruction on the Ecclesial Vocation of the Theologian*,[24] when it distinguishes among three different ways in which the magisterium can intervene, without intending to act "definitively." The first is that it "teaches a doctrine to aid a better understanding of revelation and make explicit its contents, or to recall how some teaching is in conformity with the truths of faith, or finally to guard against ideas that are incompatible with those truths." Secondly: "the magisterium can intervene in questions under discussion which involve, in addition to solid principles, certain contingent and conjectural elements. It often only becomes possible with the passage of time to distinguish between what is necessary and what is contingent." Thirdly: there are interventions in the prudential order. Of these the CDF says:

"When it comes to the question of interventions in the prudential order, it could happen that some magisterial documents
might not be free from all deficiencies. Bishops and their advisors have not always taken into immediate consideration every
aspect or the entire complexity of a question." Here the CDF has
explained, more clearly than I think it had ever been done officially before, that one rightly distinguishes among many different levels of authority exercised by the "ordinary" magisterium.

A final question to be asked in assessing the level of authority
involved in any exercise of the non-definitive magisterium has to
do with the strength of the language which the author of the document chose to use. For instance, popes have sometimes used
language, in encyclicals or other letters addressed to the whole
church, which has indicated their intention to settle a question
that was disputed among Catholics. In his encyclical *Humani
generis* of 1950, Pope Pius XII spoke of this in the following
terms: "If the supreme pontiffs, in their official documents,
deliberately pass judgment on a matter hitherto controverted, it
is evident to all that, in accordance with the mind and intention
of the same pontiffs, that question can no longer be considered a
subject for free debate among theologians."[25] The language used
by Pope John Paul II in his recent apostolic letter *Ordinatio sacerdotalis* would clearly fulfill, or even surpass, the conditions mentioned by Pius XII. In fact I am not aware of any document of
ordinary papal magisterium that uses language quite so strong as
the final sentence of this recent letter, which reads: "Wherefore,
in order that all doubt may be removed regarding a matter of
great importance, a matter which pertains to the church's divine
constitution itself, in virtue of my ministry of confirming the
brethren (Lk 22:32) I declare that the church has no authority
whatsoever to confer priestly ordination on women and that this
judgment is to be definitively held by all the church's faithful."[26]
This language comes very close to that of a solemn definition,
but we are assured by Cardinal Ratzinger that it was not the
intention of John Paul II to speak *ex cathedra*.[27*] In any case, I
would say that this statement excluding the ordination of women

---

*See the Afterword (p.181) for a discussion of the "Response" issued by the CDF on
Nov. 18, 1995.

to the priesthood would have to be put at the very top of any
scale measuring the degree of authority that has been exercised
by popes in their ordinary magisterium.

*What kind of response are the faithful expected to give to the teaching
of the ordinary, non-definitive magisterium?*

The Formula for the Profession of Faith answers this question
with the words: "I adhere with religious submission of will and
intellect." The official Latin text has: *religioso voluntatis et intellec-
tus obsequio adhaereo.* These are the terms that were used by
Vatican II in its statement on the matter, and they were repeated
in the new Code of Canon Law.[28] In rendering the Latin word
obsequio by "submission," I am in agreement with both the Abbott
and the Flannery versions of the documents of Vatican II, as well
as with the translation of the new code prepared by the Canon
Law Society of Great Britain and Ireland. However, the translation of the new code prepared by the Canon Law Society of
America translates *obsequium* as "respect," and versions in other
modern languages also vary between "submission" and "respect."
In view of the lack of agreement as to the proper translation of
the Latin word, I suggest that one should at least not give too
strong a meaning to "submission," or too weak a meaning to
"respect." In any case, the essential thing, in my view, is to note
that *obsequium* should not be translated simply as "assent."[29]
Obsequium denotes an *attitude* toward the teaching authority,
which the Congregation for the Doctrine of the Faith has
described as "the willingness to submit loyally to the teaching of
the magisterium on matters per se not irreformable."[30] This "willingness to submit" is said to be "the rule," but the Congregation
recognizes that "it can happen that a theologian may, according
to the case, raise questions regarding the timeliness, the form, or
even the contents of magisterial interventions."[31]

Further light on the meaning of this "willingness to submit
loyally to the teaching of the magisterium" is given in no. 29 of
the *Instruction*, which describes what a theologian should do who
is said to have "serious difficulties, for reasons which appear to
him well-founded, in accepting a non-irreformable magisterial
teaching." "In any case," we are told, "there should never be a
diminishment of that fundamental openness loyally to accept the
teaching of the magisterium."[32] Here again it is clear that *obse-*

quium is not to be identified with assent as such, but with a basic respect for the authority of the magisterium, and an openness to its teaching: an attitude that can well persist in people who find that they cannot give a sincere intellectual assent to a particular proposition that has been taught by this same magisterium.

The essential difference between "assent" and an attitude of willingness to accept the teaching of the magisterium is that assent is an "either-or" proposition; one either gives one's assent or one does not. On the other hand, an attitude of willingness admits of varying degrees. And these varying degrees appropriately correspond to the varying degrees of authority exercised by the magisterium when it does not teach in a definitive way.

It seems to me that an attitude of basic willingness to accept official teaching will be concretely expressed in the seriousness of one's efforts to overcome any tendency one might have simply to prefer one's own opinion, without giving serious consideration to the official teaching. In other words, an attitude of *obsequium* to the teaching authority will mean making a serious effort, proportionate to the authority which has been exercised in any particular case, to convince oneself of the truth of what has been taught. When people have made such a serious effort to accept a teaching, their attitude of *obsequium* toward the teaching authority can continue to be present, even in the case where they find themselves really unable to achieve intellectual assent to a particular proposition taught by the magisterium. In this case, it is not a lack of willingness to accept the teaching, but the strength of contrary reasons, that makes it impossible for them to give their assent. Assent is an act of the mind by which I really judge a proposition to be true. If my effort to achieve assent has been proportionate to the degree of authority that has been exercised, then I have fulfilled my obligation of *obsequium* toward the magisterium, even though I have not been able to bring myself to agree with some particular point of its teaching.

Can a theologian express his disagreement with a statement of the ordinary magisterium?

Several of the comments that appeared in the press when the CDF Instruction was published focused on the idea that it had ruled out all dissent by Catholic theologians. What was often not recognized was the specific meaning that this document was giving to the term "dissent." In Part B, under the heading "The Problem of Dissent," the Instruction described dissent as involving "attitudes of general opposition to church teaching which even comes to expression in organized groups" and "public opposition to the magisterium of the church" (32). It declared: "Dissent has different aspects. In its most radical form it aims at changing the church following a model of protest which takes its inspiration from political society" (33). Dissent is said to give rise to a "parallel magisterium," which "can cause grave harm by opposing itself to the magisterium of the pastors. Indeed, when dissent succeeds in extending its influence to the point of shaping a common opinion, it tends to become the rule of conduct. This cannot but seriously trouble the people of God and lead to contempt for true authority" (34). Other manifestations of "dissent" are: "polling public opinion to determine the proper thing to think or do, opposing the magisterium by exerting the pressure of public opinion, making the excuse of a 'consensus' among theologians, maintaining that the theologian is the prophetical spokesman of a 'base' or autonomous community which would be the source of all truth" (39).

Further light on the sense in which the Instruction used the term "dissent" was offered by Cardinal Ratzinger in a press conference which he gave concerning this document. He said: "The instruction distinguishes between healthy theological tension and true dissent, in which theology is organized according to the principle of majority rule, and the faithful are given alternative norms by a 'counter-magisterium.' Dissent thus becomes a political factor, passing from the realm of thought to that of a 'power game.' This is where a theologian's use of mass media can be dangerous."[33]

From the foregoing, it should be clear that what the CDF Instruction means by "dissent" is something quite different from the attitude of theologians who find, after careful study and reflection, that they cannot agree with some point of official teaching. The question remains: can they express their disagreement in ways that do not involve the kind of practices that have been described as "dissent"?

I find two indications in the Instruction that favor a positive answer to this question. In the context in which it speaks of tensions that can arise between theologians and the magisterium, the document says: "Even if the doctrine of the faith is not in question, the theologian will not present his own opinions or divergent hypotheses as though they were non-arguable conclusions. Respect for the truth as well as for the people of God requires this discretion....For the same reasons, the theologian will refrain from giving untimely public expression to them." From this I conclude that not all public expression is excluded, only what would be "indiscreet" or "untimely."

Another indication that the Instruction does not intend to rule out the communication among theologians of their difficulties with official teaching is given in the reference to the objections which a theologian's colleagues might offer him concerning his opinions. We are told that he should be ready, "if need be, to revise his own opinions and examine the objections which his colleagues might offer him." (29) This obviously presumes that he has shared his opinions with them in theological conventions or scholarly journals. Cardinal Ratzinger, referring to the theologian who disagrees with some official teaching, said at the same press conference: "We have not excluded all kinds of publication, nor have we closed him up in suffering. The Vatican insists, however, that theologians must choose the proper place to expound their ideas."[34] In other words, there must be a forum in which theologians can discuss with their peers the problems they might have with points of official teaching. If, in the decades prior to Vatican II, some Catholic theologians had not published their critique of certain official positions, the ground could hardly have been prepared for some of the key decisions taken by the council. It is well known how at the close of the council Pope Paul VI acknowledged the contribution made by such men as Yves Congar, Henri de Lubac and John Courtney Murray, theologians whose views had not originally been welcomed, but who were finally seen to have been courageous spokesmen of the truth.

I shall conclude this chapter where I began: with the new Catechism. I would venture to say that among its 2865 paragraphs, one could find statements that would exemplify just about every kind of doctrine taught by the magisterium and every degree of authority it has exercised in teaching it. It would be an interesting project to go through the Catechism and identify those various types of doctrines and levels of teaching authority. One would certainly find some examples of the most solemn kind: dogmas of faith. It is to these that we shall next give our attention.

3 ‖ What Is a Dogma of Faith?

Meaning of the Term "Dogma"

✝ What is true of the term "dogma" is also true of several related terms, such as "faith," "morals," and "heresy": these terms have an accepted, technical meaning in modern Catholic theology, but they have not always had this same meaning. It is a source of grave error to presume, when one finds these terms in earlier documents such as the decrees of the Council of Trent, that they have there the same meaning as they have today.

In modern Catholic usage, a dogma is a truth that must be believed with "divine and Catholic faith," as this is described in Vatican I: "All those things are to be believed with divine and Catholic faith which are contained in the word of God, written or handed down, and which by the church, either in solemn judgment or through her ordinary and universal teaching office, are proposed for belief as having been divinely revealed."[1] The faith with which such truths are to be believed is called "divine," because it is a response to God who has revealed them; it is called "Catholic," because revealed truths which have been definitively proposed for our belief by the supreme teaching authority are by that fact part of the normative faith of the Catholic Church.

A dogma, therefore, is now understood as a truth which has been revealed by God and has also been definitively taught as such by the church's magisterium. A dogma can be either defined or undefined: "definition" is a "solemn judgment" by an ecumenical council or a pope speaking *ex cathedra*; an undefined dogma is a truth that has been proposed by the ordinary universal magisterium as definitively to be held by divine faith. An example of the modern Catholic use of the term "dogma" is found in the letter *Tuas libenter* of Pius IX (1863), where the term *praefata Ecclesiae dogmata* (the aforesaid dogmas of the church) refers to both defined and undefined dogmas of faith.[2]

When modern Catholic theologians use the term "dogma," they are referring to a revealed truth which is part of the normative faith of the Catholic Church. It is important to know that the term has had this precise sense in Catholic usage only for about two hundred years. One of the first to give it this precise sense was Philipp Neri Chrismann, in his work *Regula fidei catholicae* (1792), where he described a dogma as "a divinely revealed truth which is proposed by the public judgment of the church as to be believed with divine faith, so that the contrary doctrine is condemned by the church as heretical."[3]

Since this has been the precise sense of the term "dogma" for only two hundred years, it is crucial, in interpreting previous documents, not to presume that it has the same meaning there as well. In fact, the word is found already in the New Testament, and in other ancient literature, with a variety of meanings, such as "decree, decision, ordinance, opinion, doctrine." In Lk 2:1 the "decree of Caesar Augustus that the whole world should be enrolled" is an imperial *dogma*. In Acts 16:4 the decisions taken by the apostolic council are called *dogmata*. Tenets of the various philosophical schools of antiquity were called their *dogmata*. The fathers of the church used the term *dogma* of both orthodox and heretical beliefs. So did the medieval theologians. Even after the Council of Trent, Melchior Cano could speak of "the dogmas of the Lutherans." So one must be careful not to rely on the use of the word "dogma" in writings prior to about 1800 as a sign that what is meant is what we now mean by "dogma." Of course this does not mean that before that time, theologians had no way of referring to what we now mean by "dogma." The fathers used the term "rule of faith," medieval theologians spoke of "articles of faith," and the Council of Trent spoke of "Catholic truths," with much the same meaning that the term "dogmas of faith" has today. However, there is a difference, in that the modern term puts more emphasis on the definitive proposal of the doctrine by the teaching authority of the church than the earlier terms did.

New Testament origin of dogma

Here we are referring not to the use of the term "dogma," but to the fact that already in the New Testament it is evident that membership in the Christian community required the profession of Christian faith, and that there were certain prescribed formulas in which this profession was to be made. The briefest of these is the simple "Jesus is Lord," which St. Paul insists that "no one can say except by the Holy Spirit."[4] Again, in St. Paul: "If you confess with your mouth that Jesus is Lord and believe in your heart that God raised him from the dead, you will be saved."[5] A somewhat more developed formula of faith is one that Paul himself received and handed on to the Corinthians: "that Christ died for our sins in accordance with the scriptures; that he was buried; that he was raised on the third day in accordance with the scriptures..."[6]

There is a sense, therefore, in which the Christian faith has from the beginning had a "dogmatic" character: that is, there have always been prescribed formulas in which those who belong to the Christian community must profess their faith. Needless to say, the object of Christian faith is Christ as the Word of God, and not the propositions in which Christian faith is formulated. God has definitively revealed himself to us not in many propositions, but in his one Word. As St. John of the Cross put it: "In giving us his Son, his only Word (for he possesses no other) he spoke everything to us in this sole Word—and has no more to say."[7] However, since the unity of the church has always called for professing the same faith in common, this faith necessarily has had to be formulated in propositions for all to accept, believe and profess.

The first occasion on which early Christians professed their faith was at their baptism. As described in the *Traditio Apostolica* of Hippolytus, baptism consisted of a threefold immersion, accompanied by a confession of faith in God the Father Almighty, in Christ Jesus who was crucified, died and rose from the dead, and in the Holy Spirit in the holy church.[8] This confession of faith, which in the actual reception of baptism was made by responding "I believe" to the questions put by the minister, was later given a declaratory form, such as we have in the "Apostles' Creed," to be recited by the candidates before the end

of the catechumenate. The baptismal creed was an interpretation of the foundational revelation which came to its fulfillment
in Christ, an interpretation formulated (or at least approved) and
prescribed by the bishops who presided over the catechumenate.
In that sense, it had dogmatic character. But it is important to
note that this dogmatic character was at the service of the faith,
life and worship of the Christian community. The confession of
faith in God, in Jesus Christ, in the Holy Spirit, is a way of prais-
ing and worshiping God. In that sense, the dogmatic formulation
of the faith is at the service of doxology: the praise of God.

The ongoing function of dogma in the life of the church

While the baptismal creed expressed the essential elements of
the "rule of faith" for the early church, it very soon became evident that differences would arise between Christians as to the
meaning of various articles of the creed. The unity of the church
required that authoritative answers be given to fundamental
questions about the meaning of the creed, so that Christians
could not only say the same words in professing their faith, but
really have the same faith, which depended on meaning the same
thing by the words they said. The ongoing function of dogma in
the life of the church, then, has been to provide the authoritative
answers to the questions that have kept coming up about the
meaning of what Christians profess in the creed, and thus to
make possible a common profession not only of the same words
but really of the same faith. Furthermore, our faith in the guidance of the church by the Holy Spirit gives us an assurance that
definitive answers to questions about the meaning of the faith
will also be the right answers, since otherwise they would
inevitably lead the whole church away from the truth of the
gospel. The history of the church shows that in every age there
have been, and doubtless will continue to be, new challenges to
the faith, calling for new clarifications of what the words of the
creed really mean. Hence the ongoing function of dogmatic
decisions is to make possible a common profession of the true
faith that will respond to the contemporary challenges to that
faith.

The role of dogma in tradition

The term "tradition" can refer both to what is handed on (*Verbum Dei traditum*), and to the process of handing this on. Vatican II tells us: "What was handed on by the apostles includes everything which contributes to the holiness of life and the increase in faith of the people of God; and so the church, in her teaching, life and worship, perpetuates and hands on to all generations all that she herself is, all that she believes."[9] Here the "what" that is handed on is described as "all that the church is, all that she believes." The perpetuating and handing on of this is the role of the whole church, which it performs in its teaching, life and worship. So it is evident that "what is handed on" is not only what the church believes (its doctrine) but all that it is; and the process of handing this on is not only by teaching, but also by the church's life and worship. In the church many are involved, in many different ways, in handing on the faith from one generation to the next; this handing on is by no means the exclusive role of the magisterium. But *Dei Verbum* goes on to say that the task of *authoritatively* interpreting the word of God has been entrusted exclusively to the magisterium, and it immediately explains that by "authoritatively" it means "with authority to teach in the name of Jesus Christ."[10] Vatican II also describes bishops as "teachers endowed with the authority of Christ, who preach to the people committed to them the faith they must believe and put into practice."[11] Bishops, along with many others, are engaged in the day-to-day handing on of the faith to each succeeding generation of the faithful. But they have a special role when disputes arise concerning the meaning of the faith. From the third century on, there is abundant evidence of the fact that when a dispute about the faith arose in some area of the church, the bishops of that region would gather in council to give an authoritative answer to the question. The church had already had a century of experience of such regional councils prior to the first of the great councils that we call "ecumenical," the First Council of Nicea, in 325. This council, along with the following one in 381, the First Council of Constantinople, gave definitive answers to questions about the divinity of the Word and the Holy Spirit, thus assuring the trinitarian character of Christian faith.

The following four great councils, of Ephesus (431), Chalcedon (451), Constantinople II (553) and Constantinople III (681), were all devoted to settling christological issues, especially the unity of person in Christ, and the integrity of his human nature.

Each of these councils resulted in the solemn definition of dogmas. The question we are asking is about the role that such dogmatic decisions have played in tradition, i.e. the handing on of the Christian faith. Obviously, during the long intervals between these councils, in the ordinary life of the church, the faith was being handed on by parents, catechists, and teachers, as well as by the bishops. But the dogmatic decisions taken by the councils were key moments in that tradition, crucial moments in times of crisis, when a decisive answer had to be given to questions that threatened the unity of the church in professing the true faith. In each case, an interpretation of the meaning of the gospel and of the creed was given that met the contemporary need, and at the same time marked out the direction which the teaching of the faith must take for the future on that particular question. Christian faith today is still fundamentally determined by the dogmas that were defined by the great councils of the first millennium.

The nature of a dogmatic statement

A ruling on language for confessing the faith

As we have seen, a major reason for dogmatic decisions is to make possible the common profession of orthodox faith. This necessarily involves formulating the propositions in which the common profession is to be made, and there is general agreement that dogmatic decisions have a regulative function of determining the language of faith. In his recent work, *The Nature of Doctrine*, the Lutheran scholar George Lindbeck takes the position that the function of doctrine is exclusively that of regulating the language in which Christian faith is professed.[12] Lindbeck maintains that doctrine does not have the function of making ontological truth claims; it is regulative, not informative. This would seem to mean that doctrine tells us what to say, when we profess our faith, but not that what we say is objectively true. I have no doubt that Lindbeck is personally convinced of the truth of his Christian faith, despite his view of the purely regulative function of doctrinal formulations. But, while agreeing that dogma does have a regulative function for the common profes- sion of faith, I see no reason to deny it a more basic function of expressing the truth which we believe when we profess our faith. Indeed, it seems to me that the only adequate basis for an obliga- tion to profess Christian faith in a creed is that this creed, howev- er imperfectly, says something of the truth that God has revealed to us in his Son.

Historically and culturally conditioned formulation

In its 1973 declaration *Mysterium Ecclesiae*, the Congregation for the Doctrine of the Faith made an important statement about "the historical condition that affects the expression of Revelation." The statement is as follows:

With regard to this historical condition, it must first be observed that the meaning of the pronouncements of faith depends partly upon the expressive power of the language used at a certain point in time and in particular circumstances. Moreover, it sometimes happens that some dogmatic truth is first expressed incompletely (but not falsely), and at a later date, when considered in a broader context of faith or human knowledge, it receives a fuller and more perfect expression. In addition, when the church makes new pro- nouncements she intends to confirm or clarify what is in some way contained in sacred scripture or in previous expressions of tradition; but at the same time she usually has the intention of solving certain questions or removing certain errors. All these things have to be taken into account in order that these pro- nouncements may be properly interpreted. Finally, even though the truths which the church intends to teach through her dogmat- ic formulas are distinct from the changeable conceptions of a given epoch and can be expressed without them, nevertheless it can sometimes happen that these truths may be enunciated by the sacred magisterium in terms that bear traces of such conceptions.

In view of the above, it must be stated that the dogmatic for- mulas of the church's magisterium were from the very beginning suitable for communicating revealed truth, and that as they are they remain forever suitable for communicating this truth to those who interpret them correctly. It does not however follow that every one of these formulas has always been or will always be so to the same extent. For this reason theologians seek to define exactly the intention of teaching proper to the various formulas, and in carrying out this work they are of considerable assistance to the living magisterium of the church, to which they remain subordinated. For this reason also it often happens that ancient dogmatic formulas and others closely connected with them remain living and fruitful in the habitual usage of the Church, but with suitable expository and explanatory additions that maintain and clarify their original meaning. In addition, it has sometimes happened that in this habitual usage of the Church certain of these formulas gave way to new expressions which, proposed and approved by the Sacred Magisterium, presented more clearly or more completely the same meaning.

As for the *meaning* of dogmatic formulas, this remains ever true and constant in the church, even when it is expressed with greater clarity or more developed. The faithful therefore must shun the opinion, first, that dogmatic formulas (or some category of them) cannot signify truth in a determinate way, but can only offer changeable approximations to it, which to a certain extent distort or alter it; secondly, that these formulas signify the truth only in an indeterminate way, this truth being like a goal that is constantly being sought by means of such approximations. Those who hold such an opinion do not avoid dogmatic relativism and they corrupt the concept of the church's infallibility relative to the truth to be taught or held in a determinate way.[13]

This statement of the CDF provides official clarification of the sense in which dogmatic statements can be said to be "irreformable." Irreformability is predicated of their *meaning*, which, as the CDF says, "remains ever true and constant in the church, even when it is expressed with greater clarity or more developed." On the other hand, the fact that this meaning can be expressed with greater clarity or be more developed shows that irreformability is not predicated of dogmatic formulas as such.

Several other points in the CDF statement merit a comment. The first is the recognition that considering dogmatic truth in a broader context not only of faith *but also of human knowledge* may result in giving that truth a more perfect expression. Here as an example one could invoke the influence which growth in human knowledge about the origin of the human species has had, and can still have, on our understanding and expression of the doctrine of creation and original sin. Another example is the effect which the discovery of the existence of vast populations which had never heard of Christ had on the understanding of the necessity of Christian faith and baptism for salvation.

My second observation refers to the sentence: "Finally, even though the truths which the church intends to teach through her dogmatic formulas are distinct from the changeable conceptions of a given epoch and can be expressed without them, nevertheless it can sometimes happen that these truths may be enunciated by the sacred magisterium in terms that bear traces of such conceptions." On this point I would share the reservations expressed by Karl Rahner, who has written: "The declaration says explicitly that the Church's magisterium can under certain circumstances enunciate dogmatic truths in terms which bear traces of the 'changeable conceptions of a given epoch.' We are told, however, rather curiously, that anything of this kind only happens 'sometimes' and that there are also truths of faith which could be expressed without historically conditioned terminology of this kind. Here the authors of the document are evidently still influenced by the earlier notion of 'natural' and general human terminology, which can always and everywhere be understood without further explanation, and which is independent of the wider context of the history of thought as a whole."[14]

Rahner is also critical of the declaration's insistence that dogmatic formulations cannot be described as "approximations" to the truth. He observes: "If one dogmatic statement can express the same content in a better, more living, more fruitful, more complete and more perfect way than another (as the document says), then the term *approximatio* does not necessarily have the heretical sense of a dogmatic relativism. It can also mean exactly what this document intends. If a dogmatic formula were to be totally identical with the reality meant—if, that is, it was not an *approximatio* in any way at all—how could there ever be a history of dogma, which the document itself says exists? How could we then talk about better or less adequate dogmatic formulations, let alone about formulations that have to be superseded?"[15]

While I think Rahner's critique is well founded, I also agree with him that this section on the historical character of dogmatic formulations is the best in the whole document, and that we should be glad that this teaching has at last been expressed in an official document of the holy see.[16] Since we have introduced Rahner's criticism of the statement of the CDF, it seems appropriate to see how he answered the question: "What is a dogmatic statement?" This is the title of an article which contains his answer, spelled out in five theses.[17] Here is a summary of his theses.

1. A dogmatic statement claims to be true, in the way that human statements can be true, but it can still bear the stamp of human weakness and guilt. A dogmatic statement therefore can be rash and presumptuous, since the guarantee of speaking the truth does not exclude the possibility of speaking sinfully.

2. A dogmatic statement is a statement of faith not only on the part of its object (what is believed) but also on the part of its speaker (the one who believes). There is more to the act of supernatural faith than the holding of dogmatic propositions; on the other hand, dogmatic reflection and its statement can never separate themselves from the source from which they spring: from faith itself.

3. A dogmatic statement is in a special measure an ecclesiological statement. In the church we must believe and profess our faith in common; hence there has to be an official doctrine of the church. It is the role of the magisterium to present the form of the word that is valid here and now. Hence dogmatic statements signify a ruling on terminology, even though such terminology can never be adequate to the reality it signifies. While respecting the church's ruling on dogmatic language, the theologian can be aware of its limitations, and contribute to the development of better formulations of the faith.

4. A dogmatic statement leads its hearers beyond themselves into the mystery of God. The object to which a dogmatic statement refers is only properly known when it is grasped as something infinite and incomprehensible—as a permanent mystery—in the very act of taking hold of its finite concept. While Rahner does not do so in this context, one could invoke the statement of St. Thomas that the act of faith terminates not in the proposition but in the reality which it signifies.[18]

5. A dogmatic statement is not identical with the original word of revelation and the original statement of faith. The original

statements of faith, given to us in scripture, have one thing no other statement has: they belong to that unique historical event of salvation itself to which all later proclamation and theology are referred. Scripture is the primary norm for the consciousness of faith of the church as a whole and for the church's magisterium; thus the original word of revelation and of faith is essentially distinct from every dogmatic statement. Christians will always hear the original statement in terms of its later statement by the church's magisterium and consciousness of faith. Yet they hear that original statement of faith itself, precisely because they hear it by means of the present church. For the ultimate guarantee of being able to hear the original statement is not the historical skill of man, but the exercise of faith in community with the present-day church.

We have thus summarized Rahner's answer to the question: "What is a dogmatic statement?" Other characteristics of dogmatic statements which have been mentioned elsewhere by Rahner, as well as by other theologians, are the following.

✝   *"Definitive, but also in a certain sense provisional"*
In his important work on dogma, which unfortunately is not available in English, Walter Kasper has emphasized this aspect of the nature of a dogmatic statement.[19] His approach is to insist that dogma reflects the "eschatological" situation of the church itself: that is, the "already–but not yet" situation of the present reality of salvation that is essentially directed toward a fulfillment that will take place only in the definitive kingdom of God. This "already–not yet" tension will characterize the church throughout its historical existence. So also, every historical enunciation of the church's message will be affected by the "not yet" of Christian eschatology. That means that while a dogmatic statement is definitively true, it is still provisional, and must remain open to the future, which can disclose more of the gospel than has been grasped in this interpretation of it. A dogma is a true word, but it is never the last word that can be said about a mystery of faith. Kasper insists that "dogma is under the word of God" also in this sense: that God's word will always surpass any statement, however dogmatic, that the church can say about it.

In their work *Kerygma and Dogma*, Rahner and Karl Lehmann

have expressed analogous ideas about dogma in the following way: "The dogmatic statement can only show forth in a provisional way the final state of things. It is part of the sobriety of dogmatic discourse to remain critically aware of this dual eschatological significance in dogmatic statements. Thus the seriousness which is necessary when dealing with the subject of *salvation* is preserved, but also the provisional nature of all theological formulation can remain more critically present to the mind."[20]

In dogmatic statements, revealed truth may be mingled with ideas which are not part of the binding content of the article of faith.

Here again I will follow Rahner's treatment of this aspect of dogma. He writes:

In the transmission and expression of dogmas properly speaking there may be inseparably mingled ideas, interpretations, etc., which are not part of the binding content of the article of faith concerned but which have not been explicitly separated from this article at a particular epoch in history by traditional theology or even by the Church's magisterium, and for historical reasons cannot be separated up to a certain point in time. There may be such amalgams (if we may use this admittedly problematic expression) even with dogmas properly so called. Not every idea then that was actually but without further reflection brought to bear on the elucidation of the meaning of an article of faith is in principle really an indissoluble part of this article itself...There are amalgams of this kind; in view of the historicity of truth they are simply unavoidable; they will remain (even though in such a way that the elimination of one such amalgam means that another takes its place)...If, (for instance), Pius XII still thought that monogenism is an indispensable and unrenounceable element of the Catholic doctrine of original sin, we may nevertheless hold a different opinion today and, while upholding the doctrine of original sin and its essential meaning, eliminate a monogenistic interpretation of this doctrine as an historically conditioned amalgam, even though the theology of former times and the magisterium never thought and could not have thought of this possibility.[21]

✝ *Dogma is always a partial statement of revealed truth.*

The historical circumstances that have led up to the definition of dogmas of faith have tended to focus the attention of the magisterium on certain aspects of revelation which were then being challenged. Inevitably other aspects of the truth, to which the dogmatic statement did not attend, would be left in oblivion. In interpreting dogmatic statements, therefore, it will be necessary to insert the truth defined by a particular dogma into the broader and more complete picture of revelation. One can compare a dogma to the reproduction of a particular detail in a great painting. The reproduction is useful for calling our attention to the beauty of that particular detail, but it is only when that detail is seen in its place in the whole picture that one can fully appreciate its beauty. So also the full truth of any particular dogma depends on its place in the broader picture. It may need to be balanced by other aspects of the truth which the dogma did not express.

⳨ To sum up: a dogma is an ecclesial proposition which expresses some aspect of divine revelation. Its formulation is always historically and culturally conditioned. It is a true statement, but it never says the whole truth, and it may be mixed with elements that are not part of revealed truth. As a binding ruling on the language of faith, it makes possible a common profession of faith that is vital both to the unity of the church and to its praise and worship of God. A dogma is not identical with the original word of revelation. The truth of a dogmatic statement is guaranteed by the Spirit, but it is not written under the Spirit's inspiration, as scripture is. While a dogma will always be a provisional expression of the word of God, still it leads beyond itself into the ultimate mystery, since the act of faith terminates not in the proposition but in the reality which it signifies.

4 ‖ Identifying Defined Dogmas in Conciliar Decrees

A. CRITERIA

By "defined dogma" we mean: 1) a divinely revealed truth, 2) which has been proclaimed by a solemn judgment, 3) which calls for an irrevocable response of faith and excludes the contradictory proposition as heretical. Let us consider each of these elements in detail.

Divinely Revealed Truth

The Council of Trent describes the gospel as the "source of all saving truth and rule of conduct."[1] "Divinely revealed truth," then, can be described as that saving truth which is contained in the gospel. Now the gospel here does not refer to a written book, but to the whole message of Jesus Christ, the Word of God, and to the entire saving and revealing event of his incarnation, ministry, death and resurrection. As the Tridentine decree further explains, this "saving truth" is contained in written books (the scriptures) and also in "unwritten traditions." Catholics now generally agree that this does not mean that "unwritten traditions" contain important truths of faith which are in no way to be found in scripture. Rather, tradition is to be understood as another way in which the saving truth of the gospel has been handed down and interpreted from generation to generation. Vatican II has described tradition as the process by which "the church, in her teaching, life and worship, perpetuates and hands on to all generations all that she herself is, all that she believes."[2] In this process, the church can come to know more explicitly what is only implicitly contained in the scriptures. For this reason, Vatican II says: "It is not from sacred scripture alone that the church draws her certainty about everything which has been revealed."[3] The church's *certainty* that some truth is really contained in the gospel can be the fruit of "growth in the understanding of the realities and the words which have been handed down," which can come about "through the contemplation and study of believers, who ponder these things in their hearts."[4] "Divinely revealed truth," then, will not necessarily be found explicitly stated in scripture, but it must be really, even if only implicitly, part of the "saving truth" of which the gospel is the source.

For something to be "divinely revealed truth" it is not sufficient that it can be described as a "matter of faith or morals." This expression refers to the total object of the church's teaching authority; in this total object, one distinguishes between a primary and a secondary object. As we have seen above, the latter includes truths which, while not contained in the gospel, are so necessarily connected with some revealed truth that the church needs to be able to speak definitively about them in order to defend or explain that revealed truth. The church can define such "connected truths," but it does not claim to define them as dogmas calling for the response of faith. Rather, it simply requires that Catholics accept and hold them as true.[5] The "primary object" of the magisterium consists of truths which are part of the "saving truth and rule of conduct" of which the gospel is the source; it is only such truths that can be defined as dogmas.

In order to identify a defined dogma in a document of a council, therefore, it is not sufficient to show that the council has expressed a definitive judgment about a matter; it is also necessary to show that the matter so defined belongs to the primary, and not merely to the secondary, object of the magisterium. Sometimes this will be immediately evident in the decree itself, as it is in the solemn definitions of the immaculate conception, of the assumption, and of papal infallibility. In each case, the doctrine was explicitly defined as divinely revealed.[6] However, in earlier councils it is not always so clear that the doctrine on which a definitive judgment is expressed belongs to the primary object of the magisterium. In fact, as we shall see, in some cases it will be quite evident that the matter with which a conciliar canon deals is not revealed truth. In identifying defined dogmas in the documents of earlier councils, therefore, the theologian will have to distinguish between doctrinal decrees which deal with the primary object, and those which deal with the secondary object, of the magisterium. We shall see some examples of these later on.

Proclaimed by a Solemn Judgment

Vatican I has declared that "with divine and Catholic faith all those things must be believed which are contained in the word of God whether written or handed down, and are proposed by the church either by solemn judgment or by the ordinary and universal magisterium as divinely revealed and to be believed as such."[7] Here, by "solemn judgment" is meant the kind of definitive statement that can be made only by an ecumenical council, or by a pope speaking *ex cathedra*. Obviously, not every statement made by an ecumenical council will express such a "solemn judgment." The theologian, then, must be familiar with the criteria by which to distinguish dogmatic definitions from the other kinds of statements found in conciliar decrees.

Here a basic rule is provided by canon law, which states: "No doctrine is understood as infallibly defined unless this fact is clearly established."[8] The Latin of the final phrase reads: "nisi id manifeste constiterit." The neuter pronoun *id* refers to the *fact* that a doctrine has been infallibly defined. What does it mean to say of a fact: "*constat*"? To this question, Harper's *Latin Dictionary* gives the following answer: "constat: *it is settled, established, undisputed, certain, well known.*" While the term *constat* does not specify the criteria by which a fact is recognized as "settled," it does suggest that there will be a general recognition that this is an "established fact." Synonyms such as "undisputed, well known" suggest that one can expect a consensus about a fact if one can say of it: "*constat.*" Furthermore, the canon says that no doctrine is understood to be infallibly defined unless this fact is *manifestly* established. In other words, the fact that a doctrine has been infallibly defined must not only be "settled, undisputed, well known," but must be "manifestly" such. To whom would one expect such a fact to be "manifest" if not to Catholic theologians, whose business it is to evaluate the dogmatic weight of magisterial pronouncements? I conclude that one could hardly claim that the fact that a doctrine had been infallibly defined was *manifestly* "settled, established, undisputed," if there were serious disagreement among Catholic theologians about this alleged fact.

Canon law, therefore, provides a first general criterion for identifying defined dogmas: the fact that a doctrine has been defined has to be manifestly the case, and therefore should also be something about which Catholic theologians are generally agreed. However, it is not so easy to know whether Catholic theologians are agreed on questions of this kind nowadays as it was when they wrote manuals of theology in which they would assign a theological "note" to each thesis. When they all assigned the note *de fide definita* to a thesis, it was clear that there was a consensus that a doctrine had been defined as a dogma of faith. Now that such manuals and their "notes" have gone out of style, there is no simple way to ascertain the fact of such consensus. It is up to the theologian to show, by other criteria, that it is "manifestly the case" that a doctrine has been defined. Some such criteria are the following.

Criteria from the History of the Council

From the study of the history of the council, for which its *acta* are of primary importance, it can become clear that the council was summoned to deal with a dispute about a particular point of Christian doctrine, that it did in fact issue its judgment on this question, and that in the aftermath of the council its judgment was generally received as definitive, and has continued to determine the faith of the church. Here the reception of the conciliar decision by the church at large is a key element in the discernment that its judgment was truly definitive. As an example one might cite the Council of Ephesus in 431. The council was summoned to deal with the dispute caused by Nestorius' rejection of the title "Mother of God" for the Virgin Mary. The basic issue was not Mariological, but Christological, since it implied a failure to see Jesus as one person with the Divine Word. The decision of the council was to condemn the position of Nestorius, and to approve that of his opponent Cyril of Alexandria, who insisted that the Son who was begotten of the Father before all ages was born of the Virgin Mary in time. There is no doubt about the fact that the Council of Ephesus issued a definitive judgment which has continued to determine the faith of the church on this issue.

However, while it is evident that the council decided in favor of the doctrine of Cyril against that of Nestorius, it is not at all evident that it was the intention of the council to approve of every detail of Cyril's doctrine, and, in particular, of the twelve "anathemas" which he pronounced against the doctrine of his opponents.[9] It is now generally agreed that the council did not make those twelve "anathemas" its own, and that they do not constitute conciliar definitions. Here again the basis for this conclusion is found in the *acta* of the council, and in the fact that subsequently there was no such universal reception of the doctrine of the "anathemas" as there was of the essential point on which the doctrine of Nestorius was rejected and that of Cyril approved.

The history of a council, and especially its *acta*, are prime sources for the kind of information needed to decide exactly what question the council intended to settle, and which of its statements meet the criteria for the definition of a dogma of faith. No doubt, of great importance here are indications of the intention on the part of the council to issue a definitive judgment on an issue. This has sometimes been taken to mean that one should look for indications of the intention to speak with infallibility. However, this is mistaken, since there is no evidence that the bishops who took part in the councils of the first millennium were explicitly aware of the infallibility of their decisions. The first discussion of the infallibility of conciliar definitions appears only in the ninth century.[10]

Even in the second millennium one does not find in the *acta* of western councils the expressed intention to invoke the privilege of speaking with infallibility. What one rightly looks for, however, is evidence of the intention to issue a definitive judgment on an issue of faith. In the language of St. Thomas, this meant, for instance, to formulate a new version of the creed, or to clarify a dogmatic decision taken by an earlier council. Here, as he put it, it was a question of "decisively settling matters of faith, to the end that all hold them with unshaken faith."[11] One place to look for indications of an intention to speak definitively on an issue is in the *acta* of the council. But of course one looks also in the conciliar decrees themselves.

Criteria in the Text of the Conciliar Decrees

Literary Genre

We have become accustomed to the necessity of identifying the literary genre of a book or part of a book of scripture as a first step in determining the meaning which the author intended to express. There are also a variety of literary genres in documents of councils, the recognition of which is likewise an important step in evaluating the dogmatic weight which the council intended to give to its teaching.

To begin with the most recent council: as we have seen above, Vatican II named two of its documents "dogmatic constitutions," one simply a "constitution," another a "pastoral constitution"; it called nine of them "decrees," and three of them "declarations." If the council had intended to issue any solemn dogmatic definitions, one would surely be more likely to find them in the "dogmatic constitutions" than in the "decrees" and "declarations." The fact is that in none of these documents do we find clear indications of the intention to define any doctrine as a dogma of faith. However, in the "dogmatic constitutions" we do find some important doctrinal statements, which have settled, without solemnly defining them, issues which had been disputed among Catholic theologians. Examples of this are the collegial nature of the hierarchy and the sacramentality of episcopal consecration.

In any case, one important conclusion to draw from the consideration of the documents of Vatican II is that documents of ecumenical councils may belong to the literary genre of authoritative but non-definitive expositions of Catholic doctrine. We should not be surprised to find that some of the documents of other ecumenical councils may also belong to this genre.

Distinction Between Chapters and Canons

When we examine the preceding council, Vatican I, we find that it produced two "dogmatic constitutions," each of which consists of a prologue, four chapters (*capita*), and a number of canons corresponding to the matter treated in the chapters. In the first dogmatic constitution, *Dei Filius*, on the Catholic faith, the canons are given all together at the end, with numbers that correspond to the number of the chapter to which they refer. In the second dogmatic constitution, *Pastor aeternus*, on the church of Christ, each chapter is immediately followed by one canon.

While there is some resemblance between the "chapters" of Vatican I and the chapters of a document like *Lumen gentium* of Vatican II (although those of Vatican I are much briefer and denser), there is nothing in Vatican II that corresponds to the canons of Vatican I. What is distinctive of these is that they are in the form of a sentence of excommunication pronounced against anyone who contradicts specific points of the doctrine which has been set forth in the corresponding chapter. As an illustration, let us look at the briefest of them all, the one that follows the fourth chapter of *Pastor aeternus*. It says: "But if anyone presumes to contradict this our definition—which God forbid—let him be anathema."[12] By "this our definition," the canon obviously refers to the immediately preceding conclusion to chapter 4 of the constitution, in which the council said: "We teach and define that it is a divinely revealed dogma that the Roman pontiff when he speaks *ex cathedra*...possesses that infallibility with which the Divine Redeemer wished his church to be endowed in defining doctrine of faith and morals."[13] The phrase: "let him be anathema" is an ancient way of pronouncing a sentence of excommunication.

It is obvious that pronouncing a sentence of excommunication against anyone who presumes to contradict its teaching is a good indication of the council's intention to speak in a definitive way on that issue. In this case, the text of the chapter expresses its intention to define the doctrine of papal infallibility, and the canon refers explicitly to "this our definition." There can be no doubt about the fact that in the conclusion of chapter 4 of *Pastor aeternus* we find a defined dogma of faith. It is also important to note that it is to this "definition" alone that the canon refers. This leaves the question: What about the doctrine in the rest of chapter 4? Here we find testimonies drawn from previous councils in favor of the doctrine of papal infallibility; a description of the way in which Roman pontiffs have exercised their teaching role; the citation of a text of scripture in which a promise of such infallibil-

ity has been seen; an explanation of the purpose of papal infallibility, and of the reason for defining it. What is said here provides
important indications of how the doctrine of papal infallibility is
to be understood. But there is no language in this part of the
chapter that suggests that the council intended to define what it
said there. It is an authoritative exposition of the doctrine of
papal infallibility, providing a justification and explanation of the
defined doctrine. But only that part of the chapter to which the
canon corresponds is actually a dogmatic definition.

When we examine the rest of the documents of Vatican I we
find that nowhere else has the council expressly said: "we
define." However, each of the other chapters of *Pastor aeternus* is
followed by a canon, and each of the four chapters of *Dei Filius*
has several corresponding canons. These canons pronounce the
sentence of "anathema" against those who presume to contradict
certain elements of the doctrine contained in the corresponding
chapters. The gravity of such a sentence expresses the intention
to define the positive statement whose contradiction is condemned in the canon, even though in the chapter the council
does not use the term: "we define." One can therefore identify as
doctrine defined by Vatican I only those precise statements
whose contradiction is condemned in the corresponding canons.
The rest of what is contained in the chapters is authoritative, but
non-definitive exposition of Catholic doctrine.

We must now ask whether the solemn judgments pronounced
by Vatican I meet the third requirement for a dogmatic definition:

*A solemn judgment which calls for an irrevocable assent of faith and
excludes the contradictory proposition as heretical.*

As we have seen, in its solemn definition of papal infallibility,
the council declares this to be a divinely revealed dogma; and in
Dei Filius it declares that all such dogmas are to be believed with
"divine and Catholic faith." There is no doubt, then, that this
solemn judgment calls for an irrevocable assent of faith. The
canon which pronounces "anathema" against anyone who would
"presume to contradict it" equivalently declares such a person
guilty of heresy, which canon law defines as "the obstinate denial
or doubt, after baptism, of a truth which must be believed by
divine and Catholic faith."[14]

We do not find elsewhere in the teaching of Vatican I any such explicit definition of a doctrine as "divinely revealed dogma," but, as we have seen, each chapter has one or more corresponding canons which pronounce the "anathema" against those who would contradict the key statements of the chapter. There is a good presumption that the "anathemas" mean that the contradictory proposition is heretical. This presumption is confirmed by the examination of the positive statements contained in the chapters to which the canons correspond: they are clearly taught as truths found in revelation. A further confirmation comes from the "Epilogue" of *Dei Filius* where, after its series of canons, the council says: "It is not enough to avoid the malice of heresy, unless those errors which lead close to it are also carefully avoided."[15] This indicates the judgment of the council that the errors which it has condemned in its canons would indeed involve the malice of heresy. Hence I believe one can safely conclude that Vatican I has defined as dogmas of faith those statements in its chapters to which the corresponding canons refer, and has condemned the contradictory propositions as heretical.

When we come to identify defined dogmas in the decrees of the Council of Trent, matters will be somewhat more complicated. In most of its decrees, Trent gave a positive exposition of Catholic doctrine in its "chapters," followed by canons which condemned those who would contradict certain elements of the doctrine in the chapters. As at Vatican I, this system highlights the statements in the chapters which the council intended to define, leaving the rest of what is said in the chapter as authoritative but non-definitive exposition of Catholic doctrine. However, some decrees, such as that on original sin[16] and that on the sacraments,[17] after a brief prologue, consist exclusively of canons. The canons on original sin, besides the doctrine which the council intends to define by condemning the contradictory with an anathema, also cite the scriptural texts on which the doctrine is based. There is no indication that the council intended to define the sense of those texts, so that one has to distinguish, within the canons themselves, between what is defined doctrine, and what, like the citation of biblical texts, is merely expository. The canons on the sacraments do not offer this complication.

A more serious problem, in identifying defined dogmas in the decrees of Trent, is that we cannot conclude, from the fact that

its canons pronounce "anathema" against anyone who would contradict a proposition, that this proposition is being defined as a dogma of faith. It is true that "anathema" is a sentence of excommunication, pronounced against a person judged guilty of heresy. The problem is that at Trent, and at other councils before
— Trent, the term "heresy" had a broader meaning than it has in modern canon law. It included not only the denial of a truth which must be believed with divine and Catholic faith, but also ways of believing and acting which would endanger either one's own faith or that of the community. The fathers of Trent saw such danger to the faith of the Catholic people in many things which the reformers were saying and doing, over and above their denial of what Catholics held to be divinely revealed truth. The rejection of traditional beliefs and practices sacred to Catholics also merited an "anathema" in the eyes of the bishops at Trent. There is no doubt that a number of the canons of Trent pronounce the sentence of excommunication against those who reject beliefs or practices which, while traditional, are not part of the deposit of faith. In such cases, the "anathema" does not help
— us to identify a defined dogma. It is up to the theologian, then, to determine whether, in any particular case, the proposition to which the canon refers belongs to the primary object of magisterium—in other words, whether its denial would constitute heresy in the strict sense of modern canon law or in the broader sense the term had at Trent.
— Let us look at a few examples of canons which fall into the latter category.

"If anyone says that the accepted and approved rites of the Catholic Church which are customarily used in the solemn administration of the sacraments may be despised or omitted without sin by the ministers as they please, or that they may be changed to other new rites by any pastor in the Church, a.s."[18]

"If anyone says that, when those baptized as little children have grown up, they are to be asked whether they wish to ratify what their sponsors promised in their name when they were baptized; and if they answer that they are unwilling, they are to be left to their own judgment; and if anyone says that they are not meanwhile to be forced to a Christian life by any penalty other than the exclusion from receiving the eucharist and the other sacraments until they repent, a.s."[19]

"If anyone denies that each and all of Christ's faithful of both sexes are bound, when they reach the age of reason, to receive communion once a year, at least during the paschal season, according to the precept of holy mother church, a.s."[20]

"If anyone says that confession of all sins as it is observed in the church is impossible and is a human tradition which pious people must abolish, or that it is not binding on each and all of the faithful of Christ of either sex once a year in accordance with the constitution of the great Lateran Council, and that for this reason the faithful of Christ are to be persuaded not to confess during Lent, a.s."[21]

"If anyone says that besides the priesthood there are in the Catholic Church no other orders, major or minor, by which, as by various steps, one advances toward the priesthood, a.s."[22]

"If anyone says that marriage contracted but not consummated is not dissolved by the solemn religious profession of one of the spouses, a.s."[23]

"If anyone says that the prohibition of the solemnization of marriages at certain times of the year is a tyrannical superstition, derived from pagan superstition, or condemns the blessing and other ceremonies which the church uses in solemn nuptials, a.s."[24]

While it is quite clear that in none of the canons we have just quoted is there question of divinely revealed truth, Trent's decree on the sacrament of the eucharist includes a canon which offers an interesting example of the necessity of distinguishing, within a canon, between what refers to revealed truth and what does not. The canon is as follows: "If anyone says that in the holy sacrament of the eucharist the substance of bread and wine remains together with the body and blood of our Lord Jesus Christ, and denies that wonderful and unique change of the whole substance of the bread into his body and of the whole substance of the wine into his blood while only the species of bread and wine remain, a change which the Catholic Church very fittingly calls transubstantiation, a.s."[25] Here what is defined as a dogma of faith is the "wonderful and unique change of the whole substance of bread," etc. On the other hand, that the church "very fittingly" calls this change of substance by the name "transubstantiation" is hardly something that God has revealed. From the fact that this clause is included within a canon that ends with "anathema sit" it does not follow that one would be a heretic, in the modern sense of the term, if one questioned the "fittingness" of the term "transubstantiation," provided one did not question the doctrine that Trent meant to express by the use of that term.

What is true of the broader meaning of "heresy" in earlier councils is also true of the correlative term "faith." This denoted an attitude of fidelity to the Christian tradition, which meant not only the acceptance of revealed truth, but also the acceptance of truths connected with revelation, and the rejection of whatever could endanger one's faith. Earlier councils sometimes defined, as doctrines of faith, truths that were merely connected with revelation, and condemned as heretics those who denied them. An example of this is the definition by the Council of Vienne (1311-1312) that the soul is the "form" of the body. The text is as follows:

> With the approval of the holy council we reject as erroneous and contrary to the truth of the Catholic faith any doctrine or opinion which rashly asserts that the substance of the rational and intellectual soul is not truly and of itself the form of the human body, or which calls this into doubt. In order that the truth of the pure faith may be known to all, and the path to error barred, we define that from now on whoever presumes to assert, defend, or obstinately hold that the rational and intellectual soul is not of itself and essentially the form of the human body is to be censured as a heretic.[26]

The fact that the council proposed its doctrine that the soul is the form of the body as a matter that pertains to "the truth of the Catholic faith" explains the condemnation of its denial as heresy. But at that time, it was sufficient that the doctrine "pertained" to the faith, in the sense that the council saw a *danger* to the faith in its denial. Albert Lang, a renowned medieval scholar, concludes his study of this decree as follows:

> On the sole basis of the expressions: "the truth of Catholic faith" and "heretic," one cannot conclude that the decree is a definition of faith in the sense of "divine faith." These expressions prove only that the council judged the doctrine to pertain to faith in the

broader sense, or to the "integrity of faith."...The little that remains of the acts of the council is enough to show that "faith" and "heresy" were understood by the council fathers in the broader sense that was common in those days.[27]

Another example of the use of the term "heretic" in the same Council of Vienne is the following: "If anyone should fall into the error of obstinately affirming that to practice usury is not a sin, we decree that he is to be punished as a heretic."[28] It is to be noted that, at that time, usury meant the taking of any interest whatever on a loan. It would be a mistake to conclude from the use of "heretic" by the Council of Vienne that the sinfulness of usury has been defined as a dogma.

Another term that up to the time of Trent had a broader meaning than it has in modern Catholic usage is the term "we define." As it was used by Pius IX and Pius XII in their decrees on the immaculate conception and the assumption, there is no doubt that this term expressed their intention to speak *ex cathedra* and to promulgate a dogma of faith. However, one cannot be sure that the term (often spelled *diffinimus* in earlier documents) had the same technical sense. An interesting example of the use of *diffinimus* in a conciliar decree is found in the Decree for the Greeks of the Council of Florence (1439-1445). This was a "council of reunion," which attempted to bring about reconciliation between the eastern and western churches. One of the major sources of friction was the fact that the western church had added the term *Filioque* to the common creed, expressing the western theology of the procession of the Holy Spirit from the Father *and from* the Son, whereas eastern theology taught that the Spirit proceeded from the Father *alone*, or from the Father *through* the Son. The council took up this problem, and offered a compromise solution, which we need not go into here. It concluded by saying: "Furthermore we define (*diffinimus*) that the explanatory term 'Filioque' was legitimately and reasonably added to the creed for the sake of declaring the truth and because of a need that was urgent at that time."[29] This "definition" is certainly not a dogma of faith; in fact it can scarcely be described as altogether true. The fact is that when the *Filioque* was introduced into the creed by the Frankish Church during the ninth century, the pope of the time, Pope Leo III, strenuously objected to this innovation, and refused to permit the creed to be recited in Rome with this word added to it. It was only two centuries later that the creed began to be sung in Rome with the *Filioque*. So there are good reasons to question the claim that this was "legitimately and reasonably added to the creed," and "because of urgent need"—which of course is not the same as to question the soundness of the theology involved. So the term "we define" in this statement has to be taken with a grain of salt. Perhaps what it really means here, expressing the mind of the western majority at the council, is: "We insist."

Distinction Between Doctrinal and Disciplinary Canons

While the broader meaning which such terms as "heresy" and "anathema sit" had in documents of the earlier councils obliges us to exercise caution, it remains true that in many cases conciliar canons are valuable pointers to the propositions which a council intended to define as dogmas. But this will be true only when the canons in question are doctrinal and not merely disciplinary in nature. By far the greater number of canons decreed by councils prior to Trent are of the latter kind; most of them have contributed more to the development of canon law than to the development of dogma.

To look at a few examples: the First Council of Nicea (325) concluded its creed by anathematizing those who held doctrine contrary to what the council defined about Christ. After this doctrinal decree, it issued a number of canons, all disciplinary in character. A similar procedure was followed by the First Council of Constantinople (381), by that of Chalcedon (451), and by Constantinople III (681). The attention of the medieval western councils was given more to problems of church government than to doctrinal disputes; thus the canons of the first three Councils of the Lateran (1123, 1143, and 1179) and the First Council of Lyons (1245) were exclusively disciplinary in nature. The Fourth Lateran Council (1215), which was by far the most important of the medieval ones, framed its decrees in the form of seventy "constitutions," of which the first two were doctrinal, and the rest disciplinary. The Second Council of Lyons (1274) produced two constitutions, the first of which dealt with the preparation of a crusade against the Saracens. The second constitution consisted of thirty-one chapters, only the first of which dealt with doctrine; the rest were disciplinary.

These details suggest the kind of care to be taken when one looks to conciliar canons as pointers to dogmatic definitions. In many cases they can help one to identify the dogmas which a council intended to define. But one must be sure that one is dealing with doctrinal canons, and be aware of the fact that some key terms used by earlier councils had a broader sense than they now have in Catholic usage. Failure to take this into account would lead to attributing dogmatic status to a good many propositions which in fact are not dogmas at all.

5 ‖ Identifying Defined Dogmas in Conciliar Decrees

B. APPLICATION OF CRITERIA

Our purpose in this chapter is to examine the decrees of the ecumenical councils, to identify the dogmatic definitions issued by these councils, applying the criteria we have discussed in the previous chapter. We shall, of course, look only to the doctrinal decrees, keeping in mind that not every statement in a doctrinal decree will be a dogmatic definition. We shall look for indications of a council's intention to express a definitive judgment on a doctrinal issue, to give a binding interpretation of some article of faith. In almost all cases dogmas have been defined because some article of faith was perceived as being challenged by erroneous teaching. Hence, knowledge of the controversy which occasioned the summoning of the council will be of prime importance in identifying the point of doctrine which the council intended to settle. Since doctrinal decrees were intended to exclude erroneous interpretations of the faith, in most cases the positive decrees are followed by condemnations of the opposing errors as heresies, with a sentence of excommunication (*anathema*) against those who obstinately hold them. As we have seen, such condemnations were often expressed in canons, which provide clues as to the precise points of doctrine which the council intended to define. However, not all councils added such canons to its decrees; in such cases, one must use other criteria to identify the dogmatic definitions that are contained in the conciliar decrees.

Nicea I (325)[1]

The First Council of Nicea was summoned by Emperor Constantine to deal with the controversy caused by the doctrine of Arius, who attributed to the Word of God the properties of a created being, and thus effectively denied the divinity of Christ. Using what was an already existing baptismal creed, the council added to it several terms which clearly asserted the divinity of the Son of God. I have indicated those terms by adding emphasis:

> We believe in one God, the Father almighty, maker of all things, visible and invisible.
> And in one Lord Jesus Christ, the Son of God, the only-begotten generated by the Father, *that is, from the being (ousia) of the Father*, God from God, light from light, *true* God from *true* God; begotten, *not made, one in being (homoousios) with the Father*, through whom all things were made, those in heaven and those on earth. For us men and for our salvation he came down, and became flesh, was made man, suffered, and rose again on the third day. He ascended to the heavens and shall come again to judge the living and the dead. And in the Holy Spirit.
> As for those who say: "There was a time when he was not" and "Before being begotten he was not," and who declare that he was made from nothing, or that the Son of God is from a different substance (*hypostasis*) or being (*ousia*), subject to change and alteration—these the catholic and apostolic church anathematizes.

By comparing the doctrines which the council anathematized, with the emphasized phrases of the creed, one sees exactly what the council intended to define: the true divinity of the Son of God. There is no reason to think that the council intended to define any of the other articles of the baptismal creed which it used as the vehicle for its definition. Undoubtedly those are also articles of faith, but they cannot be said to have been defined by the Council of Nicea. Many of them will remain undefined dogmas, since the church has not seen the need to define them.

The Council of Nicea was followed by several decades of bitter controversy over the council's term *homoousios*. While some objected to the term as unscriptural, a more serious charge was that it would blur or deny the real distinction between Father and Son, and thus lead to the heresy of "modalism." The distinction in God between the one *ousia* and three *hypostaseis* had still to be worked out at that time, as one can see from the use of these terms in the Nicene "anathema," where they are taken as synonymous. In any case, the dogmatic decision of Nicea prevailed over Arianism and semi-Arianism, and remains as one of the pillars of the Christian doctrine of the Trinity.

Constantinople I (381)[2]

The seven councils of the first millennium which are recognized as ecumenical by both the Orthodox and the Catholic Churches were all summoned by the emperors (not by the popes), and the bishops who took part in them were almost all from the east. However, the First Council of Constantinople is exceptional, in that no representative of the bishop of Rome or of the whole western church took part in it. It was in fact a regional council of the eastern church, and only with the passage of more than a century did it achieve ecumenical status through its reception by the western church. Its creed attained its full recognition through its confirmation by the Council of Chalcedon in 451. Subsequently this creed became the common baptismal creed of the eastern church, and then the liturgical creed of the churches of both east and west.

The decrees of the First Council of Constantinople consist of its creed and seven canons, only the first of which is doctrinal in nature. It confirms the Nicene Creed, and anathematizes the principal heretics of the day, including those known as Pneumatomachi ("opponents of the Spirit") and the followers of Apollinarius. The latter denied the full humanity of Christ, holding that, being the divine Logos incarnate, he did not have a human mind. In the post-conciliar letter which the bishops sent to Pope Damasus, they insisted that the humanity of Jesus was "not soulless nor mindless nor imperfect."[3] This affirmation by Constantinople I of the full humanity of Jesus, with the corresponding condemnation of the Apollinarian heresy, is significant for the development of Christology.

The other doctrinal problem with which the council dealt was the denial of the divinity of the Holy Spirit by the

Pneumatomachi. To refute this heresy, the fathers of the council found it sufficient to use a baptismal creed already in use, which, in its developed third article, clearly included a profession of faith in the divinity of the Holy Spirit. This was a "Nicene creed" in the sense that it included the key phrases by which the Council of Nicea had defined the divinity of the Son. At this time there was no one common baptismal creed in the east, but the various creeds were made "Nicene" by the addition of those phrases.

The original creed of Nicea had, as its third article, only the words: "And in the Holy Spirit." However, the baptismal creed which Constantinople I adopted as its own said: "And in the Holy Spirit, the Lord and giver of Life, who proceeds from the Father, who together with the Father and the Son is worshiped and glorified, who has spoken through the prophets." Here the fathers of Constantinople saw a confession of faith in the divinity of the Spirit, whose confirmation by the council would suffice to settle the question which the Pneumatomachi had raised. Hence they saw no need to do more than confirm this creed with conciliar authority. As we have seen, in their first canon they included the Pneumatomachi among those whom they anathematized.

From contemporary history we are well informed as to what this council intended to define, and we know how it accomplished its purpose. There is no reason to think that, in adopting the creed which it used, it intended to define any of the other articles of which it was composed. As confessed in an orthodox baptismal creed, these were already articles of faith, and remain such, even though some of them have never been defined. The full humanity of Jesus, and the divinity of the Spirit, are defined dogmas, which gained their full dogmatic value when the First Council of Constantinople was recognized by the west as an ecumenical council, and its decisions were confirmed by the Council of Chalcedon in 451.

Council of Ephesus (431)[4]

Since I have already described the work of the Council of Ephesus in the previous chapter, little more needs to be said here. The unique feature of this council is the fact that its dogmatic decision was expressed in the solemn approval which it gave to the doctrine of Cyril's second letter to Nestorius, and its condemnation as heretical of the doctrine of Nestorius' reply, followed by the condemnation of Nestorius in person. It is clear that the precise doctrine which it thereby defined was that the divine Son of God was truly born of the Virgin Mary according to the flesh, which meant that Mary's Son is truly divine, and Mary is rightly called *Theotokos*: Mother of God.

The council also listened to a third letter of Cyril to Nestorius, which concluded with twelve anathemas against various errors attributed to Nestorius. However, the council did not give conciliar weight to every expression of Cyril's doctrine in that third letter, or make his anathemas its own. Hence it is generally agreed that it is only the essential point of difference between Cyril and Nestorius that was the object of solemn dogmatic definition.

Council of Chalcedon (451)[5]

As we have seen, the first two councils settled the doctrinal disputes which they were summoned to resolve by solemnly proposing a profession of faith in which the dogma they intended to define was included. One of the canons of the Council of Ephesus decreed: "It is not permitted to produce or write or compose any other creed except the one which was defined by the holy fathers who were gathered together in the Holy Spirit at Nicea."[6] In view of this canon, the fathers at Chalcedon were very reluctant to issue their decision in the form of a creed. Yet it had become clear that a further definitive statement was needed to clarify the meaning of the creed. For this purpose, Chalcedon issued not a new creed, but a "definition of faith," in which it *taught* how the faith was to be confessed.

The controversy that led to the Council of Chalcedon was rooted in the different approaches to the mystery of Christ taken by the two great theological schools of the ancient church: Alexandria and Antioch. Alexandria stressed the unity of Christ in the one divine person of the Word; Antioch stressed the distinction of natures, with special emphasis on the free human will of Christ. While Antiochenes spoke of two natures (*physeis*) in Christ, the Alexandrians, following Cyril, spoke of "one incarnate nature of the Word." Cyril himself understood this formula in a way that recognized the existence in the incarnate Word of divinity and humanity as truly distinct. In his second letter to Nestorius, which was approved as orthodox by the Council of Ephesus, Cyril insisted that the distinctness of the natures was not destroyed by their union.[7] However, after Cyril's death, his followers stressed the "one incarnate nature" formula to the point that this seemed to mean that in Christ the humanity was so "divinized" by the hypostatic union as to be really absorbed by the divinity. In any case, they claimed that only Nestorians would speak of two *physeis* in Christ.

The most vigorous proponent of "monophysism" was an aged and venerable monk of Constantinople, Eutyches, whose doctrine was condemned by a synod led by the bishop of Constantinople, Flavian, in 448. When Cyril's successor as bishop of Alexandria, Dioscorus, protested against this condemnation, Flavian appealed to Leo I, bishop of Rome, for support, and received the famous "Tome to Flavian" in which Pope Leo strongly suppported the doctrine of two natures in Christ.[8] However, Emperor Theodosius II sided with Eutyches and Dioscorus, and summoned a council, held in Ephesus in 449, in which Eutyches was absolved and Flavian was condemned. This has come down in history as the "robber synod," so named by Leo I, who denounced it as illegitimate and rejected its decisions.

The death of Theodosius II and the enthronement of Marcian as his successor meant the end of imperial support for Dioscorus and his party. Marcian, with the approval of Pope Leo, summoned the Council of Chalcedon, which renewed the condemnation of Eutyches, and approved the doctrine of Leo's Tome to Flavian. Given the history of the controversy, it is clear what the council intended to define. On the one hand, it confirmed the doctrine of the first, authentic council of Ephesus, rejecting the Nestorian division of Christ into two persons. But it likewise clearly defined the existence of two distinct natures in Christ, expressing this in the following terms: "We confess that one and the same Lord Jesus Christ, the only-begotten Son, must be acknowledged in two natures, without confusion or change, without division or separation. The distinction between the natures was never abolished by their union but rather the character proper to each of the two natures was preserved as they came together in one person (*prosopon*) and one *hypostasis*."[9]

The council concluded its "Definition of Faith" with a last paragraph (not a separate doctrinal canon), warning of the penalties that would be imposed on anyone who would think or teach otherwise than is laid down in this definition. Sad to say, a great many Christians would continue to think and teach otherwise, since the bishops of Alexandria, followed by the Egyptian and some other eastern churches, continued to insist that the doctrine of two *physeis* was really Nestorian, and that Cyril's formula, "One incarnate *physis* of the Word," was the orthodox one. This led to a long-lasting breakdown of the unity of both the church and the empire in the east, which Emperor Justinian, in the sixth century, tried to heal by an action which he thought would appease and reconcile the Monophysites. This was the condemnation of three long-dead bishops whom the Council of Chalcedon had accepted as orthodox, but whom the Monophysites judged guilty of Nestorianism because, among other reasons, they had dared to criticize the doctrine of Cyril of Alexandria. This leads us to the next council.

Constantinople II (553)[10]

This is known as the "Council of the Three Chapters," these three being the doctrine and person of Theodore of Mopsuestia, and some writings of Theodoret of Cyrrhus and Ibas of Edessa. The council's decree consists of fourteen canons all ending with a sentence of anathema. The first ten spell out in further detail the doctrine of the Councils of Ephesus and Chalcedon, condemning both Nestorianism and Monophysism, occasionally mentioning Theodore of Mopsuestia among the Nestorians. The language used favors the Alexandrian rather than the Antiochene school, and care is taken to give an orthodox explanation of Cyril's formula: "One incarnate nature of God the Word." While these canons are doctrinal in nature, they do not define any new dogma. The eleventh canon is a global condemnation of various heresies that had already been condemned. The twelfth condemns Theodore and his writings as heretical, giving various examples of doctrines attributed to him which would show him guilty of Nestorianism.

The thirteenth condemns the writings of Theodoret in which he had criticized the doctrine, and especially the twelve anathemas, of Cyril of Alexandria. The fourteenth condemns a letter of Ibas in which he had dared to do the same.

The pope of the time, Vigilius, had condemned various propositions attributed to Theodore of Mopsuestia, but he refused to condemn him as a heretic, or to condemn the writings of the other two, since they had been approved as orthodox by the Council of Chalcedon. For his refusal to go along with Justinian and the council which the emperor had summoned for the express purpose of condemning the "Three Chapters," Vigilius was excommunicated by the council and imprisoned by the emperor until he eventually gave in to the pressure and signed the conciliar decree. Because Pope Vigilius actually confirmed the action of the council, even under duress, his successors in Rome upheld the validity of the council, but a great many bishops of the west refused to accept it, and broke off communion with Rome as a result. It took over a century to heal the schism that followed.

The "Council of the Three Chapters" certainly does not go down as a glorious chapter in the history of councils or of the papacy. What about the dogmatic value of its decrees? Its first eleven canons, while doctrinal in nature, do not define any distinctively new dogmas. In some respects they clarify the meaning of the dogmas of Ephesus and Chalcedon, giving them a somewhat more "Alexandrian" formulation. The canons condemning the "Three Chapters" certainly contain no new dogma. Furthermore, it is now generally agreed that Theodoret and Ibas were orthodox, as the Council of Chalcedon had recognized them to be, and that while there were defects in the doctrine of Theodore of Mopsuestia that made him sound like a Nestorian, one must keep in mind that he died three years before the Council of Ephesus, in good standing as a bishop in the church. He certainly was not guilty of heresy in the modern sense of the term. It is questionable whether his doctrine should be called heretical, since it represented a stage in the development of doctrine when it had not yet become clear how one could attribute human birth and death to the divine person of the Word without thereby attributing such things to his divine nature. The fact is that no one nowadays takes these condemnations seriously. They certainly do not involve the infallibility which ecumenical councils have when they define dogmas of faith.

Constantinople III (681)[11]

While the continued rejection of the doctrine of the Council of Chalcedon on the part of several great churches of the East kept them alienated from the rest of Christendom and the Roman empire, a tendency toward a mitigated form of monophysism on the part of some in the east led to the doctrine that in Christ there was only one mode of activity and only one will. This doctrine was held by Sergius, the patriarch of Constantinople, who wrote a letter to Pope Honorius seeking papal approval of his view. Honorius did not see the question as having serious theological consequences, and in two letters written in 634 replied that it was one for grammarians to decide.[12] Unfortunately, Honorius badly underrated the importance of the controversy, which after his death was settled at the Third Council of Constantinople by its solemn confirmation of the decision of Pope Agatho[13] and a Roman synod[14] in favor of the doctrine of two modes of activity and two wills in Christ. There is no doubt about the fact that the council defined this doctrine as a dogma of faith in its "Exposition of Faith" promulgated on September 16, 681.[15] In an earlier session, after condemning Sergius along with several of his successors in the see of Constantinople as heretics, the council went on to anathematize Pope Honorius, on the grounds that in his letters to Sergius he had "confirmed that man's impious opinions."[16] Of course, by this time Honorius was in his tomb, so it was a question of damning his memory.

Agatho's successor, Leo II, confirmed the decrees of the council, including its condemnation of Honorius, who, as he said, had "allowed the immaculate faith of this apostolic church to be stained by an unholy betrayal."[17] Obviously, Honorius was not guilty of heresy in the modern sense of the term, nor had he even remotely intended to issue a definitive decision on the matter in his letters to Sergius. So there is question of the exercise of infallibility neither on his part, nor on the part of the council in issuing its anathema against him. But it did issue a dogmatic definition on the doctrinal question, and thus brought to a close the series of ecumenical councils which determined the basic elements of our Trinitarian and Christological faith.

Second Council of Nicea (787)[18]

A series of Christian emperors, from 730 to 780, forbade the veneration of images, and cruelly persecuted the Christians, especially the monks, who resisted their edicts. In 753 one of these emperors, Constantine V, summoned a council of more than 300 bishops and got them to condemn the veneration of images as idolatrous. When Irene, the widow of the last "iconoclast" emperor, came to power, she lost no time in calling for a new council to reverse the decision of the previous one. With the approval of Pope Adrian I, the council took place in 787 and issued a solemn decree approving the veneration of images and distinguishing such veneration from the worship that is due to God alone. It further explained that one who venerates an image venerates the person represented by it. The bishops also saw the veneration of images representing Jesus as a confirmation of the Christological dogma concerning his true humanity.

If one asks in what sense the council's condemnation of iconoclasm and approval of the use of sacred images involves revealed truth, I believe one could answer that it is an interpretation of the biblical commandment against idolatry, defining that the veneration of sacred images that is traditional in the church does not constitute the sin of idolatry forbidden by this commandment. In that sense its definition can be understood as a dogma of faith.

Fourth Council of Constantinople (869-701)[19]

This council is not recognized by the Orthodox as ecumenical, and is actually of doubtful ecumenicity, since Pope John VIII (872-882) declared it to be abrogated.[20] Its principal action was to depose Photius, patriarch of Constantinople. Its only canon of a doctrinal nature anathematized those who held that the human person has two souls.[21] While it condemned this opinion as heretical, it would seem that here the term was used of an opinion that was seen to endanger the faith, rather than as one clearly contradicting a revealed truth. Hence it would not involve a dogma of faith.

Medieval General Councils

For the Orthodox and other Eastern Christians, an ecumenical council must involve the participation and consensus of the five patriarchal churches: Rome, Constantinople, Alexandria, Antioch and Jerusalem. Hence they insist that no ecumenical council has taken place in the second millennium. In the west also, for many centuries after the break with the east, an ecumenical council was still thought to require the participation of both east and west. However, by the twelfth century, it became clear that there was need of holding general councils to discuss and decide the affairs of western Christendom. These councils were summoned by the pope, and not only bishops and abbots from all regions of Europe but also secular rulers took part in them, since they dealt more often with disciplinary and political matters than with doctrine. Three such councils were held in Rome in the twelfth century: Lateran Councils I, II and III. Since these councils issued only disciplinary decrees, we shall pass over them, and go directly to the following one, which issued an important doctrinal decree.

Fourth Lateran Council (1215)[22]

This council, over which Pope Innocent III presided, issued its decrees in the form of seventy constitutions, of which only the first two are doctrinal in nature. The first of these, entitled "On the Catholic Faith," is also known by its first word: *Firmiter*. It is a conciliar profession of faith, beginning: "We firmly believe and simply confess..."[23] It has the structure of the baptismal creed, devoting a paragraph to matters concerning each of the three articles, but going well beyond both the Roman creed and the Creed of Constantinople in the way it spells out the elements of doctrine in each article. The contents are totally positive in nature; no explicit mention is made of any contrary doctrine which the council intended to condemn. Needless to say, a great deal of what this profession of faith affirms had already been defined as dogma by the earlier councils, or was professed as an article of faith in the creed. The question we are asking is whether Lateran IV, in this constitution, defined the points of doctrine in which it clearly went beyond what the creeds said or what earlier councils had defined. Unfortunately for us, it did not add canons to its constitution, condemning the heresies that would contradict its doctrine. However, there is no doubt that it — did have a number of heresies in mind, against which it was directing its positive presentation of Catholic faith. The first sentence of the third constitution makes this clear. It says: "We excommunicate and anathematize every heresy raising itself up against this holy, orthodox and Catholic faith which we have expounded above."[24]

While the conciliar document does not describe these heresies, we know enough about the contemporary situation to be able to identify them. This first constitution is given the title: "Definition against the Albigensians and Cathari," and there is every reason to believe that the decree was aimed primarily at them. Moreover, Pope Innocent III had just recently issued a decree against the Waldensians,[25] and there is hardly any doubt that the council had them in mind as well. When we compare the tenets of these heretics with the doctrines in which the decree *Firmiter* goes beyond the previous dogmas, it is clear that the council proposed these doctrines precisely with a view to affirming the Catholic beliefs which the heretics were denying. For this reason, one can conclude that the intention of the council was to teach, in a definitive way, those doctrines of Catholic faith which the Waldensians, Albigensians and Cathari were denying. In other words, one can recognize as dogmas of faith defined by Lateran IV those propositions of its decree *Firmiter* which contradict the distinctive beliefs of the contemporary adversaries of the Catholic faith.

It is not to our purpose here to identify those dogmas in detail, but merely to establish the criteria on which this can be done. Suffice it to say that against the Manichaean dualism of the Albigensians and Cathari, Lateran IV defined that there is only one God, who created both material and spiritual beings, all of which, as they came from God, were good. Against those heretics, and also the Waldensians, it defined the necessity of the church for salvation, along with doctrines concerning the sacraments of eucharist, baptism, penance and matrimony. When we find in the decree *Firmiter* statements of Catholic faith that contradict doctrines held by the Albigensians, Cathari or Waldensians, we can conclude that we are dealing with defined dogmas of faith.

It is, then, a dogma that "there is one church of the faithful, outside of which no one at all is saved."[26] On the other hand, it is obvious that we do not now understand this dogma in the way that medieval Christians did. I have traced the history of the interpretation of this dogma in another book.[27]

A question can be raised whether Lateran IV intended to define not only those elements of Catholic faith that were denied by the sectarians, but also other elements which they did not dispute. For instance, the Albigensians and Cathari denied that God created material things but admitted that he created spiritual beings. *Firmiter* says that God "created from nothing both spiritual and corporeal creatures, that is to say, angelic and earthly."[28] Since the heretics did not deny that God created angelic creatures, we cannot be certain that the council intended to define this, although it presumed its truth as a matter of common belief. Hence it is questionable whether the existence of angels has been defined as a dogma of faith by this council. And as we have seen, canon law insists that "nothing is understood as infallibly defined unless this is manifestly established."[29]

Apropos of this decree, it is interesting that St. Thomas Aquinas wrote a commentary on it, seeing it as a conciliar exposition of the doctrine of the creed.[30] He did not describe it as a "dogmatic definition," but one cannot expect him to use those terms as we would today. He clearly recognized that the council proposed its doctrine as a response to various heresies. But, with one exception, he referred to heresies of the ancient church, such as those of Arius, Nestorius and Eutyches, rather than to heresies of his own day. The only exception came when he referred to the Waldensians (using their older name: "the poor men of Lyons") as those against whom the council taught that no one can celebrate the eucharist except a properly ordained priest.

During St. Thomas' lifetime, in 1245, the First Council of Lyons took place, which issued no doctrinal decrees. St. Thomas was invited by Pope Gregory X to take part in the Second Council of Lyons, but fell ill and died on his way to the council.

Second Council of Lyons (1274)

In a letter commemorating the seventh centenary of this council, Pope Paul VI referred to it as "the sixth of the general synods held in the west."[31] While the pope did not explain his reason for using this terminology, it would seem to denote a recognition of the difference between the ecumenical councils of the first millennium, and the "general synods held in the west."

Two documents of this council merit our attention. The first is a statement on the procession of the Holy Spirit.[32] As we have seen, the Frankish church introduced the term *Filioque* into the creed in the ninth century, and by the thirteenth this had been accepted everywhere in the west. Among the objections to this on the part of the eastern church was that it would mean there were "two principles" and "two spirations" in the origin of the Spirit. In reply to this, Lyons II issued a decree condemning not only those who would speak of "two principles" and "two spirations," but also those who would deny that the Holy Spirit proceeds from Father and Son. Thus, it not only condemned an erroneous interpretation of the *Filioque*, but also the denial of the *Filioque* itself. This would seem to justify the conclusion that for the western church it is a defined dogma that the Holy Spirit proceeds from the Father and the Son, which would make it a heresy to hold that the Spirit proceeds from the Father *alone*. However, it is another question whether this would exclude the opinion that the Spirit proceeds from the Father *through* the Son. This question will come up again at the Council of Florence.

The other document from Lyons II to be considered is the "Profession of Faith of the Emperor Michael Palaeologus."[33] This was cited at Vatican I, in its chapter on the infallibility of the pope, as evidence of previous conciliar recognition of the supreme teaching authority of the Roman pontiff. Vatican I introduced it with the words: "Furthermore, with the approval of the Second

Council of Lyons, the Greeks professed..."[34] However, this introduction claims too much for the document. It is actually the text of
a profession of faith which, six years before, the preceding pope,
Clement IV, had sent to Emperor Michael, as a condition for the
restoration of his empire's communion with Rome. Hoping for
political and military support from the west, the emperor signed
this profession of faith and sent it in a letter which was publicly
read at the Second Council of Lyons, but no conciliar action was
taken on it. As Neuner and Dupuis say in their introduction to this
text, "This document was not written at the council, nor was it
accepted by the Greeks as a basis for a doctrinal agreement with
the Latins. It was neither promulgated, nor even discussed by the
council fathers, but simply read from a letter sent by the Byzantine
emperor."[35] This profession of faith, therefore, does not have conciliar but rather papal authority, as imposed by Clement IV. The
other decrees issued by Lyons II had to do with plans for a crusade, and with other non-doctrinal matters.

Council of Vienne (1311-1312)

John Peter Olivi (1248-1298) was a Franciscan theologian, the
intellectual leader of the "Spirituals" in their controversy with
the rest of the Franciscan commmunity about the interpretation
of their vow of poverty. His opponents not only attacked his
views on poverty, but also a number of other opinions which he
had defended in his theological writings. Three of his opinions
were the object of the only doctrinal decree of the Council of
Vienne: the Constitution *Fidei catholicae.*[36] The first of these had
to do with the kind of unity existing between the intellectual soul
and the body (a question with consequences for the unity of the
humanity of Christ). Against Olivi's position (though without
naming him in the decree) the Council of Vienne, summoned by
Pope Clement V, defined that the intellectual soul is the "form"
of the human body. Since we have already discussed the dogmatic value of this definition, we can omit it here.[37]

The second of Olivi's opinions was a curious one: he had
claimed that the piercing of Jesus' side, described in John 19:24,
took place while Jesus was still alive on the cross. Against this,

Pope Clement V, *sacro approbante concilio*, "declared that John the apostle and evangelist held to the right order of what took place, when he narrated that it was Christ already dead whose side one of the soldiers pierced with a lance." This would seem to be a case where a council has solemnly declared the sense of a text of scripture, at least in one respect. Presumably the importance of this question was due to the idea, also expressed in the decree, that the outpouring of blood and water from the side of Christ signified the birth of the church. It would seem likely that Olivi's curious reading of the Johannine text is due to a refusal to attribute so important a role to the dead body of Christ.

The third of Olivi's opinions concerned the effect of infant baptism. The more common view of medieval theologians was that baptism confers grace and infused virtues on infants as habitual gifts, which remain merely such until the child reaches the use of reason. Olivi, with others, denied this effect of baptism on infants. On this point the council did not issue a definitive decision, but declared its preference for the more common opinion "as more probable and more in harmony with the words of the saints and of modern doctors of theology." Here we have an interesting example of a doctrinal conciliar decree which merely expresses its preference between two theological opinions. No doubt the opponents of Olivi had wanted more than this, but the council chose not to define an issue that was controverted among Catholic theologians.

Council of Constance (1414-1418)

We come now to the most controversial of councils, and the most controversial of decrees of councils, in the history of the church. This council has the merit of having brought an end to the disastrous schism which had divided the western church for almost forty years. The cardinals who had elected Urban VI in 1378 soon afterward denounced his election as invalid, claiming they had acted under duress. They then elected another pope, Clement VII, who took up residence at Avignon, while Urban stayed on in Rome. For the next thirty years, the church was divided between adherents to the two rival popes and their successors. In 1408 the cardinals of both sides summoned a council which took place at Pisa, and attempted to end the schism by deposing both rival popes, and electing a new one, who took the name Alexander V. However, the popes of Rome and Avignon refused to step down, so the successor of Alexander V, John XXIII, was persuaded by Emperor Sigismund to summon a new council, which began in Constance in 1414. When John XXIII saw himself in danger of being deposed by this council for his notorious crimes, he fled, hoping thereby to bring the council to an end. However, Emperor Sigismund persuaded the bishops to carry on and resolve the schism. They saw that this could be done only by invoking the thesis commonly held by medieval canonists, that a general council can judge a heretical or schismatic pope, and declare him deposed. Prior to taking action against the three rival popes, all of whom they considered guilty of prolonging the schism by their refusal to resign, the council decided first to declare its own competence to take such action. For this purpose, on April 6, 1415, it enacted the decree *Haec sancta*, whose text reads as follows.[38]

> This holy synod of Constance, which is a general council, for the eradication of the present schism and for bringing unity and reform to God's church in head and members, legitimately assembled in the Holy Spirit to the praise of almighty God, ordains, defines, decrees, discerns and declares as follows, in order that this union and reform of God's church may be obtained the more easily, securely, fruitfully and freely.
>
> First it declares that, legitimately assembled in the holy Spirit, constituting a general council and representing the Catholic Church militant, it has power immediately from Christ; and that everyone of whatever state or dignity, even papal, is bound to obey it in those matters which pertain to the faith, the eradication of the said schism and the general reform of the said church of God in head and members.
>
> Next, it declares that anyone of whatsoever condition, state or dignity, even papal, who contumaciously refuses to obey the past or future mandates, statutes, ordinances or precepts of this sacred council or of any other legitimately assembled general council, regarding the aforesaid things or matters pertaining to them, shall be subjected to well-deserved penance, unless he repents,

and shall be duly punished, even by having recourse, if necessary, to other supports of the law.

This decree raises a great many questions, to practically all of which conflicting answers have been given. To discuss all these questions would require a long book. Here we shall ask only one question: What doctrinal weight does this decree have?

Joseph Gill judges this decree to be simply invalid, on the grounds that at the time it was enacted Constance was not yet an ecumenical council, since it had not been summoned by a legitimate pope, and the subsequently elected pope, Martin V, never gave the needed papal confirmation to *Haec sancta*.[39] However, others argue that, given the actual circumstances, a general council could act without the approval of a pope, since this was the only way the schism could be brought to an end. The principle here was the sound one, that if the actions of a pope tended to tear down the church rather than to build it up,[40] the church could not lack an adequate remedy, which a general council would have authority to apply. Obviously, in such a case, the council's authority could not depend on papal convocation or approval, but would have to come, as *Haec sancta* says, immedi- ately from Christ.

I believe that, given the actual situation, Constance was correct in describing itself as a general council, with authority from Christ to do what had to be done to resolve the schism. For this purpose, it had first to declare its own competence to act as it intended to do. That necessarily involved declaring that everyone, even of papal dignity, was bound to obey it in matters that pertained to the faith and the eradication of the said schism. (It is another question whether the decree went too far in including "matters which pertain to the reform of the church," and in extending this also to "any other legitimately assembled general council.") We shall focus our question on the dogmatic weight of *Haec sancta*: Did the council define its authority over "everyone, even of papal dignity" as a dogma of faith?

On this question I agree with several noted scholars, including such experts on medieval and conciliar history as Hubert Jedin and Brian Tierney, who agree that Constance did not intend to issue this decree as a dogma of faith. Tierney puts it this way:

Haec sancta is not cast in the form of a solemn dogmatic definition. It does not demand belief, like a dogmatic definition; it exacts obedience, like a decree of positive law. In its preamble, *Haec sancta* does not purport to define an article of faith. It does not appeal to scripture or tradition. It does not pronounce anathemas against unbelievers. We cannot be sure that it was intended as an immutable dogmatic decree, and in such cases it would surely be wise to adopt a variation of Ockham's razor and abide by the principle that "Infallibilities are not to be multiplied without necessity."[41]

Hubert Jedin agrees with this view, and notes also that when the schismatic Council of Basel attempted to define conciliar supremacy over legitimate popes as an article of faith, it was raising a new issue that had not been raised at Constance.[42]

Tierney and Jedin, along with other scholars,[43] agree in seeing *Haec sancta* not as a dogmatic definition, but as a legislative decree, applying a generally accepted principle of medieval canon law to the actual situation in which the church found itself, and extending this principle to similar situations if they should occur in the future. There is a good deal of ambiguity in the way Constance expressed this decree, and scholars will no doubt continue to differ in their interpretation of it. But there is good authority for holding that while it is a valid decree, it is not a dogmatic definition. One could also raise the question whether, at the time it enacted this decree, Constance possessed the authority to define a dogma of faith. It certainly had the authority to do what had to be done to resolve the schism. But for that, it was not necessary to settle a dogmatic issue. In my opinion, Constance did not have the authority to define a dogma of faith until later on, when its judgment could be confirmed by a certainly legitimate pope.

Prior to electing such a legitimate pope, the council had issued two doctrinal decrees, condemning a number of propositions of John Wycliff and John Hus. Martin V, the pope elected by the council, subsequently issued a bull which contained all those propositions and called upon persons suspected of favoring the opinions of Wycliff or Hus to declare that they rejected them. The papal bull confirmed the conciliar judgment concerning the opinions of Wycliff and Hus that "some of them are notoriously heretical, some erroneous, others rash and seditious, others offensive to pious ears."[44] Since such a "global censure" does not identify which propositions are condemned as heretical, one cannot identify which propositions the council intended to define as dogmas of faith. Hence, while the conciliar decrees — against Wycliff and Hus received explicit papal confirmation, they do not contain any dogmatic definition.

The other important decree of Constance was the one obliging the pope to summon general councils at regular intervals: — the decree *Frequens*.[45] This is clearly a legislative decree, which soon fell into desuetude. But it did result in the summoning of the next great council: begun at Basel, continued at Ferrara and Florence, and concluded in Rome.

Council of Florence (1439-1445)

If one takes the term "ecumenical council" to refer only to those in which both the eastern and the western churches took part, then the Council of Florence is the only truly ecumenical council of the second millennium. It was summoned by Pope Eugenius IV as a council of reunion, and there was a very significant presence of the east, in the persons of the Byzantine emperor, the patriarch of Constantinople and other major prelates. There was a serious and prolonged discussion of the principal issues that divided the churches. The fruit of that discussion, the bull *Laetentur caeli*, issued on July 6, 1439, was hailed as the achievement of reunion between the Latin and the Greek churches.[46]

The last section of the bull is a dogmatic decree, commonly — referred to as the "Decree for the Greeks."[47] Its first paragraph is the fruit of the effort of the council to resolve the dispute between east and west concerning the procession of the Holy Spirit.[48] In the third volume of his work *I Believe in the Holy Spirit*, Yves Congar has studied the solution reached by the council in detail. He recognizes it as a binding dogmatic decision, but is critical of the way that it favors the Latin over the Greek way of understanding and expressing the dogma. For instance, he says: "At Florence, a Greek point of view was reduced to a Latin point of view, without the other Greek points of view having been really effectively taken into consideration."[49] "It reduced the Greek expression to the fundamentally western meaning of its Latin equivalent: *per Filium* is Catholic if it is interpreted in the sense of *Filioque*."[50]

As I have observed in a previous chapter, I would not describe as "dogma" the final sentence of the first paragraph of the decree, which "defines" that "the *Filioque* was added legitimately and with good reason for the sake of clarifying the truth and under the impact of a real need at that time."[51]

The second paragraph declares that in the eucharist one may use either leavened or unleavened bread: a decision that resolved a conflict, but is hardly a dogma of faith.[52]

The third paragraph deals with the "last things," concerning which the Latin doctrine of purgatory had been the main issue.[53] It repeats the doctrine contained in the profession of faith which Clement IV had imposed on Emperor Michael Paleologus, which was read at the Second Council of Lyons.[54] The decree of Florence gave to that doctrine the full dogmatic weight which the reading of the emperor's profession of faith at Lyons had not given it. There has been further development with regard to what it says in its final paragraph about the fate of those who die in the state of original sin alone. No Catholic nowadays would say that such persons (e.g. infants dying unbaptized) are condemned to hell, as this decree does.[55]

The fourth paragraph, on the Roman primacy,[56] was quoted as "the definition of the ecumenical Council of Florence," in the constitution *Pastor Aeternus* of Vatican I, as proof that, in its doctrine on the papacy, Vatican I was "following the express and definite decrees of the general councils."[57] Here one must recognize a defined dogma, expressed in the terms of the Latin rather than the Greek idea of the Roman primacy.

The final paragraph merely confirms the traditional order of dignity and precedence of the five patriarchal sees.[58] There is no dogma here. The inclusion of the final phrase, which assured the eastern patriarchs that all their privileges and rights remained intact, was one of the very few concessions the Latins made to the Greeks at Florence. As Congar put it: "Florence was too great a victory for the Latins—and for the papacy—for it to be a full council of union."[59] In fact, the reunion was short-lived. Once back home, Mark of Ephesus, the prelate who had strongly opposed the agreements at the council, stirred up general opposition to them. A key factor in bringing the emperor and patriarch to Florence was the hope of receiving help from the west to prevent Constantinople from falling to the Turks. Despite the reunion at Florence, such help never arrived, and only four years later Constantinople was captured and the Byzantine empire came to an end. Feeling betrayed by Rome and the west, the Greek church repudiated the agreements that had been made at Florence.

While that council was still going on, delegates from two Monophysite churches, among whom Franciscan missionaries had been working, arrived seeking reunion with Rome. Without much discussion, documents were presented for them to accept and sign, which began with the dogmatic decrees of the great councils of the first millennium, and continued with an exposition of Catholic doctrine in typically western terms. The first of these is the "Decree for the Armenians";[60] the second is the "Decree for the Jacobites," also called the "Decree for the Copts."[61]

Yves Congar has described the "Decree for the Armenians" in the following way: "This text is taken from Thomas Aquinas, sometimes literally; see his *De art. fid. et Eccl. sacr.* It is not a dogma, but merely theology and, what is more, only one theology."[62] It is obvious that by "only one theology" Congar means "only Latin theology." In this judgment, Congar agrees with a very detailed study which had been made of the same decree over sixty years before by Joseph de Guibert.[63] De Guibert said: "The term which best seems to characterize the nature of this document is that of a *declaration or doctrinal exposition of the Council of Florence on the sacraments.* If one were looking for something comparable among the recent acts of the Holy See, one could think of certain doctrinal encyclicals of Pius IX or Leo XIII."[64] I suggest that nowadays one could look to the dogmatic constitutions of Vatican II as well.

Joseph Gill has described the process leading up to the Decree for the Jacobites in the following way. "The visitors [from Egypt] were not only interrogated, they were also instructed, and the result of this double process was codified in the Bull *Cantate*

Domino, promulgated in solemn session on 4 February 1442, and accepted by the Egyptians in the name of their Patriarch and of their Church."[65] This decree is really a lengthy "instruction" in the doctrine of the Roman church. Yves Congar has referred to the "Decree for the Jacobites" in a similar vein, saying of it: "This decree is a statement of classical Scholastic theology."[66]

The recognition of the very limited doctrinal authority of these two decrees relieves us of any need to uphold some statements that are found in them. For instance, the Decree for the Armenians says that the "matter" of the sacrament of holy orders is the handing over of the instruments, such as the chalice and paten, in ordination to the priesthood.[67] This doctrine was much controverted until Pius XII settled the question in his apostolic constitution *Sacramentum Ordinis* of 1947, determining that the only "matter" of the sacrament of holy orders is the imposition of hands.[68]

The Decree for the Jacobites makes its own the atrocious statement of a sixth-century bishop, Fulgentius of Ruspe, that "no one remaining outside the Catholic Church, not only pagans, but also Jews, heretics or schismatics, can become partakers of eternal life, but they will go to the eternal fire prepared for the devil and his angels, unless before the end of their life they are received into it."[69] Obviously, the Catholic Church does not recognize a dogma of its faith in that statement, which can be understood only in the light of the medieval persuasion that all such people were guilty of the sin of infidelity.[70]

Fifth Lateran Council (1512-1517)

This has come down in history as the council that failed to undertake the reform which the church so badly needed, thus paving the way for the reformation, whose beginning is usually seen in Luther's attack on indulgences, which took place in the same year that this council came to a close. Its one doctrinal decree defined the immortality of the individual soul as a dogma of faith.[71]

The next council was that of Trent, which lasted almost twenty years, beginning in 1545 and ending in 1563. In the previous chapter we have already discussed the criteria for identifying defined dogmas in the decrees of Trent and Vatican I.

Thus we conclude our survey of the councils that are generally recognized as "ecumenical," applying the criteria by which we can identify defined dogmas in their decrees. The fact that this survey has meant recalling a great many details of church history brings out the fact that one cannot evaluate or interpret the decrees of a council without a good knowledge of its historical context, and without taking account of the specific challenges to the faith which each council had to face. We shall next consider papal documents, to ask which of them also contain dogmatic definitions. As we shall see, the answer is: fewer than one might think!

6 | Identifying Defined Dogmas in Papal Documents

Vatican I defined that the pope speaks infallibly under the following conditions: "when he speaks *ex cathedra*, that is, when, acting in the office of shepherd and teacher of all Christians, he defines, by virtue of his supreme apostolic authority, a doctrine concerning faith or morals to be held by the universal church."[1] It is important to note that not every solemn papal definition will result in a dogma. This would be true if the formula had said: "a doctrine concerning faith or morals to be *believed* by the universal church." For, as we have seen above, a dogma is a doctrine that must be believed with "divine and Catholic faith." The reason why not every solemn papal definition will result in a dogma is that Vatican I left open the possibility that the pope might define a truth that is not revealed, but connected with revelation, or, in other words, a truth pertaining to the secondary object of infallibility. Such a truth can be defined, if its definition is necessary for the defense or explanation of some revealed truth. However, even if defined, it would not become a doctrine to be believed with divine faith, and therefore would not be a dogma.[2] The following case will illustrate the difference between defining a dogma and defining something connected with revelation.

In 1653, Pope Innocent X condemned five propositions which had been extracted from the book *Augustinus*, written by Cornelius Jansen and published after his death.[3] The pope censured each of these propositions as heretical, and it is generally recognized that he thereby defined the contradictory of each of them as a dogma of faith. Subsequently, the Jansenists objected

80

that while these propositions might be heretical, they did not express the meaning which Jansen had intended in his book, where they were said to be found. To meet this objection, Pope Alexander VII, in 1656, defined that those five propositions were found in *Augustinus*, and were condemned in the sense intended by the author.[4] Now this is obviously not a truth revealed by God, but one deemed necessary for the defense of the truths previously defined by Pope Innocent X. Theologians speak of this as an example of a "dogmatic fact," that is, a fact that is connected with dogma in such a way as to justify its infallible definition. Thus, there are two definitions involved, but only that of Innocent X resulted in defined dogma.

Besides the condition that the matter involved in dogma must be revealed truth, other conditions laid down by Vatican I have to be verified in order to identify defined dogmas in papal documents. The pope must be speaking *ex cathedra*, that is, acting in his public capacity as teacher of all the faithful, exercising his supreme apostolic authority, issuing a definitive decision on a matter of faith or morals, obliging all Catholics to give their irrevocable assent of faith. It is important to note that a dogma concerning "morals" must be drawn from divinely revealed truth. This could be a truth knowable by natural reasoning, but to be capable of definition as a dogma it must be confirmed by revelation. It does not seem that any moral truth has actually been defined as a dogma.

One might think that it should be relatively easy to determine whether all the above conditions are fulfilled, and that therefore there should be general agreement among Catholic theologians as to which papal statements have been solemn dogmatic definitions. There is, in fact, general agreement that the definitions of the immaculate conception by Pius IX and that of the assumption by Pius XII meet all the conditions for defining dogmas of faith. And there is good reason to be assured that any future dogmatic definition will employ language similar to that used by those two popes, so that there will be no doubt about the pope's intention to define a dogma.

However, when we look to the past and attempt to determine which papal statements in the course of history have met the conditions for dogmatic definitions, matters are much more complicated. First of all, while it is hardly likely that a modern pope

would use the term "we define" other than in a solemn definition, or fail to use it in such a definition, one cannot presume
that this term always had such a specific meaning in documents
of the past. In older documents, neither the presence of the term
"we define," nor its absence, would be decisive for determining
the intention of a pope to speak *ex cathedra*.

The identification of *ex cathedra* statements in papal documents involves the possibility of distinguishing not only between
the private opinions of popes and their official teaching, but also
between their solemn dogmatic definitions and their other official teaching which falls short of being dogmatically definitive.
Brian Tierney, in his study of the origins of the doctrine of papal
infallibility, has expressed the opinion that this latter distinction
would not have been understood by earlier popes and hence cannot be used now to identify their *ex cathedra* pronouncements.[5]
However, the terms used by St. Thomas Aquinas and other
medieval theologians show that they understood the difference
between a definitive and a non-definitive exercise of papal teaching authority. St. Thomas, for instance, speaks of the kind of
decision by which a pope would "definitively (*sententialiter*) settle
matters of faith, so that they would be held by all with unshaken
faith."[6] Similarly, the fourteenth century Carmelite bishop,
Guido Terreni, who was one of the first to attribute infallibility
to the papal exercise of teaching authority, insisted that the pope
would teach infallibly only when he determined a matter of faith
for the whole church after having consulted the college of cardinals.[7] So, while one cannot simply rely on the presence of the
term "we define," there can be other indications of an intention
to pronounce a definitive judgment on a matter of faith for the
whole church. This, of course, does not mean that one will find
evidence of the pope's consciousness of speaking with infallibility, as this idea was not expressed as such even in the recent papal
definitions.

To my knowledge, there have been two attempts made in
recent years to identify defined dogmas in the documents of
popes: one by the Catholic members of the Lutheran-Catholic
Dialogue in the USA[8] and the other by the German church histo-
rian Klaus Schatz.[9] It seems profitable to compare the results of
these two studies.

According to the Catholic members of the Lutheran-Catholic Dialogue, "there are only two papal pronouncements which are generally acknowledged as having engaged papal infallibility: the dogma of the immaculate conception (1854) and that of the assumption of the Blessed Virgin (1950). Several other types of papal pronouncements have, however, been thought by some to be infallible. With an eye to the teaching of twentieth century theological manuals, several prominent examples may here be mentioned: the solemn canonizations of saints, the condemnation of certain doctrines, papal teaching concerning certain moral matters, and the decision concerning Anglican ordinations." They then offer their reasons for rejecting all the latter as genuine examples of infallible papal teaching.

While it is true that some Catholic theologians can be cited who recognize papal definitions in each of these kinds of teaching, I agree with the members of the dialogue in denying that popes have defined dogmas in canonizing saints, in their teaching concerning moral matters, and in the decision regarding Anglican ordinations. Some Catholic theologians did see solemn definitions in *Apostolicae curae* (Leo XIII's decision on the validity of Anglican orders) and in *Casti connubii* (Pius XI's encyclical on birth control), but their opinion has not prevailed.[10]

On the other hand, there are reasons to question the view of the Catholic members of the dialogue that there have been no other papal definitions than those of the immaculate conception and the assumption. First, I think the members of the dialogue are mistaken when they claim that no papal condemnation of doctrine as heretical has fulfilled the conditions required for infallibility, and that consequently none has defined a dogma. They say: "For the infallible character to be clearly manifest, the condemnation would have to claim infallibility for itself and would have to fall within the scope of papal infallibility as set forth by the two Vatican Councils. In point of fact, none of the papal documents condemning doctrinal errors evidently meets these two criteria."[11] As I have already pointed out, it is a mistake to require that a dogmatic definition explicitly claim infallibility for itself. If this were really required, most conciliar decrees which are universally recognized as dogmatic definitions would also be discounted, since none of them explicitly claims infallibility. With regard to the second criterion mentioned, I would agree that some examples of papal condemnations of doctrinal errors do not meet the conditions laid down by Vatican I for a dogmatic definition. Referring to the papal condemnation of the errors attributed to Martin Luther in the bull *Exsurge Domine* (1520) of Leo X,[12] the Catholic members of the dialogue correctly observe that "it embodies propositions of unequal theological weight." In fact, the censure which follows is a "global" one, which does not specify which errors it condemns as heretical.[13]

For this reason I would agree that *Exsurge Domine* does not meet the requirements for a dogmatic definition. However, I would maintain that when a pope has solemnly condemned a specific proposition as heretical, and it is clear that the matter involved is one of revealed truth, we can conclude that he has defined the contradictory proposition as a dogma.

My second objection to the position taken by the Catholic members of the dialogue is that they do not consider several examples of positive doctrinal decisions taken by popes in the past, which have been considered by many theologians to constitute papal dogmatic definitions. Perhaps in these cases also they find lacking an explicit claim to speak with infallibility. In any case, I believe that Klaus Schatz has provided a more thorough study of this question than have the Catholic members of the Lutheran-Catholic dialogue.

Schatz asks: Where have Catholic theologians seen papal dogmatic definitions in documents issued prior to Vatican I? He finds lists of such definitions in two works written near the beginning of this century: in Louis Billot's *Tractatus de Ecclesia Christi*[14] and Edmond Dublanchy's article on infallibility in the *Dictionnaire de Théologie Catholique*.[15] Both these authors recognized dogmatic definitions in the following twelve papal documents:

1. The "Tome to Flavian" of Pope Leo I on two natures in Christ (449).
2. The letter of Pope Agatho on two wills in Christ (680).
3. The final sentence of Boniface VIII's *Unam sanctam* (1302).
4. The bull *Benedictus Deus* of Benedict XII on the beatific vision of the just prior to final judgment (1336).

5. *Exsurge Domine* of Leo X condemning the errors of Luther (1520).

6. *Cum occasione* of Innocent X, condemning five propositions of Jansen as heretical (1653).

7. *Caelestis pastor* of Innocent XI, condemning the "Quietism" of Molinos (1687).

8. *Cum alias* of Innocent XII, condemning the errors of Fénélon (1699).

9. *Unigenitus* of Clement XI condemning errors of Quesnel (1713).

10. *Auctorem fidei* of Pius VI condemning errors of the Synod of Pistoia (1794).

11. The definition of the immaculate conception by Pius IX (1854).

12. *Quanta cura* of Pius IX against various errors of his day (1864).

Schatz shows that in this century, the list of such commonly recognized papal definitions has gradually been reduced, until, as we have seen, the Catholic participants in the Lutheran-Catholic Dialogue in the USA recognized only the two Marian dogmas as such. Schatz suggests that the reason for present doubt that earlier papal decisions fulfill the conditions for infallible definitions is that it is difficult to be sure that those popes had the intention to invoke their power to define the issue with infallibility. However, as he observes, it is a mistake to look for such an explicit intention to speak with infallibility.

I believe Schatz is right in observing that while it may be difficult to determine, in some earlier documents, that the pope intended to issue a solemn dogmatic definition, one can recognize that certain papal decisions in matters of faith have actually settled a doctrinal question in a definitive way, as can be seen in the subsequent reception of their decisions by the church. On the significance of the reception by the church of doctrinal decisions, he appeals to the authoritative study of the ecumenical councils by H.J. Sieben.[16] Sieben has shown that the clearest sign that a conciliar decision was definitive is seen in the reception of that decision by the whole church. He insists that such reception is not the source of the definitive authority of the decision, but it is the most effective witness to it. Schatz proposes that, analogously, one can also look to the reception of papal decisions for evidence that they have truly been definitive for the faith of the church. Invoking this criterion of reception, that is, the evidence that a papal decision has actually determined the faith of the church, Schatz offers the following list of papal documents in which he would recognize dogmatic definitions.

1. Leo I's "Tome to Flavian," which was received by the Council of Chalcedon.[17]

2. Pope Agatho's decision on two wills in Christ, received by the Third Council of Constantinople.[18]

3. *Benedictus Deus* of Benedict XII on the beatific vision.[19]

4. The condemnation of five propositions of Jansen as heretical, by Innocent X.[20]

5. The condemnation of seven Jansenist propositions of the Synod of Pistoia as heretical, by Pius VI.[21]

6. The definition of the immaculate conception by Pius IX.[22]

7. The definition of the assumption by Pius XII.[23]

It is of course true that the first two of these became conciliar definitions when they were confirmed by the respective councils. That would leave only five instances in the course of church history when a pope, acting independently of an ecumenical council, exercised his teaching authority to define dogmas of faith. That would seem to relativize the importance of papal infallibility in the church's life of faith. However, I believe Schatz is correct when he points out that the more important exercise of papal teaching authority has been the contribution that popes have made to the dogmatic decisions of councils, both ecumenical and regional, as well as their participation in the "ordinary universal magisterium." The fact is that, with few exceptions, our Catholic faith is based not on dogmas defined by popes, but on those that have been defined by councils, and on those that have never been formally defined, but are part of the faith which we profess when we participate in the liturgy.

It would be instructive now to look more closely at the papal documents in which Billot and Dublanchy recognized dogmatic definitions, but which Schatz has not included in his list, with a view to seeing in what respect they fail to meet the requirements for dogmatic definitions. We take them in chronological order.

The first is the bull *Unam sanctam* of Boniface VIII. Schönmetzer's note distinguishes the final sentence of this bull from the rest of the document, describing only this last sentence as a "dogmatic definition." Neuner and Dupuis do likewise, calling only the conclusion to the bull a "doctrinal declaration." The sentence reads as follows: "Furthermore we declare, state and define that for every human creature it is necessary for salvation to be subject to the Roman pontiff."[24] It is clear that this final sentence expresses the pope's intention to define a dogma. What is not so clear is what doctrine he intended to define. The problem is to determine in what precise sense Boniface VIII intended the term "to be subject to the Roman pontiff." For, in the light of the rest of the bull, two different senses are possible.

The bull begins with a profession of faith in the oneness of the church, outside of which there is no salvation. This was no new doctrine, as it was the consistent doctrine of the fathers of the church, and had been solemnly declared in the profession of faith of the fourth Lateran Council.[25] In enunciating this traditional doctrine, Boniface put particular emphasis on the role of the pope as head of the church, with the consequence that no one can be a member of Christ's flock who is not under its visible shepherd. Schönmetzer takes the final sentence of the bull to be a definition only of the traditional doctrine presented in its first part, interpreting the term "to be subject to the Roman pontiff" in the light of a statement of St. Thomas (with which Boniface could well have been familiar) in which the necessity of being subject to the Roman pontiff was simply another way of expressing the necessity of being in the communion of the Catholic Church in order to be saved.[26] If this is what Boniface intended to define, there is no doubt that his doctrine was received by the church, as the necessity of being in the Catholic Church for salvation is still the doctrine of Vatican II, even though its interpretation has developed in a way that Boniface could hardly have foreseen.[27]

On the other hand, the term "to be subject to the Roman pontiff" would receive quite a different interpretation if it were understood in the light of the main section of the bull, in which Boniface developed a medieval theory about the supremacy of the spiritual power over the temporal power, giving the pope as head of Christendom the authority to "institute and to judge" temporal rulers. This theory is obviously dependent on the cultural situation of Europe in the middle ages, when kings and emperors were crowned by popes, and as Christians were subject to their spiritual authority. It also reflects the contemporary conflict between Boniface VIII and Philip the Fair of France, in which the pope was attempting to exercise his spiritual supremacy over the temporal power of the king. If the phrase "to be subject to the Roman pontiff" is taken in this sense, then one would have to say that this doctrine of Boniface VIII was not universally received, even in his own day, and it certainly has not become a permanent part of the faith of the Catholic Church.

In a paper which he presented in the course of the Lutheran-Catholic dialogue on papal primacy, George Tavard discussed the question we have been considering here, and concluded that what Boniface intended to define was the central doctrine of his bull, namely the supremacy of the spiritual over the temporal power. But Tavard ruled this out as a genuine exercise of papal infallibility, on the grounds that this doctrine was not generally received, and has not been maintained as the doctrine of the Catholic Church.[28] Without referring to Tavard's study, Klaus Schatz likewise interprets the phrase "to be subject to the Roman pontiff" in the light of Boniface's medieval theory, and sees this as an instance of non-reception from which one can conclude that this papal statement did not meet all the conditions necessary for the definition of a dogma of faith.

The idea that a papal statement should be recognized as a dogmatic definition by the way it has been received, and by the fact that it has been decisive for the faith of the church, might seem to be in conflict with the statement of Vatican I that a papal definition is "irreformable of itself, and not from the consensus of the church."[29] To this objection one can reply that the pope can define as dogma only a truth that is revealed, and that must therefore be contained at least implicitly in the faith of the church. The eventual failure of any papal doctrine to be received by the church as an article of its faith would show that that doctrine was not contained in the deposit of faith, and hence was not capable of being defined as dogma.

In a work which he published in 1969, Joseph Ratzinger made a statement which seems to me to be consonant with the approach that Schatz has taken on this issue. Ratzinger wrote: "Criticism of papal pronouncements will be possible and even necessary, to the extent that they lack support in scripture and the creed, that is, in the faith of the whole church. When neither the consensus of the whole church is had, nor clear evidence from the sources is available, an ultimately binding decision is not possible. Were one formally to take place, the conditions for such an act would be lacking, and hence the question would have to be raised concerning its legitimacy."[30]

One could also argue, as Bishop Christopher Butler did, from the statement of Vatican II that "the assent of the church can never be wanting" to definitions that result from the exercise of the supreme teaching authority.[31] From this he drew the conclusion that "if a definition failed in the end to enjoy such a 'reception' on the part of the church, this would prove that the definition had not in fact met the stringent requirements for an *ex cathedra* pronouncement."[32]

Of the twelve papal definitions listed by Billot and Dublanchy, seven involve papal condemnations of various erroneous propositions. Of these Schatz retains only two: the condemnation of five propositions of Jansen by Innocent X in *Cum occasione*;[33] and the condemnation of seven Jansenist propositions of the Synod of Pistoia by Pius VI in *Auctorem fidei*.[34] In both of these documents, Jansenist propositions were explicitly condemned as heretical, and there is no doubt that the contradictory of each of them is a doctrine of Catholic faith. On the other hand, the other five documents consist of a list of erroneous propositions, followed by a "global" censure, which does not specify which censure is attached to which proposition.[35] In some cases this global censure includes the most severe one, "heretical," but it does not say which ones deserve that condemnation. I agree with Schatz that since this form of censure does not explicitly condemn any particular proposition as heretical, one cannot conclude that the contradictory of any of the condemned propositions is a defined dogma. Such documents, therefore, are to be seen as examples of the ordinary, non-definitive exercise of papal magisterium.

Papal Professions of Faith

Among the papal documents in which he recognizes dogmatic definitions, Schatz has not mentioned any of the "professions of faith" which have been promulgated by popes. However, since such professions of faith are clearly doctrinal in nature, and give the impression of being rather solemn pronouncements, it seems worthwhile to consider some examples of them, with a view to assessing the level of authority which popes have exercised in them.

During the first millennium it was customary for newly-elected popes and patriarchs to announce their election to one another, and to include in such letters their profession of faith. Such a profession of faith was sent by Pope Leo IX to Peter, patriarch of Antioch, in 1053 (the year before the break of communion between east and west).[36] Among other things, Pope Leo professes his acceptance and veneration of seven universal councils (a number which suggests that he did not recognize the Fourth Council of Constantinople of 869-70 as ecumenical). He also includes the *Filioque*, which had been introduced into the creed at Rome only fifty years before this, after two centuries of resistance.

We have already mentioned the profession of faith which Pope Clement IV had imposed on Emperor Michael Palaeologus, and which was read as part of the emperor's letter to the Second Council of Lyons in 1274.[37] After an exposition of Trinitarian doctrine, which, as one might expect, includes the *Filioque*, there follow several items of doctrine on which eastern theology was thought to be weak, such as purgatory, eternal punishment of the damned, the seven sacraments, and the Roman primacy. This was standard Roman doctrine, and there is no reason to think that Clement IV intended to define any of it by including it in the profession of faith he imposed on the emperor.

The Council of Trent enacted a law that obliged all prelates in the church to make a profession of faith. The year after the conclusion of the council, Pope Pius IV promulgated the formula in which such a profession of faith was to be made. This is often called "Tridentine," even though it was not formulated by the council.[38] However, the name can be justified by the fact that the doctrine which it contains is largely that of Trent. However, it would be a mistake to conclude that every doctrine which it contains is a dogma of faith defined by the council. For, among other things, the formula obliged one to "accept and embrace the apostolic and ecclesiastical traditions, and all other observances and constitutions of the same church,"[39] and to "admit and accept the rites received and approved in the Catholic Church for the administration of the sacraments."[40] As the council had anathematized those who rejected such things, so also Catholic prelates were obliged to profess their acceptance of them; in neither case was there question of dogmas of faith. But of course many other statements in this profession were dogmas of faith, some defined by previous councils, others by Trent. In promulgating his profession of faith, Pius IV did not define any new dogmas. Some new ones were added to it after 1870, when dogmas defined by Vatican I were inserted into it.

While that profession was obligatory only for prelates, Pius X, in his struggle against "Modernism," required all members of the clergy engaged in pastoral work or teaching to take an oath, which was really a profession of faith in the doctrines which were threatened by Modernist errors.[41] So, from 1910 until 1967, when Pope Paul VI abrogated it, most members of the clergy were obliged to take the "Oath against Modernism" annually. Despite the solemn nature of such an oath, there is no reason to believe that any doctrine which was not already a dogma of faith became such by its inclusion in this document.

When Pope Paul VI abrogated the "Oath against Modernism" in 1967, he prescribed a new formula for the profession of faith which certain members of the clergy were obliged by canon law to make.[42] This was a brief formula, which, after the creed used at the Sunday liturgy, expressed faith in a global way in all the dogmas, defined or undefined, mentioning specifically only "those which refer to the mystery of the holy church of Christ and its sacraments, the sacrifice of the mass, and the primacy of the Roman pontiff." Unlike the "Tridentine" formula of Pius IV, this post–Vatican II formula of Paul VI required the acceptance only of divinely revealed truths calling for the response of faith.

The year after the promulgation of this formula to be used in making the canonically required profession of faith, Paul VI concluded the "Year of the Faith" with a liturgical celebration in the course of which he made a much lengthier profession of faith "in the name of the whole people of God."[43] He explained that it was not his intention to define the doctrine in this creed, but to include in it, besides the major doctrines of Vatican II, "some developments called for by the spiritual condition of the times." What the creed says on such matters gives us the mind of Paul VI on some contemporary theological issues, but does not settle any question in a dogmatically definitive way.

The brief profession of faith decreed by Paul VI in 1967 was replaced in 1989, when the CDF promulgated a new formula for the canonically required profession of faith.[44] To this was added the text of an "Oath of Fidelity" to be sworn by all those obliged to make the profession of faith.[45] Unlike the "Oath against Modernism" of Pius X, this new "Oath of Fidelity" is not equivalent to a further profession of faith, and therefore does not concern us here.

As we have seen in Chapter 2, those obliged by canon law to make the profession of faith according to the new formula must not only profess sincere belief in all the dogmas of the church, both defined and undefined, but must also profess that they "embrace and hold" other doctrines which are not revealed, but connected with revelation, and have been proposed as definitively to be held. They are further required to express their "religious submission" to doctrines taught by the ordinary, non-definitive magisterium. Neither of these last two paragraphs of the new profession of faith calls for a response of faith, in the proper sense of the term. As we have seen, there was a precedent for this, in the "Tridentine" profession of Pius IV, which called not only for the response of faith to the dogmas defined by the Council of Trent, but for the acceptance of ecclesiastical traditions, observances and rites as well.

To sum up: despite the solemn nature of such obligatory professions of faith, imposed by papal authority, they do not fulfill the conditions required for *ex cathedra* pronouncements, and while they contain many dogmas of faith, no doctrines have become defined dogmas by being included in them.

7 || Undefined Dogmas

The Hierarchy of Truths

In its Decree on Ecumenism, Vatican II urged Catholic theologians to "remember that in Catholic teaching there exists an order or 'hierarchy' of truths, since they vary in their relationship to the foundation of the Christian faith."[1] Since we have been dealing up to now with doctrines that have been defined by ecumenical councils or by popes, the impression may have been given that defined dogmas must rank highest in that "hierarchy of truths" of which the council spoke. This, however, is not the case. The criterion for assigning truths their place in this hierarchy is their "relationship to the foundation of Christian faith," that is to say, their intrinsic importance for our life of faith. Some truths which have never been defined are much more closely related to the foundation of Christian faith than some others which have been solemnly defined. One could hardly think of truths more basic to the faith than those mentioned by St. Paul when he said: "If you confess with your lips that Jesus is Lord and believe in your heart that God raised him from the dead, you will be saved."[2] No doubt, Christ's lordship and resurrection are basic dogmas of our faith, but they have not been the object of any solemn definition.

In most cases, truths have been defined because they were being threatened by erroneous teaching. The development of dogma reflects the historical circumstances that required the church to take a definitive stand on certain issues. Nothing in this history suggests a deliberate intention to give priority to the more important truths of faith by defining them. Nothing sug-

93

gests an intention to make sure that all the most important articles of faith would become defined dogmas. In respect to some basic truths of our faith, we are still in the same situation as the early church was, before any dogmas had been defined.

The "Rule of Faith" in the Early Church

Writing a century and a half before the first ecumenical council, Irenaeus, bishop of Lyons, often mentioned the "rule of faith" or "canon of truth" which Christians followed in their profession of faith. The following passage from his great work — *Against the Heresies* tells us what he meant by this "rule of faith."[3]

> Suppose there arise a dispute relative to some important question among us, should we not have recourse to the most ancient churches with which the apostles held constant intercourse, and learn from them what is certain and clear in regard to the present question? For how should it be if the apostles themselves had not left us writings? Would it not be necessary to follow the course of the tradition which they handed down to those to whom they committed the churches? To which course many nations of those barbarians who believe in Christ do assent, having salvation written in their hearts by the Spirit, without paper or ink, and carefully preserving the ancient tradition, believing in one God, the Creator of heaven and earth, and all things therein, by means of Christ Jesus, the Son of God; who, because of his surpassing love toward his creation, condescended to be born of the virgin, he himself uniting man through himself to God, and having suffered under Pontius Pilate, and rising again, and having been received up in splendor, shall come again in glory, the Savior of those who are saved, and the judge of those who are judged, and sending into eternal fire those who transform the truth, and despise his Father and his coming.

In this passage we see both the formal principle of the "rule of faith," namely, the tradition preserved in the apostolic churches, and the contents of this "rule," namely, the basic truths of faith which Christians professed. An essential feature of this "rule of faith" was that it was common to all the churches that were faithful to the apostolic tradition. Irenaeus insists: "It is within the power of all, in every church, who may wish to see the truth, to contemplate clearly the tradition of the apostles manifested throughout the world."[4]

The "rule of faith" was not simply identical with the baptismal creed; in fact, at this period there was no creedal formula common to all the churches. The introductory section of DS gives the text of a considerable number of early baptismal creeds from both eastern and western churches.[5] Here one can see that, despite their variations, their contents represent the same "rule of faith" that was common to all the churches. The consensus of all the churches in the profession of the same faith continued to be recognized as the reliable criterion of the truth in the patristic period. An outstanding exponent of this criterion is St. Augustine, who again and again expressed it in his famous phrase: *securus iudicat orbis terrarum*, which can be translated: "One can rely on the judgment of the whole world."[6] For Augustine, the sure test of orthodoxy was the "consensus of the universal church."[7] In most cases, such a consensus was obtained through the practice of communicating the decisions of regional councils to the other churches for their approval and reception.

Consensus by "Reception"

There was an extraordinary amount of communication among the Christian churches during the patristic period. Newly elected bishops would send their profession of faith to the bishops of other major churches. Bishops would keep one another informed about heresies that had arisen in their region, and of how their authors were dealt with, so that others would also deny communion to those condemned as heretics. It was through such a process of mutual communication and reception that a consensus was reached on so fundamental a question as the canon of the New Testament. The Council of Trent was the first ecumenical council to issue a definitive decree about the canon of scripture; until then it was a matter of consensus. Similarly, the baptismal formula that we know as the Apostles' Creed came to be received in the whole western church by such a consensus. It was originally the baptismal creed of the Roman church, and was received by the other local churches of the west. However, it came to be more fully developed in the churches of northern Europe, and eventually that augmented formula came to be received in turn by the church of Rome. This final form of the Apostles' Creed, which offers a striking example of "reception," is appropriately known as the *textus receptus*.[8]

Taking the Apostles' Creed as the most basic expression of Christian faith, medieval theologians distinguished in it twelve "articles," in which they recognized the essential elements of Christian doctrine. Where we now speak of "dogmas," St. Thomas and the other medieval theologians would speak of "articles of faith." For a doctrine to be termed an "article of faith," it did not have to have been defined by one of the great councils; it sufficed that it was included, at least implicitly, in the creed.[9] Not every article of the creed had been defined by St. Thomas' day, and it is still true that not every article of the creed has been defined. But it can hardly be doubted that every article of the creed is a dogma of faith. So if one is looking for "undefined dogmas," the first place to look is to those articles of the Apostles' Creed which have never been defined. In my judgment, this applies not only to the baptismal creed, but also to the conciliar creeds of Nicea and Constantinople. We know which dogmas those councils intended to define; there is no reason to think that they intended to define other articles of faith which at that time were not in dispute.

Reception of the Decrees of Regional Councils

In the patristic period several important doctrinal issues were settled by regional councils, whose decisions were received so widely that a genuine consensus was reached without having the question decided by an ecumenical council. The following are some examples of such regional councils. The decision of the synod of Antioch in 268 which condemned Paul of Samosata was so widely received that its criticism of his heretical use of *homoousios* subsequently became a serious problem for the Council of Nicea when it chose to use the same term in an orthodox sense. The judgment of the Council of Carthage of 418 against Pelagianism was received as a dogma of faith, but it remained undefined until it was confirmed by the Council of Trent.[10] The same could be said for the doctrine of the Second Council of Orange (529) on grace.[11] Though mainly concerned with a Christological issue, the Lateran Council of 649 also played a key role in the history of Mariology, especially regarding the doctrine of the perpetual virginity of Mary.[12] The profession of faith of the Eleventh Council of Toledo (675) is acknowledged as one of the most important formulations of Trinitarian doctrine by any council.[13] Two regional councils of the ninth century Frankish church, of Quierzy and Valence, were decisive in maintaining the doctrine of the universal salvific will of God against heretical views on predestination.[14]

Of the doctrines we have mentioned, some have subsequently been solemnly defined, others have not. But even independently of such definition, they all became part of the faith of the church by virtue of their universal reception. I would class those that have not been defined as good examples of what I mean by undefined dogmas.

Infallibility of Consensus of the Universal Church in Faith

While the first known reference to the infallibility of ecumenical councils dates from the ninth century,[15] and the first reference to the infallibility of popes to the thirteenth century,[16] the conviction that the consensus of the universal church in its faith is an infallible norm of truth goes back to the second century, with Irenaeus, and is a consistent element of Christian belief. St. Thomas Aquinas shared this belief, which he expressed by saying: "It is certain that it is impossible for the judgment of the universal church to err in matters that pertain to faith."[17] In the sixteenth century St. Robert Bellarmine spelled this out in more detail, saying: "When we say that the church cannot err, we understand this both of the entire body of the faithful and of the entire body of the bishops, so that the meaning of the proposition that the church cannot err is this: that what all the faithful hold as of faith is necessarily true and of faith; and likewise what all the bishops teach as of faith is necessarily true and of faith."[18] Here it is obvious that in speaking both of what the faithful hold and what the bishops teach, Bellarmine is not talking about different truths, but of two criteria by which we can be certain that something is true and is *de fide*, i.e., to be believed as divinely revealed. A universal consensus of the faithful in their belief and of the bishops in their teaching are both infallible criteria of revealed truth.

Here Bellarmine was enunciating the principle which the Council of Trent put into practice in its deliberations and invoked again and again in its dogmatic decrees. We shall quote just a few of the many places where Trent expressed its confidence in the reliability of a consensus of the whole church on a matter of faith.

In the introduction to its decree on original sin, Trent declares that it will base its decree on "the testimony of the sacred scriptures, the holy fathers and the approved councils, and the judgment and consensus of the church."[19] In the course of this decree, it insists that the statement of St. Paul in Romans 5:12 "is not to be understood otherwise than as the Catholic Church throughout the world has always understood it."[20] In the introduction to its decree on justification the council declares its intention to expound the true and sound doctrine which "the Catholic Church, under the guidance of the Holy Spirit, has always held."[21] In this decree it insists that the words of St. Paul about justification by faith "are to be understood in that sense which the perpetual consensus of the Catholic Church has held and expressed." Again, in the introduction to its decree on the eucharist, Trent declares its intention to hand on "that sound and pure doctrine which the Catholic Church, instructed by Jesus Christ our Lord himself and his apostles, and taught by the Holy Spirit...has always retained, and will keep to the end of time."[22] In this decree Trent speaks of those who deny the true presence of the flesh and blood of Christ in the eucharist as distorting the sense of the words of Christ "against the universal consensus of the church."[23] The words of Christ at the last supper must be understood in the way that "the Catholic Church has always understood and taught."[24]

This repeated appeal of Trent to the consensus of the Catholic Church as warrant for its dogmatic decrees demonstrates beyond any doubt that the bishops at the council shared the view later expressed by Bellarmine, that "what all the faithful hold as of faith is necessarily true and of faith; and likewise what all the bishops teach as of faith is necessarily true and of faith." In view of this evident fact, one could reasonably conclude that a good many of the doctrines defined by Trent were already dogmas of Catholic faith prior to being solemnly defined. Trent obviously did not invent them; it found them already there in the universal teaching, belief and practice of the Catholic Church.

Pius IX on the "Ordinary Magisterium"

The term "ordinary magisterium" first appeared in an official document of the Catholic Church in the letter *Tuas libenter* which Pius IX addressed to the archbishop of Munich on December 21, 1863.[25] In this letter the pope expressed his concern about a meeting of Catholic theologians which had taken place in Munich earlier that year, organized by Ignaz von Döllinger. It had been reported to the pope that in the course of that meeting the opinion had been aired that Catholic theologians were bound to hold only those truths of faith which had been solemnly defined. To this Pius IX replied:

> We want to persuade ourselves that they do not wish to limit the obligation by which Catholic teachers and writers are bound, only to those things which have been proposed by the infallible judgment of the church as dogmas of faith to be believed by all. And we are persuaded that they did not wish to declare that that perfect adherence to revealed truths which they acknowledge to be absolutely necessary for the genuine progress of science and for the refutation of errors can be had if faith and assent is given only to the expressly defined dogmas of the church. For even if it is a matter of that subjection which must be given in the act of divine faith, it must not be limited to those things which have been defined by the express decrees of councils or of the Roman pontiffs and of this apostolic see, but must also be extended to those things which are handed on by the ordinary magisterium of the whole church dispersed throughout the world as divinely revealed, and therefore are held by the universal and constant consensus of Catholic theologians to pertain to the faith.[26]

In the study which John P. Boyle has made of this letter,[27] he has demonstrated the likelihood that it owes much of its language to a memorandum concerning the Munich congress, which was given to the pope by Cardinal Reisach, who in turn was indebted to the work of the Jesuit theologian Joseph Kleutgen. In his book *Die Theologie der Vorzeit*, Kleutgen had distinguished between the extraordinary magisterium, exercised by ecumenical councils in defining doctrine, and the "ordinary and perpetual" magisterium exercised by the popes with the bishops when they are dispersed around the world.[28] He had insisted that many traditional Christian doctrines had already been taught as dogmas of faith by this ordinary magisterium prior to their solemn definition, and that therefore obligatory faith could not be limited to what had been defined. He also suggested that the consensus of Catholic theologians that a doctrine was *de fide* would indicate that it had been taught as such by the ordinary magisterium.

Boyle is no doubt correct in seeing the link between Kleutgen's theology and the doctrine of Pius IX. Kleutgen's distinction between "extraordinary" and "ordinary" magisterium seems to have been a new way of expressing the matter. It certainly made its first appearance in official ecclesiastical language in *Tuas libenter*. But the idea which it intended to express can hardly be described as new. It is essentially the same as what Augustine meant by "*securus iudicat orbis terrarum*," what St. Thomas meant by saying: "It is impossible for the judgment of the universal church to err in matters that pertain to faith," and what Bellarmine meant by saying: "What all the bishops teach as of faith is necessarily true and of faith." It is likewise what the bishops at Trent had in mind when they appealed to "what the Catholic Church has always believed and taught" as the sure ground for their dogmatic decrees. It is absurd to think that the Tridentine dogmas were merely pious opinions until the council defined them.

Two points in the statement of Pius IX are especially worth noting. First, he limits it to matters which are taught by the ordinary magisterium throughout the world *as divinely revealed*. Second, he suggests how it can be known which doctrines have been taught in this way: namely by the universal and constant consensus among Catholic theologians that certain doctrines are matters of faith, even though they have not been solemnly defined. It was not difficult to ascertain this fact, when Catholic theologians in writing their manuals qualified each of their theses with a theological "note," giving to some dogmas the note *de fide definita* and to others the simple *de fide*. It is also worth noting that in *Tuas libenter* Pius IX used the term *dogmata* referring both to defined dogmas and those which had been proposed for belief by the ordinary universal magisterium.[29]

Vatican I on the "Ordinary Universal Magisterium"

The teaching of Pius IX on this point was incorporated into the dogmatic constitution *Dei Filius* of Vatican I, when it said: "All those things are to be believed with divine and Catholic faith which are contained in the word of God, written or handed down, and are proposed by the church either by a solemn judgment or by its ordinary and universal magisterium as divinely revealed and to be believed as such."[30] The reference to the teaching of the ordinary magisterium was introduced into the text at the urging of Bishop Senestrey. The first draft including this reference said: "All those things are to be believed by divine and Catholic faith which are contained in the Word of God, written or handed down, and are proposed by the church for belief either by solemn judgment or by the ordinary magisterium."[31] From the concilar discussion of this text it is clear that the term "ordinary magisterium" was an unfamiliar one to many of the bishops. Some thought it referred to papal teaching, and objected that it prematurely raised the issue of papal infallibility. Others wanted it to be made clear that the statement referred only to divinely revealed truths. To clarify the text, two additions were made. "Ordinary magisterium" became "ordinary and universal magisterium," and the words "as divinely revealed" were added. It was explained to the bishops that the term "universal magisterium" referred to the teaching of the whole episcopate along with the pope, and not to the teaching of the pope alone, even when this was directed to the universal church.[32]

The question has been raised whether this statement of Vatican I defines the *infallibility* of the ordinary universal magisterium. It certainly does not do so explicitly, nor is it likely that it was the intention of the council to define it in this document, which is the Constitution on the Faith, since questions about the magisterium were still to be treated in the Constitution on the Church. However, it might be said to follow as a theological conclusion from the obligation on all the faithful to believe what is proposed as divinely revealed in this way, in view of the basic truth that the whole church cannot be led into error in what it is obliged to believe. The question of infallibility did come up, however, at the Second Vatican Council.

Vatican II on the Ordinary Universal Magisterium

The statement of Vatican II on the ordinary universal magisterium concerns precisely the question as to the conditions under which it enjoys the privilege of infallibility. The text is as follows:

> Although the individual bishops do not enjoy the prerogative of infallibility, they do nevertheless proclaim Christ's doctrine infallibly even when dispersed around the world, provided that while maintaining the bond of communion among themselves and with Peter's successor, and teaching authoritatively on a matter of faith or morals, they are in agreement that a particular judgment is to be held definitively.[33]

Two points are noteworthy concerning the history of this text. Where the final text says "while...teaching authoritatively on a matter of faith or morals," the earlier draft had said "in handing on the revealed faith." This means that originally the text would have spoken of the ordinary universal magisterium as infallible only when it proposed a doctrine as divinely revealed and calling for the response of faith. In this it would have followed the lead of Pius IX and Vatican I, which had likewise spoken of the ordinary universal magisterium only in reference to its teaching revealed truth. However, just as the insistence of Archbishop Manning and Bishop Senestrey at Vatican I brought it about that papal infallibility was defined in such a way that it was not limited to defining dogmas of faith,[34] so also at Vatican II some bishops insisted that the infallibility of the ordinary universal magisterium should not be so limited. To satisfy their request, the restriction to matters of "revealed faith" was removed, so as to allow for the possibility of infallible teaching on a matter of faith or morals that was not revealed, but connected with revelation.[35] This is also the reason for the use of the term "to be held," which does not necessarily mean "by divine faith."

At the same time, another important emendation was made to the text: the term "to be held" was qualified with the adverb "definitively." This clearly limits the infallibility of the ordinary universal magisterium to what it proposes in such a way as to call for the definitive assent of the faithful. This means that from the fact that the bishops around the world concurred in teaching a doctrine which the pope had taught in an encyclical, it would not follow that the doctrine was being taught infallibly, unless it were also clear that both pope and bishops were proposing this doctrine as one to be held definitively. But this raises a problem, because, normally, the ordinary exercise of magisterium, while it requires a response of "religious submission," does not propose a teaching as definitive, and consequently does not call for definitive assent.

By allowing for the infallible teaching of the ordinary universal magisterium on matters that are only connected with revelation, Vatican II has gone beyond what Pope Pius IX and Vatican I had said. In referring to this magisterium, they had spoken only about the teaching of revealed truth that called for the assent of faith. Vatican II has opened the door to the claim that norms of the natural law, even those not confirmed by revelation, have been infallibly taught by the ordinary universal magisterium. But this raises, in a more acute way, the basic problem regarding this particular kind of magisterium, which is the difficulty of proving not merely that the bishops in the whole world are agreed in teaching some doctrine along with the pope, but that they are all proposing this same doctrine "as to be held definitively."

As we have seen, Pius IX suggested a sign by which one could know that a doctrine had been taught by the universal magisterium as a matter of faith: it was the "universal and constant" consensus of Catholic theologians that the doctrine was *de fide*. It is surely significant that Pius IX described such a consensus not only as "universal" but also as "constant." The Latin word he used is *constans*, which the Latin dictionary translates as "steady, firm, unchanging, immovable." This suggests that the kind of consensus by which we can conclude that a doctrine has been infallibly taught must be one that perseveres and remains unchanged. On the other hand, if it becomes evident that there is no longer a consensus on some point of doctrine about which, in former times, there was a consensus, it would seem necessary to conclude that this is not the kind of *constant* consensus that points to infallible teaching.

To give an example: both draft documents on Catholic doctrine that were prepared for the First Vatican Council proposed that the council define, as a dogma of faith, that the whole human race descended from a single couple.[36] It was repeatedly noted in the *Acta* that there was no opposition to such a projected definition.[37] Although the interruption of the council prevented conciliar discussion and action on this proposal, the unanimity in the commission that prepared those *schemata* suggests that prior to Vatican I there was a consensus among Catholic bishops and theologians that the descent of all men from Adam was definable doctrine, and that the theory of polygenism was contrary to the Tridentine decree which speaks of the "sin of Adam as one in origin and transmitted by propagation."[38] Eighty years after Vatican I, Pius XII, in his encyclical *Humani generis*, still insisted that Catholic theologians were not to hold the theory of polygenism, "for it is not at all apparent how such a view can be reconciled with the data which the sources of revealed truth and the documents of the church propose concerning original sin, namely, that it originates from a sin truly committed by one Adam, is transmitted to all through generation, and is in each, proper to him."[39] However, the fact that in 1950 Pius XII felt the need to tell Catholic theologians that they were not free to hold a theory of polygenism indicates that in the intervening years the former consensus on this point had begun to weaken. Indeed, within another twenty years that consensus had weakened to the point that Karl Rahner could write: "We may surely say that the development of Catholic theology since 'Humani generis' has made such advances (advances that have been tolerated by the church's *magisterium*) that the opinion that polygenism is not irreconcilable with the doctrine of original sin is no longer exposed to the danger of being censured by the authorities of the church."[40]

Here we have an instance of a consensus that seemed strong enough in 1870 to justify defining a doctrine as a dogma of faith, but which has not remained constant and is no longer universal. It would hardly seem reasonable to argue that since the former consensus had fulfilled the conditions required for the infallible exercise of ordinary universal magisterium, the subsequent lack of consensus could not nullify the claim that the doctrine had already been infallibly taught.

Here is another example, in the field of moral teaching. In their article "Contraception and the Infallibility of the Ordinary Magisterium," John C. Ford and Germain Grisez claimed that the official teaching on artificial contraception fulfilled the conditions laid down by Vatican II for the infallible exercise of the ordinary universal magisterium.[41] To show that the condition of "universal consensus" was fulfilled, they appealed to the fact that this teaching "was universally proposed by Catholic bishops up to 1962."[42] They also cited the historical study of contraception by John T. Noonan, Jr., as offering "substantial evidence for the universality of the Catholic Church's teaching on contraception up to 1962."[43] They concluded that "the historical evidence shows that Catholic bishops dispersed throughout the world agreed in one judgment on the morality of contraception, a judgment which remained substantially the same and which was universally proposed at least until 1962."[44] They also appealed to "a constant consensus of Catholic theologians in modern times," and gave the references to a very large number of works of moral theology of the nineteenth and twentieth centuries which maintained this doctrine; none of these works, however, is dated after 1962.

The repeated reference to consensus "until 1962" indicates that Ford and Grisez did not claim that in the late 1970s, when they were writing their article, there was still a universal consensus in the Catholic Church on the moral wrongness of contraception. However, in their view, the pre-1962 consensus was sufficient to fulfill the condition required for infallible teaching. They wrote: "Another point about the required universality [of consensus] is that if this condition has been met for some period in the past, it is not nullified by lack of present consensus among Catholic bishops."[45] In their view, it does not matter that the previous consensus has weakened or disappeared. In a recent article, Germain Grisez has reiterated the argument which he and John Ford had proposed, saying: "Since the previously existing ecclesial consensus was absent in 1978, we also argued that, once something has been taught infallibly, subsequent dissent cannot negate it."[46] It is true, of course, that if something was indeed taught infallibly, subsequent dissent cannot negate it. But, to fulfill the conditions required for the infallible teaching of the ordinary universal magisterium, the consensus must not only be universal; it must also be *constant*. If the argument advanced by Ford and Grisez were valid, one would have to hold that the incompatibility of polygenism with the dogma of original sin was infallibly taught, and that it makes no difference that there is no such consensus on that point today.

Another question that is pertinent to this problem is whether the prescription of canon law which says that "no doctrine is understood to be infallibly defined unless this fact is clearly established"[47] also applies to the recognition of infallible teaching by the ordinary universal magisterium. On this point there is a difference between the 1983 Code and the previous one. The 1917 Code said: "Nothing is understood to be infallibly defined or declared unless this is clearly established." Here the words "or declared" would seem to apply to the infallible teaching of the ordinary universal magisterium. From the fact that the 1983 Code omits the words "or declared," Germain Grisez has argued that the fact has to be "clearly established" only when it is a question of judging that a doctrine has been infallibly defined.[48] Perhaps this is the only requirement that is now recognized in canon law. However, I would argue on theological grounds that it is also true that no doctrine should be understood as having been infallibly taught by the ordinary universal magisterium unless this fact is clearly established.

My argument is based on the consequences for the faithful of the fact that a doctrine has been infallibly taught, whether this is by solemn definition or by the ordinary universal magisterium. According to Vatican I[49] and the 1983 Code,[50] doctrine proposed as divinely revealed must be believed with "divine and catholic faith," whether it has been solemnly defined, or infallibly taught by the ordinary universal magisterium. According to the new Formula for the Profession of Faith, if a doctrine has been infallibly proposed as divinely revealed, whether this was by solemn definition or by the ordinary universal magisterium, the obligation on the faithful is the same: they must believe it with firm faith. According to the 1983 Code, a person who is guilty of obstinate denial or doubt regarding a doctrine which must be believed with divine and Catholic faith is guilty of heresy.[51] No distinction is made between doctrine which has been solemnly defined, and that which has been infallibly taught by the ordinary and universal magisterium.

From the fact that the consequences for the faithful are the same whether doctrine has been solemnly defined or infallibly taught by the ordinary universal magisterium, I conclude that on theological grounds, the principle is equally true that no doctrine should be understood as having been infallibly proposed unless this fact is clearly established, whether the doctrine has been defined or taught by the ordinary universal magisterium.

As we have seen above,[52] the language used in the Code: *nisi id manifeste constiterit*, means that the fact that a doctrine has been infallibly defined must not only be "settled, undisputed, well known," but must be "manifestly" such. One could hardly claim that the fact that a doctrine had been infallibly defined was manifestly established if there were no consensus among Catholic theologians about this alleged fact. On the same grounds, I would say that one could hardly claim that a doctrine had been infallibly taught by the ordinary universal magisterium if there were no consensus among Catholic theologians on this point. On the other hand, their *constant and universal* consensus would be a reliable basis for judging that it had actually been taught in that way. As we have seen above, this is the criterion that Pope Pius IX himself proposed in *Tuas libenter*. It is true, of course, that it is not so easy nowadays to establish the fact of such a consensus among Catholic theologians as it was when they wrote manuals and assigned a theological "note" to each of their theses.

Conclusion

I have entitled this chapter "Undefined Dogmas." It can hardly be doubted that there are some dogmas of faith that have never been defined. Some articles of the creed are such; some dogmatic issues have been settled by regional councils, and their decisions have been universally received. Many of the doctrines of Trent were already dogmas of Catholic faith prior to being defined. Pius IX surely had good reason to object to the idea that a Catholic is obliged to believe only such dogmas as have been solemnly defined.

On the other hand, when one is dealing with a controversial issue, I believe one rightly applies two principles: 1) that the consensus required for infallible teaching of the ordinary magisterium must be a constant and enduring one; 2) that no doctrine is understood as having been infallibly taught unless this fact is clearly established, and this fact can hardly be clearly established if there is no consensus among Catholic theologians that the doctrine has indeed been infallibly taught.

8 || The Interpretation of Doctrinal Texts

There is broad agreement among theologians nowadays that ⊕ theology is an essentially hermeneutic endeavor. Hermeneutics is the science of interpretation. As an historical religion, Christianity relies heavily on written documents from the past: on sacred scripture, the writings of church fathers, liturgical texts, and documents produced by councils and popes. Its principal means of access to its own tradition is through such texts, which preserve the record of how the church has lived and confessed its faith throughout its history. Since scripture provides the normative expression of divine revelation, its interpretation is crucial for the faith of the church. For this reason, the science of hermeneutics has been developed primarily with a view to the interpretation of scripture. Only more recently have Catholic theologians come to realize how necessary it is to apply the science of hermeneutics also to the study of church documents.

The science of hermeneutics is especially concerned with the interpretation of texts which come from a time and culture that are distant from that of the contemporary reader. Fundamentalism is the practice of reading sacred scripture or other ancient documents, without paying attention to the consequences of the fact that they come from another time and culture than that of the reader. Fundamentalists presume that the "plain meaning" that the text has for them must be the meaning intended by the original author. They fail to see how the literary genre of a text will affect its meaning. They ignore the difference between the context in which the document was written, and the context in which they are reading it. They overlook the fact that a statement has meaning in its context, and that in a different context what is apparently the same statement may have quite a different meaning. In contrast to a fundamentalist reading, a hermeneutical reading pays attention to all the factors that make up the context in which the text was written, and in which it has its original meaning.

Five Steps in the Interpretation of a Doctrinal Text

The first step is to familiarize oneself with the historical factors which are significant elements of the context in which the text was written.

The second step is the study of the text itself. Here one will apply the pertinent rules of exegesis which biblical scholars have developed for the interpretation of scriptural texts.

The third step is to see how the doctrinal statement functions as an interpretation of the biblical message, and how it is integrated into the broader context of revealed truth found in scripture.

The fourth step is to look to the subsequent history of the doctrine contained in the dogmatic text, taking account of the further development of the church's understanding of the doctrine in its ongoing tradition.

Finally, theologians, whose vocation is to seek a contemporary understanding of the faith, will seek to express that understanding in concepts and terms that are meaningful to the faithful of their own day.

Let us now consider what is involved in each of these five steps, in somewhat more detail.

1. The Historical Context

With rare exceptions, dogmatic statements have been made because some article of Christian faith was being challenged by an erroneous teaching. Dogmas are the church's answer to a specific question that was being put to it at the time. One will not understand the answer unless one has a clear idea of what the question was. This calls for the study of the available sources, which throw light on the nature of the problem that the church had to face, and on the efforts that had been made, prior to the dogmatic decision, to resolve it.

As Juan Alfaro points out, "Dogmas always rise out of a prior theology whose concepts and language the dogmas make their own. The interpretation of dogmas therefore requires a knowledge of the theology in question, of the limitations proper to the problematic of such a theology, of the kind of thinking that its categories reveal, and of the varied and even contrary positions taken on the same question."[1]

As Alfaro also points out, besides determining what the concrete teaching was which the church meant to condemn as erroneous, and how this teaching was understood by its proponents and its adversaries, the interpreter will also seek to determine whether some aspects of the question were overlooked or simply omitted, what theological opinions were left open (neither rejected nor approved), what presuppositions, not recognized at the time, may have exercised a hidden (but decisive) influence on the way the church's doctrine was formulated. Alfaro insists: "These varied questions are not arbitrarily put down here, for they express concrete aspects of the historical conditioning which no human thinking can escape."[2]

2. Exegesis

In previous chapters we have looked at the criteria to be employed in evaluating the dogmatic weight of the various documents of the magisterium. We noted the importance of recognizing the different literary genres that are present in such documents. Obviously, in the exegesis of a magisterial text, the question of the literary genre will also be of primary importance. Is the text in question a profession of faith, an exposition of Catholic doctrine, a conciliar canon ending with *anathema*, a conciliar constitution, decree, or declaration?

In every kind of document, there will always be a distinction to be made between the principal assertions and the accessory material which does not have the same importance. In the major documents of ecumenical councils, the key distinction to be made is between the statement which actually defines a dogma of faith, and the rest of the document, which provides a justification or explanation of what is defined. Once the definitory statement is identified, it is the work of the exegete to determine as precisely as possible the meaning of the defined proposition.

This will call for a careful analysis of the terms that are used, keeping in mind that terms will reflect the meaning which they had in the period in which the document was written—a meaning which may well not be the same as the meaning which the same terms have in modern usage. This calls for a knowledge of the contemporary theological language as it is found in other sources of the same period.

As we have seen above, many dogmas have been defined by the condemnation of an erroneous doctrine as heretical. To arrive at the meaning of a dogma defined in this way, one must first determine the exact point which the council or pope intended to condemn, and then determine what positive proposition is the exact contradictory of the one that is condemned. Careful attention must be given to other elements in the doctrinal decree that may shed further light on the meaning, both of the heretical position and of the defined dogma, keeping in mind, however, the distinction between the central assertion which is defined, and other elements which do not have the same doctrinal weight. Among other things, these would include the biblical texts which are cited in support of the defined doctrine. There is a good presumption that councils and popes do not intend to define the sense of particular biblical texts which they cite in favor of their teaching; one would need clear evidence to judge that they had such an intention.

For some councils, we have not only the final decrees, but also the previous drafts, which show us what changes were made in the text during the course of the conciliar deliberations. In some cases, as for both Vatican Councils, we have the official reports (*relationes*) which explain the reasons why certain emendations were accepted and others rejected. While the *acta* of councils vary in the amount of data they provide, in many cases they provide information that is crucial for determining the meaning of the conciliar texts. Few theologians will be able to become thoroughly familiar with the *acta* of all the councils, or even of one council such as that of Trent; but in dealing with conciliar documents, one would be unwise not to consult the findings of those who have made such research their "functional specialty."

A major effort of the theologian in interpreting a dogmatic text will be to distinguish between the precise assertion of faith which the council or pope intended to define, and other elements in the statement which were part of the "world-view" or cultural conditioning of people at that time, and were inevitably presupposed in formulating the doctrine. It is quite possible that this distinction could not have been made at the time the doctrine was defined, and that only in the light of further knowledge does it become clear that certain elements in the dogmatic statement are presuppositions which need to be distinguished from the assertion of faith.

3. Interpreting Dogma in the Light of Scripture

Since a dogmatic statement is an authoritative expression of some revealed truth, an important step in its interpretation will be to seek an understanding of the defined truth precisely as revealed. This is not a question of looking for "proof-texts" in support of the dogma, but of inserting this particular truth into the broader context of revelation, especially as this is found in scripture. By reason of the fact that dogmas are defined in response to specific historical challenges to the faith, they are inevitably limited to particular and partial aspects of the total content of revelation. Since the full truth of any such partial aspect of revealed truth depends on its insertion into the whole, the interpretation of any dogma will demand that it be understood not as an isolated truth, but as an integral part of what God has revealed. This will mean recognizing that dogmas not only interpret scripture, but in turn must be interpreted in the light of scripture. One example of this is Vatican I's definition of faith as "a supernatural virtue whereby we believe that which God has revealed is true because of the authority of God who has revealed it."[3] Faith does, of course, include such an intellectual assent, but this description of it has to be understood in the light of the more comprehensive biblical notion of faith as a total response of the human person to God.

In seeking to understand a dogmatic statement precisely as expressing a revealed truth, the theologian will return to scripture, not only to identify the biblical foundation of the dogma, but also to seek the further light which scriptural exegesis can shed on its meaning. The idea that the meaning of dogma can be clarified by a return to scripture was not mentioned by Pius XII when he spoke of the theologian's return to the sources in his encyclical *Humani generis*. There he said:

> It is true that theologians must always return to the sources of divine revelation, for it is their task to show how what is taught by the living magisterium is found, whether explicitly or implicitly, in sacred scripture and in divine tradition...Along with these sacred fonts, God has given to his church the living magisterium for the sake of clarifying and spelling out what is contained only obscurely in the deposit of faith...Now if the church performs this task of hers, as in the course of the centuries she has often done, whether by the ordinary or the extraordinary exercise of her magisterium, it is evident how wrong a method it is to explain what is clear from what is obscure; rather it is the exactly contrary procedure that all should follow. Wherefore Our Predecessor of immortal memory, Pius IX, when teaching that it is theology's most noble function to demonstrate how doctrine defined by the church is contained in the sources, not without grave reasons added those words: "in the very same sense in which it has been defined."[4]

Joseph Ratzinger expressed his dissatisfaction with this view of the role of theology in no uncertain terms, in his commentary on the dogmatic constitution *Dei Verbum* of Vatican II, where he said:

> The risk of a false orientation cannot be dismissed when *Humani generis* (which incidentally quotes Pius IX on the point) declares that it is obviously wrong to seek to clarify what is clear by the help of what is obscure...which means in the context that it is not the teaching office that can be clarified by scripture, but only, on the contrary, scripture by the teaching office. This is then developed to the point at which the task of theology is described as that of showing how what the teaching office has established is contained in the sources..."and that precisely in the sense in which it has been defined." One can hardly deny that the point of view which sees only scripture as what is unclear, but the teaching office as what is clear, is a very limited one and that to reduce the task of theology to the proof of the presence of the statements of the teaching

office in the sources is to threaten the primacy of the sources which (were one to continue logically in this direction) would ultimately destroy the serving character of the teaching office.[5]

4. Interpreting Dogma in the Light of Ongoing Tradition

The theologian seeks a contemporary understanding of his faith, and therefore has to interpret dogmas of the past in the light of any fuller understanding of them which the church may have achieved in the course of its ongoing tradition. Since a dogmatic statement is an interpretation of some aspect of the biblical message, further developments in the church's understanding of scripture can have an impact also on our understanding of dogma. An obvious example of this is the impact which a better understanding of the literary genre of the early chapters of Genesis has had, and continues to have, on the interpretation of the dogma of original sin.

In its declaration *Mysterium Ecclesiae*, the Congregation for the Doctrine of the Faith has observed that a dogmatic truth which was at first expressed in an incomplete way can, when considered in a broader context of faith or human knowledge, receive a fuller and more perfect expression.[6] Such a "more perfect expression" of a dogmatic truth will reflect the better understanding of it which has been achieved in the light of that broader context of faith or human knowledge. This means that scientific discoveries can also contribute to our better understanding of revealed truth. Such discoveries, for example, in the sciences which deal with the origin and development of the human species, cannot be ignored in our interpretation of the dogmas of creation and original sin.

Another example of the impact which growth in human knowledge can have on the interpretation of dogma is had in the case of the dogmatic statement: "Outside of the church there is no salvation." In the thirteenth century, when this was defined by the Fourth Lateran Council, and even in 1442, when it was even more rigidly asserted by the Council of Florence,[7] the world known to the council fathers was practically limited to Christendom and Islam. With no idea of the vast multitudes of human beings living in the continents still to be discovered, they believed that everyone had had an opportunity to hear the gospel and respond to it, and so they considered those who were "outside the church," such as the Jews and Moslems, guilty of rejecting the offer of salvation. It was only in the light of new knowledge about the extent of the earth and its human population, achieved in the late fifteenth and sixteenth centuries, that Catholic theologians came to realize that they could no longer interpret that doctrine in the same way that medieval Christians had done. This led to the search for a new understanding of the necessary role of the church in the divine plan of salvation, the fruit of which one finds in the documents of Vatican II.[8]

5. Communicating a Contemporary Understanding of the Faith

It is the task of theologians not only to seek a contemporary understanding of the faith, but also to render that understanding accessible to the contemporary faithful. While the "charism of infallibility" given to the magisterium guarantees that its dogmatic definitions are not erroneous, it does not guarantee that its dogmas are formulated in such a way that they will remain intelligible in every time and culture. In fact, the historical conditioning which affects the formulation of doctrine makes it highly improbable that any dogmatic statement will be free of the limitations which make its meaning less accessible to people of a different time and culture. Such limitations affect the way in which the question was originally asked, the presuppositions which influenced the way people of that time thought about the question, and the concepts then available for responding to it. The consequence of such historical conditioning is that the mere repetition of the original dogmatic formulas in a changed cultural setting could result in a "breakdown of communications," with the risk that the profession of faith would become a mere recitation of words. An important part of the theologians' task is to make the church's dogmas meaningful to the faithful of their own time.

The attitude with which a theologian should undertake this task of communicating a contemporary understanding of the faith is well described as one of "creative fidelity." Fidelity describes the theologian's effort to grasp the authentic meaning of a dogma, and to preserve that same meaning in any reconceptualization and reformulation of it. "Fidelity," then, has to do primarily with the meaning of dogma, rather than with its verbal expression. However, there is a sense in which the theologian's "fidelity" also includes a certain respect for the traditional language in which the faith has been expressed and is professed. Differing views as to what such "respect for traditional language" involves are found even in official documents of the magisterium.

In the encyclical *Humani generis*, Pope Pius XII warned theologians against departing from the traditional formulas in which the church has expressed its faith, on the grounds that this would lead to dogmatic relativism.[9] Pope Paul VI in his encyclical *Mysterium fidei* was critical of attempts made by some theologians to express the mystery of the eucharist in terms other than those used by the Council of Trent. Referring to the Tridentine formulas, he said:

> These formulas—like the others that the Church has used to propose the dogmas of faith—express concepts that are not tied to a certain specific form of human culture, or to a certain level of scientific progress, or to one or another theological school. Instead they set forth what the human mind grasps of reality through necessary and universal experience and what it expresses in apt and exact words, whether it be in ordinary or more refined language. For this reason, these formulas are adapted to all men of all times and all places.[10]

Although this encyclical was contemporary with Vatican II, it does not seem to reflect the new approach which the council had taken to this question. In the Decree on Ecumenism, referring to differences between eastern and western formulations of doctrine, the council said: "In the investigation of revealed truth, east and west have used different methods and approaches in understanding and proclaiming divine things. It is hardly surprising, then, if sometimes one tradition has come nearer than the other to an apt appreciation of certain aspects of a revealed mystery, or has expressed them in a clearer manner. As a result, these various theological formulations are often to be considered as complementary rather than conflicting."[11] Likewise, in its Pastoral Constitution on the Church in the Modern World, the council urged theologians "to seek continually for more suitable ways of communicating doctrine to the men of their times. For the deposit of faith or revealed truths are one thing; the manner in which they are formulated, without violence to their meaning and significance, is another."[12]

Avery Dulles, writing in 1970, remarked: "There seems to be, prima facie, a difference in emphasis, if not in teaching, between two sets of documents. Some documents, such as *Humani generis* and *Mysterium fidei*, accent the universal and timeless value of the church's concepts and formulas. Others, such as *Unitatis redintegratio* and *Gaudium et spes*, allow for, and even encourage, a variety of formulations in accordance with the mentality and traditions of different peoples and ages."[13] If Dulles had written this after 1973, he would probably have remarked an even greater contrast between *Humani generis* and *Mysterium fidei*, on the one hand, and the CDF declaration *Mysterium Ecclesiae* on the other.[14]

It is instructive to see how the International Theological Commission handled the apparent conflict between those documents, in its statement "On the Interpretation of Dogmas."[15] Having summarized the position taken by Pius XII and Paul VI in their encyclicals, the commission described the Second Vatican Council as having "presented the previous teaching of the church in a broad context and in the process asserted the historical dimension of dogma...Its exposition of the pastoral character of the teaching office directed attention to the distinction between the immutable deposit of faith (or truths of faith) and the way in which they are expressed. This means that the teaching of the church—to be sure always with the same meaning and the same content—must be transmitted to people in a manner that is alive and appropriate to the exigencies of the day."[16]

Here the commission would seem to have distanced itself from the position taken in *Humani generis* and *Mysterium fidei*. However, in a later section of its document, it took up the question of the balance to be maintained between "the need for a contemporary interpretation" and the "permanent validity of dogmatic formulations."[17] It began by observing that "a contemporary interpretation of dogmas must take into account two, at first sight, contradictory principles: the abiding validity of the truth, and the actuality of the truth."[18]

However, in the following section, it is not only truth, but also dogmatic formulations, that are said to have abiding validity. The commission began its discussion of this point by agreeing that "without doubt, the permanent and valid content of the dogmas is to be distinguished from the way in which they are formulated. In any age the mystery of Christ surpasses the possibilities of formulation and thus eludes any final systematization."[19] On the other hand, the Commission insists:

> No clear-cut separation can be made between the content and form of the statement. The symbolic system of language is not mere external apparel, but to a certain extent the incarnation of a truth...As a community of faith, the church is a community in spoken confession (of that faith). Consequently, unity in the fundamental verbal expressions of faith belongs to the unity of the church diachronically and synchronically. And those expressions are not revised if one does not wish to lose sight of the "reality" manifested in them. However, in a multiplicity of ways in which it is proclaimed that "reality" must be appropriated ever anew and given further expression. For this an occasion and obligation are provided by Christianity's taking root in other cultures. The truth of revelation nevertheless remains always the same "not only in its real substance (content), but also in its decisive linguistic formulations."[20]

One could wish that the commission had further explained how the obligation of appropriating the reality of faith ever anew and giving it further expression in other cultures is compatible with the idea that the truth of revelation remains always the same not only in its content but also in its decisive linguistic formulations. I suggest that to resolve this dilemma it would be helpful to distinguish, as Karl Rahner has done, between unity of creed and pluralism of theologies. Here is a passage where he has explained what this distinction involves.

> The inevitable pluralism of theologies which exists today must not and need not surrender the unity of the Church's creed even at the verbal level. In the theology of the Church and in the mind and heart of the individual believer there must be a pluralism in

the interpretation of any given dogma...But all this does not exclude the fact that there must be unity of creed within the church and, moreover, that this can be established in sufficient measure. On any Catholic understanding of the faith this unity cannot consist merely in the unity of that reality which is ultimately signified but is beyond words, and to which the various theological statements refer. There must also be a unity in the verbal creed itself within the one church...In order that there shall be a unity of one and the same creed within the church in a context of insuperable pluralism with regard to the understanding of the faith, and in order to uphold the verbal expression of the truth in its presentation at the social level, it is inevitable and legitimate to have a certain linguistic norm...The Christian and the theologian must adopt a policy which has nothing to do with any cowardly or facile ecclesiastical conformism, namely to strive in a spirit of sincerity and self-criticism to ensure that a verbal formulation of the creed expressing the one faith of the church is really preserved. And to this end they must ever anew bring their own interpretation of the faith (however justified or indeed necessary it may be in itself) into conformity with the one creed of the church, and help to promote this one creed. Otherwise in the long run the danger of real heresies arising in the church can no longer be excluded.[21]

Accepting Rahner's distinction between unity of creed and pluralism of theologies, one could say that the "creative fidelity" which theologians are to exercise in interpreting dogmas includes respect for the traditional language in which the church professes its faith, along with freedom to express a contemporary understanding of the faith in modern patterns of thought and language—a freedom which is limited by the requirement that their interpretation be faithful to the meaning of the creed.

This, of course, raises the crucial question: Who is to judge whether a new interpretation of a dogma is faithful to its meaning? Here an important distinction is to be made between scholarly judgment and official judgment. The former is the responsibility of theologians; the latter is the responsibility of the bearers of official teaching authority. The frank exchange of critical opinion among competent theologians concerning new interpretations of dogma is an essential part of the theological enterprise. Karl Rahner has written of the theologian's "right and duty to question the orthodoxy of another theologian's theory, even if the latter was published by episcopal permission," adding that "insofar as this does not happen enough, the wrong opinion grows up that everything which appears beneath an *Imprimatur* is orthodox and may not be doubted." He went on to deplore the reluctance of theologians to exercise a critical function toward one another's theories: "It is a false politeness and collegiality when theologians are too concerned to take pains to be 'indulgent' with one another. The indisputable decline in theological criticism is to be deplored in this respect, and it is an extremely dangerous situation."[22]

While Rahner urged theologians to exercise their scholarly judgment on the orthodoxy of opinions expressed by their peers, he also recognized that there can come a point when an intervention of the official teaching authority is required. This is how he put it:

> It must not be thought that today one can either leave each question alone or that it can be cleared up in a purely scholarly dialogue with the agreement of all theological parties, without the teaching office having to step in authoritatively. The bearers of doctrinal authority (each according to his fundamental and respectively different authority and according to the importance of the matter in hand) must have the courage to say No under certain circumstances, even if they have not been able to 'convince' each and every person beforehand by exhortation, theological discussion of the issue itself, etc. After all, the church *has* a common confession of faith which must be protected; the church is more than a theological debating society...What is "indispensable" and what is not is decided in the final analysis by the theology of the magisterium, not by the theology of the theologians.[23]

9 ‖ Some Examples of Interpretation

My intention in this chapter is to offer a few examples of the way that respected Catholic theologians have interpreted some documents of the magisterium. Obviously, this will be but a small sample of the kind of work that has been done, and is being done, by theologians to determine the precise meaning of doctrinal texts, and to express that meaning in terms that make sense to people today. Perhaps not all Catholic theologians will be in complete agreement with the conclusions reached by those whose interpretations will be presented here. However, I am confident that their work exemplifies that "creative fidelity" which should characterize the efforts of theologians to apply the principles of hermeneutics to the study of doctrinal texts. I shall begin with a text in the decree of Trent on the Eucharist.

On Transubstantiation[1]

The text reads as follows:

Because Christ our Redeemer said that it was truly his body that he was offering under the species of bread (cf. Mt 26:26ff; Mk 14:22ff; Lk 22:19f; 1 Cor 11:24ff), it has always been the conviction of the church of God, and this holy council now again declares, that by the consecration of the bread and wine there takes place a change of the whole substance of bread into the substance of the body of Christ our Lord and of the whole substance of wine into the substance of his blood. This change the holy Catholic Church has fittingly and properly named transubstantiation.

122

To this "chapter" there corresponds canon 2:[2]

If anyone says that in the holy sacrament of the eucharist the sub-stance of bread and wine remains together with the body and blood of our Lord Jesus Christ, and denies that wonderful and unique change of the whole substance of the bread into his body and of the whole substance of the wine into his blood while only the species of bread and wine remain, a change which the Catholic Church very fittingly calls transubstantiation, *anathema sit*.

A preliminary observation on these texts is to note the differ-ence between the final clause in both chapter and canon, affirm-ing that the Catholic Church very fittingly calls the change from bread to the body of Christ "transubstantiation," and the central affirmation about the change itself. It is obvious that only the cen-tral affirmation defines a dogma of faith. To question or deny the "fittingness" of the term "transubstantiation" would involve heresy only if it was equivalently a denial of the dogma which that term intends to express. Furthermore, to agree that up to the time of Trent this term was "very fitting" does not exclude the possibil-ity that, in another time and culture, this might not be the most fitting term, and that another term might be preferable to it. But, of course, the fundamental question here is to determine exactly what Trent meant by "transubstantiation," because any other term would have to be faithful to that meaning.

An example of a modern Catholic interpretation of the mean-ing of transubstantiation in the Tridentine decree is found in the article of Karl Rahner: "The Presence of Christ in the Sacrament of the Lord's Supper."[3] It is a rather long article, and obviously I cannot attempt to do it justice here. But I shall present what I take to be the essentials of his interpretation, using Rahner's own words, by quoting the following passages of his article.

The council finds proof of this doctrine in the fact that Christ declares that what he offers (the apostles) under the appearance of bread *is* his body. This means that if the words of consecration are to be taken in their strict and literal sense, and if they bring about the event of the presence of the body of Christ, then what Christ offers his apostles is not bread, but his body. This state-ment, as it stands, must be accepted by all who refuse to give a vague, figurative meaning to the words of Christ.[4]

First I should wish to make a conceptual distinction of a fundamental nature, which I shall make use of later. I should like to distinguish between a logical and an ontic explanation of a matter, and try to explain this distinction. The *logical* explanation of a statement about a given matter would be a statement which makes the statement to be explained clear, that is, more definite and unmistakable, by interpreting it on its own terms, that is, without appealing to matters distinct from the matter to be explained. The logical explanation—to put it crudely for the moment—explains by giving precisions, but does not affirm anything else in explanation of the matter in hand...The *ontic* explanation of a statement about a given matter would be the explanation which asserts *something else* than the matter in question, but something which is capable of rendering it intelligible, and so preserving it from misunderstandings, by giving for instance indications of its cause, of the precise, concrete way in which it came about, and so on.[5]

Presupposing this distinction, I should like to put forward the thesis that the dogma of transubstantiation (insofar as it is really strict *dogma*) is a logical and not an ontic explanation of the words of Christ taken literally...It intends to say exactly what Christ says: that what he gives is his body and no longer bread, though bread had been there, because his declaration effectively changes the reality and produces what it affirms: the reality of the body of Christ instead of the substance of the bread. I call the doctrine of transubstantiation [a] logical [explanation] on account of its relationship to the words of Christ, which are to be explained and guarded against all misunderstandings that would weaken or deny their sense. By this I mean that the doctrine of transubstantiation tells me no more than do the words of Christ when I take them seriously. The function of this doctrine is not to explain the real presence by accounting for *how* it takes place, so that the manner of its coming, understood in itself as *another* process, would explain how the real presence came to be. Transubstantiation, as a dogma, means more than just any sort of a real presence, but it does not affirm anything more than the real presence which is there when what is given is understood as the presence of the body of Christ...The dogma rests solely on the words of Christ, and implies only the possibility of what is implied in these words of Christ; it does not imply *other* matters which can only be known by presupposing a given philosophical system.[6]

Further light on the meaning of transubstantiation is given by
Joseph Ratzinger, when he explained the eucharistic change in
the following way:

> The eucharistic change, by definition, concerns not what appears,
> but what cannot appear (i.e. the "substance"). This change takes
> place outside the physical realm. That means that, as far as
> physics and chemistry are concerned, *nothing* happens to the
> bread and wine. Physically and chemically, they are the same after
> the change as before.[7]

If I understand Ratzinger correctly here, he distinguishes
between the species as the empirical reality and the substance as
the meta-empirical reality. What our senses reach is the empirical reality. What a thing "really is" is its substance, and this is not
reached by the senses. Thus in the eucharist the empirical reality
of bread remains but not the substance of bread, because after
the consecration what it "really is" is not bread but the body of
Christ. If one takes the term "substance," as Trent did, simply to
mean "what something really is," then the change from really
being bread to really being the body of Christ, from one reality
to another reality, can fittingly be called a change from one substance to another substance, or transubstantiation. To say that
the substance of bread does not remain means that what was
bread is no longer really bread, but is the body of Christ. This
truth, which is knowable only to faith, is not denied by the fact
that there has been no change in the empirical reality of the
bread, which remains as the sacramental sign.

All of this is based on the premise that "substance" is understood to mean "what something really is," and that this is not identical with the empirical reality. The problem with the traditional
language of transubstantiation today is that most people now
would understand the term "substance" to mean what physical or
chemical analysis would determine something to be, and this is
precisely what is meant by the empirical reality. It is hard for people nowadays to think of a change as "substantial," if it is such as to
leave the elements physically and chemically unchanged. The fact
that the term "transubstantiation" describes the eucharistic
change as "substantial," even though no physical or chemical
change takes place in the elements, suggests that it might be wise

to look for another way of expressing this mystery that would make it more meaningful and intelligible to the modern mind.

An example of a modern attempt to express this doctrine without using the term "substantial change" is found in the agreed statements on "Eucharistic Doctrine" of the First Anglican–Roman Catholic International Commission (ARCIC).[8] The original statement expressed the doctrine on eucharistic change in the following way:

> Communion with Christ in the eucharist presupposes his true presence, effectually signified by the bread and wine, which, in this mystery, become his body and blood. (Footnote here: "The word *transubstantiation* is commonly used in the Roman Catholic Church to indicate that God acting in the eucharist effects a change in the inner reality of the elements. This term should be seen as affirming the fact of Christ's presence and of the mysterious and radical change which takes place. In contemporary Roman Catholic theology it is not understood as explaining how the change takes place.")[9]

> The Lord's words at the last supper: "Take and eat; this is my body," do not allow us to dissociate the gift of the presence and the act of sacramental eating. The elements are not mere signs; Christ's body and blood become really present and are really given. But they are really present and given in order that, receiving them, believers may be united in communion with Christ the Lord.[10]

> According to the traditional order of the liturgy the consecratory prayer (*anaphora*) leads to the communion of the faithful. Through this prayer of thanksgiving, a word of faith addressed to the Father, the bread and wine become the body and blood of Christ by the action of the Holy Spirit, so that in communion we eat the flesh of Christ and drink his blood.[11]

In response to comments made on their original statement on the Eucharist, ARCIC I added the following "Elucidation":

> Criticism has been evoked by the statement that the bread and wine become the body and blood of Christ in the eucharist. The word *become* has been suspected of expressing a materialistic conception of Christ's presence, and this has seemed to some to be confirmed in the footnote on the word *transubstantiation* which

also speaks of *change*. It is feared that this suggests that Christ's presence is confined to the elements, and that the Real Presence involves a physical change in them...

Becoming does not here imply material change. Nor does the liturgical use of the word imply that the bread and wine become Christ's body and blood in such a way that in the eucharistic celebration his presence is limited to the consecrated elements. It does not imply that Christ becomes present in the eucharist in the same manner that he was present in his earthly life. It does not imply that this *becoming* follows the physical laws of this world. What is here affirmed is a sacramental presence in which God uses realities of this world to convey the realities of the new creation: bread for this life becomes the bread of eternal life. Before the Eucharistic Prayer, to the question: "What is that?" the believer answers: "It is bread." After the Eucharistic Prayer, to the same question he answers: "It is truly the body of Christ, the Bread of Life."[12]

In their *Response to the Final Report of ARCIC I*, the Bishops' Conference of England and Wales made the following comment on what ARCIC had said about the real presence of Christ in the eucharist.

Real Presence. The statement clearly maintains the real and true presence of Christ. The substantial nature of the change of the bread and wine is clearly asserted by the repeated use of the word "become," as in the statement that "they become his body and blood," by reference to the transforming action of the Spirit, by use of the language of change in the footnote on transubstantiation, and by the careful description of the role of faith within the individual. In the light of this we accept the statement as an expression of Catholic faith in the real presence.[13]

Six years later, the Vatican issued its official response to the Final Report of ARCIC I.[14] Here is the Vatican comment on ARCIC's treatment of the doctrine of the real presence:

27. The affirmations that the eucharist is "the Lord's real gift of himself to his church," and that the bread and wine "become" the body and blood of Christ, can certainly be interpreted in conformity with Catholic faith. They are insufficient, however, to remove all ambiguity regarding the mode of the real presence which is due to a substantial change in the elements.[15]

In its Elucidation, ARCIC had to respond to the idea that to say that in the eucharist bread and wine *become* the body and blood of Christ, and that a "mysterious and radical *change*" takes place, would imply a physical or material change of the elements, or a materialistic conception of Christ's presence in the eucharist. This manifests the ambiguity that is involved in speaking of a "substantial" change, in an age when people are conditioned to think of "substance" as what chemical analysis would determine a thing to be. Who nowadays would be likely to call a change "substantial" if they knew it would involve no physical or chemical change in the elements? It seems to me (and evidently also to the bishops of England and Wales) that ARCIC has found an apt way to express the mystery of the eucharist without using the terms "substance" or "substantial change." I presume that this choice was motivated by their realization of the ambiguity which these terms present to the modern mind, when used of a change that leaves bread and wine chemically the same as they were before.

The bishops of England and Wales judged that, without using the term "substantial change," the ARCIC statement clearly asserted the substantial nature of the change that takes place in the eucharist. The Vatican Response, on the other hand, insists that in order to remove ambiguity from ARCIC's statement, the term "substantial change" must be used. In my opinion, the use of this term would have the contrary effect of introducing the very ambiguity which ARCIC has successfully avoided.

Trent's Canon on Preparation for Receiving the Eucharist[16]

The text reads as follows:

If anyone says that faith alone is a sufficient preparation for receiving the sacrament of the most holy eucharist, *anathema sit.* And, lest so great a sacrament be received unworthily and hence unto death and condemnation, this holy council determines and decrees that those whose conscience is burdened with mortal sin, no matter how contrite they may think they are, must necessarily make first a sacramental confession if a confessor is available. If anyone presumes to teach, or preach, or obstinately maintain, or

defend in public dispitation the opposite of this, he shall by the
very fact be excommunicated.

The first sentence, the only one which ends with *anathema sit*,
condemns as heretical the Lutheran opinion that faith alone is a
sufficient preparation for receiving the eucharist. Hence it is
defined dogma that faith *alone* would not *always* be a sufficient
preparation. In the light of the rest of this canon, as well as of
what is said in the second paragraph of Chapter 7 of this
decree,[17] it is clear that what is at stake here is the further preparation that would be required if a person were conscious of being
in the state of grave sin. It is a dogma of faith that, at least in that
case, something more than faith alone is required as preparation
for receiving the eucharist.

The rest of the canon answers the question: What more than
faith is required, if a person's conscience is burdened with mortal sin? The answer is clear: contrition, no matter how perfect the
person may judge it to be, is not a sufficient preparation. One
must necessarily first make a sacramental confession if a confessor is available. But has the council defined the necessity of
sacramental confession in such a case as a dogma of faith?

One indication of how this question should be answered is the
difference between the language which the council used in the
first sentence of this canon, and which it used in the rest of the
canon. The first sentence, ending with *anathema sit*, clearly condemns a doctrinal position as heretical. But in the second sentence, the council *determines and decrees* that those whose
conscience is burdened with mortal sin *must necessarily* first make
a sacramental confession. The terms used here are not those of a
statement of doctrine, but rather of a legislative decree: they do
not prescribe what must be believed, but what must be done.
However, the final sentence might seem to define the issue, since
it declares excommunicated anyone who presumes to teach,
preach or obstinately maintain or publicly defend the opposite of
what is prescribed here. If the council intended to condemn such
a person as guilty of heresy, one could conclude that it intended
to define as dogma the necessity of confession before communion for one conscious of mortal sin. But if it had intended to
condemn anyone teaching the opposite as a heretic, why did it

not use the term *anathema sit* here, as it did in the first sentence? Was it the mind of Trent that one who teaches the opposite of what is prescribed here is really contradicting a doctrine of faith?

Here is a case where it would be helpful to have contemporary evidence as to exactly what the intention of the council on this matter was. Maurice Bévenot has found such evidence in the writing of Melchior Cano, a Dominican theologian who took part in the Council of Trent. Cano explains the background of this decree as follows. It was well known at Trent that a prominent Catholic theologian, Cajetan, held the opinion that for a person conscious of mortal sin, perfect contrition was a sufficient preparation for receiving communion; sacramental confession was not strictly required. The great majority of the fathers at Trent strongly disapproved of this opinion, seeing it as likely to lead to grave abuse of the sacrament. It was for this reason that the council issued a sentence of excommunication against anyone who would propagate this opinion. But Cano insists that Trent did not intend to condemn Cajetan's opinion as heresy, and Cano was certainly in a position to know the mind of Trent on the matter.[18] We can therefore resolve the doubt that might remain as to the meaning of the final sentence of the canon, in the light of reliable information provided by a theologian who took part in the council. It is not a dogma of faith that a person conscious of mortal sin must make a sacramental confession before receiving communion if a confessor is available.

However, from the condemnation as heresy of the view that faith alone suffices, it is dogmatically certain that something more than faith is required, at least if a person is conscious of mortal sin. Since it is not a dogma that sacramental confession is required, then the dogma must be that contrition for mortal sin is required, in addition to faith, as a preparation for receiving the Eucharist.

The Code of Canon Law specifies the obligation in the following way:

> Anyone who is conscious of grave sin may not celebrate Mass or receive the Body of the Lord without previously having been to sacramental confession, unless there is a grave reason and there is no opportunity to confess; in this case the person is to remember

the obligation to mak^ an act of perfect contrition, which includes the resolve to go to confession as soon as possible.[19]

Trent's Canon on Sacramental Character

The question of sacramental character is treated in the Decree on the Sacraments, in the ninth of the Canons on the Sacraments in General. Canon 9 reads as follows:

> If anyone says that in three sacraments, namely, baptism, confirmation and order, a character is not imprinted on the soul, that is, a kind of indelible spiritual sign by reason of which these sacraments cannot be repeated, anathema sit.[20]

At first sight, this would seem to define, as a dogma of faith, the doctrine that these three sacraments imprint a character in the soul. However, as we have seen above, for a doctrine to be defined as a dogma of faith, it must be a divinely revealed truth. In his article, "The Sacramental Character at the Council of Trent,"[21] Piet Fransen has studied the discussion and deliberations concerning this question at Trent, and has come to the following conclusion: "The doctrine of the sacramental character belonged at the time of Trent to the commonly accepted and officially recognized body of doctrine of the western church. This universality and this recognition is a guarantee that this doctrine is not contrary to the reality of revelation. But whether it is part of revelation itself cannot be inferred from the discussions at Trent."[22] In other words, in Fransen's opinion, Trent's doctrine on sacramental character is not defined as a dogma of faith since it is not certain that Trent intended to define it as divinely revealed doctrine. At Trent, the contumacious denial of a commonly accepted and officially recognized doctrine of the Catholic Church justified condemnation as heresy; this did not necessarily mean denial of divinely revealed truth.

The Canon of Trent on the Indissolubility of Marriage

The question at issue was whether the marriage bond can be dissolved on account of the adultery of one of the spouses. This is treated in the seventh of the canons on the sacrament of matrimony, which reads as follows:

> If anyone says that the church is in error for having taught and for still teaching that, in accordance with the evangelical and apostolic doctrine (cf. Mk 10:1; 1 Cor 7), the marriage bond cannot be dissolved because of adultery on the part of one of the spouses, and that neither of the two, not even the innocent one who has given no cause for infidelity, can contract another marriage during the lifetime of the other, and that the husband who dismisses an adulterous wife and marries again and the wife who dismisses an adulterous husband and marries again are both guilty of adultery, a.s. [23]

This has often been understood as defining the infallibility of the church in teaching this doctrine, with the consequence that the doctrine is taken to have been defined as a dogma of faith. However, Piet Fransen concluded, from his study of the Acts of the Council, that this was not the intention of the Fathers at Trent. In a series of scholarly articles, Fransen published the details of his painstaking examination of the discussions that led up to this decree.[24] He subsequently summed up the fruit of this study in the paper which he read at the symposium on "Problems of Authority" held at Bec in 1961. Here are the conclusions to which his study led him.

> I have studied the Council of Trent's Session on Marriage, especially Canon 7 on divorce in the case of adultery. It is formulated in a very complicated way, and for a very simple reason. All that was desired was a condemnation of the position taken up by Luther and defended in the *De Captivitate Babylonica*. At the same time and at the request of the Venetian ambassadors and the Venetian bishops in the Greek islands, it was also desired to avoid condemning a different practice in the Eastern Church...That is why, in the end, a very subtle formula was adopted: *Si quis dixerit Ecclesiam errare, cum docuit et docet...*
>
> The meaning of this canon has been under discussion for centuries. A conclusion exactly opposite to that intended by the Council has often been drawn, for instance, that the Greeks were condemned by the canon!...it was commonly claimed that the canon defined the inerrancy of the Church in this particular matter and, logically enough, the impossibility of divorce in cases of adultery. When we read the Acts of the Council today...we can

easily recognize that ᵗʰis aspect of the question was hardly considered at all by the Fathers of the Council. And so a historical misunderstanding has arisen.

Errare, which occurs several times during the Session on
Marriage, had a wider meaning, due to the contrary teaching of
Luther. Luther's central position in regard to marriage was that
marriage was outside the jurisdiction of the Church. The whole of
Canon and Pontifical Law was therefore simply *an abuse of power*.
Hence *errare* formally indicated in this context of thought: to
usurp a jurisdiction which the Church did not possess...As is
proved by the statements of the bishops of the Greek islands during the final solemn Session, which formally "defines" a conciliar
text, the contrary practice of the Greeks was *not* condemned.[25]

It is clear from Fransen's study of the conciliar *acta* that since
Trent did not intend to condemn the practice of the Greek
church as heretical, it did not define as a dogma of faith the doctrine that marriage cannot be dissolved on the grounds of the
adultery of one of the spouses. What it strictly condemned was
the position of Luther that the church has no authority to make
laws about marriage. If Fransen's interpretation is correct, it follows that in this canon Trent did not define the indissolubility of
marriage as a dogma of faith. But if it did not define it in this
canon, it did not define it at all, for there is no other decree of
Trent that can be understood to have done so.

In his book *Faithful Dissent*, Charles Curran has published the
correspondence between himself and the Congregation for the
Doctrine of the Faith, which culminated in the letter of July 25,
1986, signed by the prefect, Cardinal Joseph Ratzinger, which
informed Fr. Curran of Rome's decision that he would "no
longer be considered suitable or eligible to exercise the function
of a Professor of Catholic Theology."[26] In giving the reasons for
this decision, Cardinal Ratzinger wrote:

> Your basic assertion has been that since your positions are con-
> vincing to you and diverge only from the 'non-infallible' teaching
> of the Church, they constitute 'responsible dissent,' and should
> therefore be allowed by the Church. In this regard, the following
> considerations seem to be in order...It is clear that you have not
> taken into adequate account, for instance, that the Church's posi-
> tion on the indissolubility of sacramental and consummated mar-

riage, which you claim ought to be changed, was in fact defined at the Council of Trent and so belongs to the patrimony of the Faith.[27]

Two days after receiving this letter, Charles Curran issued a public statement in which, referring to Ratzinger's charge that he disagreed with a dogma that had been defined by Trent, Curran said: "All Catholic theologians recognize that the teaching of the Council of Trent does not exclude as contrary to faith the practice of *economia* in the Greek Church. I have maintained that the position I propose on the indissolubility of marriage is in keeping with this tradition."[28]

Of the two positions in contrast here, Curran's is the one that is supported by the research that Piet Fransen has done on the meaning of Trent's decree about divorce on the grounds of adultery.

The Decree of Trent on Original Sin[29]

Zoltan Alszeghy and Maurizio Flick, colleagues of mine for many years on the faculty of the Gregorian but now deceased, offered a masterful example of the interpretation of a conciliar decree in their article "Il decreto tridentino sul peccato originale."[30] Since many will not have read this article in the original Italian, I think it would be worthwhile to give the key sections of it here, in my translation. A further justification for this lengthy quotation is that, in giving their interpretation, they also explained the hermeneutical principles which guided their work.

> The question we propose is: In what sense and within what limits must this decree be received by a believer today as the norm of his own faith? We must say clearly that no one would have proposed this question as we have put it if the current state of the natural sciences and of biblical exegesis did not present serious difficulties to the believer of today in accepting *sic et simpliciter* the story of the origin of original sin, as it is presented by the Councils of Carthage and the Council of Trent. For the fathers of Trent (and also for their Protestant adversaries) it was altogether natural to take the story in Genesis 2–3 as literally true. The believer of today knows that the way in which Genesis and the corresponding

passage in the letter to the Romans were read in the sixteenth century is exegetically questionable, and does not correspond to the
findings of science about the history of the human race. On the
other hand, a faithful Catholic does not want to abandon as erroneous the dogmatic definition of an ecumenical council, which
his church presents to him as the rule of faith. Intellectual hon-
esty, therefore, demands that he ask to what extent the various
assertions of the decree of Trent are to be considered unchange-
able truths.[31]

What unconditionally demands our faith is the *message* which
the council intended to teach, and not, in the same way or to the
same degree, the *individual statements* by which the message is
proposed.[32]

The message of faith is always and necessarily formulated in reference to the way in which, at a particular time, the world is conceived; otherwise, the message would not be intelligible. But if the
intelligibility of the message demands that it be expressed in terms
of a cosmic system taken as true in the contemporary culture, the
validity of the message is not inseparably linked to that system of
thought. The person speaking is usually not aware of the possibility
of separating the content of his message from the system carrying
it, because the system is used not merely as a verbal means of
expressing his proposition, but as a conceptual means for thinking
it. The possibility of this distinction becomes an object of conscious
reflection only when the vision of the world which is implied in the
statement of faith becomes questionable to a person who wishes to
adhere faithfully to its saving content. Such principles have for a
long time now been applied in biblical exegesis. Because they
depend on the intrinsic nature of every human statement, especially such as refer to the mystery of salvation, they have to be applied
also in the interpretation of documents of the magisterium.[33]

The etiological assertions of Canon 1,[34] which describe the origin of original sin are particularly problematic. They use the language of Genesis, tacitly supposing that it is to be taken literally as
history. But the problematic nature of that narrative was not taken
into account, because at the time of Trent (not to speak of
Carthage and Orange) the problem of the evolutionary development of the human race was unthinkable...It would be faulty
hermeneutics to attribute to the council the settling of a controversy which remained totally beyond its horizon, and whose solution
has no direct bearing on the question which the council intended
to decide. Judging that the probable function of this canon is to

explain, in the light of its origin, the sin which Canon 5 will say does not remain in us after baptism, the minimal and indispensable meaning of the canon is to affirm a sinful catastrophe of such a nature that it explains why all men are in need of the grace of pardon. The council conceives of this catastrophe and expresses it in terms of the drama of Eden, and could not have imagined it otherwise. However, it seems to us that the council does not answer questions such as: Was the one responsible for this catastrophe the father of all humanity? Was it a single person? Or was it a group of humans? What the text does affirm is a catastrophe, capable of explaining why all men come into existence in a state that is contrary to the original idea of the Creator.[35]

Summing up our dogmatic interpretation of the decree of Trent, we shall distinguish those assertions which, in our opinion, demand the assent of faith, from those problems which remain open, whose solutions require further elucidation.

A. In the justified person there remains no sin in the true and proper sense. However, further clarification is needed about the nature of concupiscence, that force which is described as the effect and cause of sin, and which does not render hateful to God the person in whom it exists, as long as he resists it.

B. Justification, even in those who have not committed personal sin, has the character of a pardon; it is preceded by a state which can, not just metaphorically, be called "sin." But it remains to be clarified in what sense the notion of "sin" is verified in a person who is not justified but is personally innocent, and why this disaster affects every member of the human race. The function of biological descent in the transmission of this evil remains particularly obscure.

C. The condition in which all members of the human race are conceived does not correspond to the plan of God, but is caused by man himself, who from the beginning of human history abused his freedom. However, the council does not define to what extent the story of the drama of Eden as recounted in Genesis corresponds to historical fact, not even with regard to the person of the unique Adam, as father of all men.[36]

This article by Alszeghy and Flick was published in 1971. Needless to say, it was not to be the last word on this extremely complex question, nor was it my intention to suggest that their interpretation of the decree of Trent is the only one that does justice to the text. However, in my opinion, their work was worth quoting, even at length, as an instructive example of the way that Catholic dogmatic theologians nowadays are applying modern hermeneutics to their study of conciliar decrees.

Doctrinal Statements Concerning the Virginity of Mary

Apostles' Creed: "who was conceived by the Holy Spirit, born of the Virgin Mary."[37]

Creed of Constantinople I (381): "by the power of the Holy Spirit he was born of the Virgin Mary."[38]

"Tome to Flavian" of Pope Leo I (449): "He was conceived by the Holy Spirit in the womb of the Virgin Mother, who gave him birth without losing her virginity as she conceived him without losing her virginity."[39]

Second Council of Constantinople (553): "If anyone does not confess two births of the Word of God, one from the Father before the ages which is timeless and incorporeal, the other in the latter days when the same Word, descending from heaven, was made flesh from Mary, the holy and glorious Mother of God ever virgin, and was born of her, *anathema sit.*"[40]

Council of the Lateran (649): "If anyone does not, according to the holy fathers, confess truly and properly that holy Mary, ever virgin and immaculate, is Mother of God, since in this latter age she conceived in true reality without human seed, from the Holy Spirit, God the Word himself, who before the ages was born of God the Father, and gave birth to him without corruption, her virginity remaining equally inviolate after the birth, let him be anathema."[41]

Pope Paul IV, Constitution *Cum quorundam hominum* (1555): "We question and admonish all those who...have asserted, taught and believed...that our Lord...was not conceived from the Holy Spirit according to the flesh in the womb of the Blessed Mary ever Virgin but, as other men, from the seed of Joseph...or that the same Blessed Virgin Mary is not truly the Mother of God and did not retain her virginity intact before the birth, in the birth, and perpetually after the birth."[42]

Second Vatican Council: "the birth of Our Lord did not diminish his mother's virginal integrity but sanctified it."[43]

In the foregoing documents of the magisterium, it is necessary to distinguish three distinct Marian doctrines, which have different degrees of dogmatic weight. The three are the following: 1) the virginal conception of Jesus; 2) the perpetual virginity of Mary; 3) Mary's virginity in giving birth to Jesus. I shall offer some comments on each.

The Virginal Conception of Jesus

This is primarily a Christological doctrine, but it obviously also concerns the virginity of Mary. It is the only one of the three doctrines concerning her virginity that has a clear basis in the New Testament (Mt 1:18-25; Lk 1:34-35), and that is affirmed in the major Christian creeds. However, in none of the documents which affirm this truth does one find evidence of the intention, on the part of an ecumenical council or a pope, solemnly to define this doctrine as a dogma of faith. However, it was certainly a matter of Christian belief from the earliest centuries, and while it is now denied by some Christians, it is the consistent teaching and belief of the Catholic Church. Raymond E. Brown, who has studied this question from both the exegetical and the doctrinal points of view, has written: "Despite some modern claims to the contrary, I think the majority of Roman Catholic theologians would agree with me that the virginal conception is a doctrine infallibly taught by the Church's ordinary magisterium."[44] Brown sees no contradiction between holding this, and also agreeing with the ecumenical group of scholars who wrote *Mary in the New Testament* that "the historicity of the virginal conception could not be settled by historical critical exegesis."[45] He believes that while biblical criticism cannot by itself settle the issue, it does favor the historicity of the virginal conception, and that infallible church teaching can resolve the ambiguity left by historical criticism.[46] I number myself among the "majority of Catholic theologians" mentioned by Brown who hold that the virginal conception of Jesus is a doctrine infallibly taught by the ordinary universal magisterium. It is a good example of a dogma of faith professed in the creed, but never solemnly defined.

The Perpetual Virginity of Mary

In contrast to the virginal conception, the doctrine of Mary's perpetual virginity is not clearly found in scripture; in fact, the references to the "brothers and sisters of Jesus" in the Gospels offer the strongest argument used by those who contest this belief. Nor do the common creeds affirm this doctrine; the first creedal reference to it is found in the "longer form" of the creed of Bishop Epiphanius of Salamis (374), where Mary is described as *aeiparthenos* ("ever-virgin").[47] Among third century church writers, Tertullian held that after Jesus' birth, Mary and Joseph lived a normal married life,[48] but Origen affirmed that Mary remained a virgin, explaining the "brothers and sisters of Jesus" as children of Joseph by a previous marriage.[49] The high esteem for celibacy and its widespread practice among Christians in the fourth and fifth centuries had a positive influence on belief in the perpetual virginity of Mary, who was portrayed as the perfect model of this state. The objections raised by Helvidius against this belief were vigorously refuted by Saint Jerome.[50] A homily attributed to St. Basil expressed the common Christian attitude, saying: "The friends of Christ refuse to admit that the Mother of God ever ceased to be a virgin."[51]

At the beginning of this section I have quoted a few of the conciliar and papal documents which affirm this belief; they could easily be multiplied. While none of them has defined it, they witness to the constant and universal belief and teaching of the Catholic Church that Mary remained "ever-virgin." In my judgment, the grounds for recognizing Mary's perpetual virginity as an undefined dogma on the basis of the church's consensus in belief about this are at least as strong as were the grounds for defining her immaculate conception and assumption as dogmas of faith.

Mary's Virginity in Giving Birth (Virginitas in Partu)

Many fathers of the church and Catholic theologians have held that the perfection of Mary's virginity involved the miracle of her giving birth without losing the physical integrity normal in a virgin. Some of the documents quoted above would most likely have meant that.[52] However, in Karl Rahner's judgment, this tradition is not uniform or constant enough to have truly dogmatic weight. Here is his interpretation of *virginitas in partu*:

All we say is this: Church doctrine affirms, with the real substance of tradition, that Mary's child-birth, as regards both child and mother, like the conception, is, in its total reality, as the completely human act of this "virgin," in itself (and not just by reason of the conception), an act corresponding to the nature of this mother, and hence it is unique, miraculous and "virginal." But this proposition, which is directly intelligible, does not offer us the possibility of deducing assertions about the concrete details of the process, which would be *certain* and *universally* binding.[53]

Walter Kasper, the prominent Catholic theologian who is now bishop of Rottenburg-Stuttgart, approves of this interpretation of *virginitas in partu*, and notes that other Catholic theologians do so as well. Referring to the article we have quoted, he says: "In the fourth volume of his *Schriften*, Karl Rahner has already said all that is necessary on this subject, and as far as I can ascertain, Catholic theology has accepted it without contradiction."[54]

Concluding Remarks

It should be evident that the theologians whose work we have considered have all taken the magisterial documents seriously. At the same time, they have not been satisfied merely to repeat the older formulas, but have taken account of further developments in biblical exegesis and other areas of human knowledge that have cast new light on the meaning of the texts. They see their work as a service to the faith of the people of God, seeking an understanding of the faith that is appropriate for people of our time, aware of how damaging fundamentalism can be to their faith, whether it be a fundamentalist reading of scripture or of church documents. At the same time, they are aware of the difference between understanding and judgment. They offer to the church the fruit of their work of "seeking to understand the faith," prepared to submit their understanding of the faith to the judgment of their peers, and ultimately to the judgment of the church.

10 ‖ Documents of the Ordinary Magisterium

My intention in this chapter is to give some examples of the way that Catholic theologians have evaluated and interpreted some documents of the ordinary magisterium. In Chapter 2 I have explained that within the category of authoritative but non-definitive teaching, many different degrees of authority can be identified. First of all, such magisterium can be exercised by an ⌐ ecumenical council, a pope, a regional or national council, a Roman congregation, an episcopal conference, or a local bishop. Second, different kinds of documents will manifest different levels of teaching authority. Third, there are different kinds of interventions, some of which aim to defend or explain revealed truth, others involve contingent and conjectural elements, and still others are merely of the prudential order. Fourth, the degree of authoritativeness can be assessed from the language that is used and the insistence with which a teaching is repeated. All of these factors must be taken into consideration in evaluating the doctrinal weight of any particular exercise of the ordinary magisterium. As I have also pointed out, the response which a Catholic gives to such teaching should be proportionate to the degree of authority that is exercised.

I believe it should be instructive to see how responsible Catholic theologians have assessed the doctrinal weight of some documents of the ordinary magisterium, and how they have applied principles of hermeneutics in interpreting them. Obviously only a few examples will be given here. I shall begin with some documents that are found in Denzinger-Schönmetzer.

The "Syllabus of Errors" of Pius IX[1]

In 1864, when Pius IX had already been pope for eighteen years, he published an encyclical letter, *Quanta cura*, condemning a number of opinions which he described as "the errors of the age." Along with this letter, the papal secretary of state, Cardinal Antonelli, sent to each bishop a copy of a document with the title: "Syllabus containing the most important errors of our time which have been condemned by Our Holy Father Pius IX in allocutions, at consistories, in encyclicals and other apostolic letters." There were eighty errors in all, with each of which was given a reference to the papal document in which it had been condemned. While the individual papal documents had caused no great stir when each of them was issued, the publication of the Syllabus, listing no less than eighty errors at once, did make a profound impression on public opinion, both within and outside the Catholic Church.

This impact on public opinion is the more understandable when one reads the text of some of those "errors." Here are some examples. "Every man is free to embrace and profess the religion which, led by the light of reason, he thinks true."[2] "The church ought to be separated from the state and the state from the church."[3] "The Roman pontiff can and should be reconciled and come to terms with progress, liberalism and modern civilization."[4]

Another factor contributing to the controversy aroused by the Syllabus was the fact that the five years which followed its promulgation were the years leading up to the First Vatican Council. The question of papal infallibility was in the air, and many of those who wanted the coming council to define this as a dogma looked for a definition that would mean that each error in the Syllabus had been infallibly condemned.[5] On the contrary, those opposed to such a definition were concerned that it would really mean just that. In the end, of course, it did not. As John Henry Newman said in a private letter he wrote shortly after the council had adjourned: "They hoped to get a decree that would cover the Syllabus, and they *have not* got it."[6]

Five years later, Newman had another occasion to write about the Syllabus, this time in a letter he wrote for publication: his famous "Letter to the Duke of Norfolk."[7] The occasion was a pamphlet which the prime minister, William Gladstone, had published, in which he had claimed that the newly defined dogma of papal infallibility, and the doctrines made obligatory for Catholics by the Syllabus, had made it impossible for Roman Catholics to be loyal citizens of a modern state. Gladstone's interpretation of papal infallibility resembled that of Archbishop Manning, which up to then Newman had criticized only in private correspondence with his friends. Newman gladly took advantage of the occasion to reply to Gladstone, since it gave him the opportunity at the same time to refute Manning's extreme interpretation of papal infallibility, without mentioning his name.

My purpose here is to present Newman's reply to Gladstone's attack on the Syllabus as a classic example of the interpretation of a document of the ordinary magisterium. Newman's treatment of this subject is too long to quote in full; I shall give the gist of it in his own words.

> The Syllabus is to be received with profound submission, as having been sent by the Pope's authority to the Bishops of the world. It certainly has indirectly his extrinsic sanction; but intrinsically, and viewed in itself, it is nothing more than a digest of certain errors made by an anonymous writer.[8]
>
> The Syllabus then has no dogmatic force; it addresses us, not in its separate portions, but as a whole, and is to be received from the Pope by an act of obedience, not of faith, that obedience being shown by having recourse to the original and authoritative documents, (Allocutions and the like,) to which the Syllabus pointedly refers. Moreover, when we turn to those documents, which are authoritative, we find the Syllabus cannot even be called an echo of the Apostolic Voice; for, in matters in which wording is so important, it is not an exact transcript of the words of the Pope, in its account of the errors condemned, just as would be natural in what is an index for reference.[9]
>
> The Syllabus, then, is a list, or rather an index, of the Pope's Encyclical or Allocutional condemnations...drawn up by the Pope's orders, out of his paternal care for the flock of Christ, and conveyed to the Bishops by his Minister of State. But we can no more accept it as *de fide*, as a dogmatic document, than another index or table of contents.
>
> The value of the Syllabus, then, lies in its references; but of these Mr. Gladstone has certainly availed himself very little. Yet, in

order to see the nature and extent of the condemnation passed on any proposition of the Syllabus, it is absolutely necessary to turn out the passage of the Allocution, Encyclical, or other document, in which the condemnation is found; for the wording of the errors which the Syllabus contains is to be interpreted by its references.[10]

It seems to me that it would be difficult to find an example of the evaluation and interpretation of a document of the ordinary magisterium, more respectful of the authority of the source from which it came, more balanced in assessing its doctrinal weight, or more accurate in interpreting its meaning, than Newman's treatment of the Syllabus of Errors.

Decrees and Responses of the "Holy Office"

The body of the Roman curia still often referred to as the "Holy Office," but whose official name is now "Congregation for the Doctrine of the Faith," was founded by Paul III in 1542 for the purpose of defending the church against heresy. Its original name was "Sacred Congregation of the Holy Office of Universal Inquisition." (The Latin word *inquisitio* means "investigation," so that the name *Officium Universalis Inquisitionis* means roughly the same as "Federal Bureau of Investigation.") When giving it its current name, Pope Paul VI also redefined its purpose, adding the role of promoting sound doctrine to its historic one of defending the faith against error.

As I have mentioned above, it is the official doctrine of the Holy See that documents issued by this Congregation participate in the ordinary magisterium of the pope.[11] In his letter *Tuas libenter* of 1863, Pius IX reminded Catholics of their obligation to submit to doctrinal decisions that are issued by the pontifical congregations.[12] When the First Vatican Council likewise spoke of the obligation to observe the decrees by which dangerous opinions have been condemned by the Holy See, it no doubt included decrees issued by the Holy Office.[13] Hence there is no doubt about the fact that such decrees share in the pope's teaching authority, and therefore call for a response proportionate to the authority which they enjoy. In determining the proper response to such decrees, a theologian should keep the following things in mind.

Since the Holy Office was founded to defend the church against heresy, a great many of its decrees have involved the condemnation of propositions which were judged erroneous or dangerous to the faith. In most cases, a list of such propositions has been followed by a "censure" specifying the gravity of the errors being condemned. Among such "censures" one finds not only the most grave, like "heretical," but others like "scandalous and harmful in practice,"[14] "at least rash and novel,"[15] "false, scandalous and harmful,"[16] and "rash and close to error."[17] Obviously the response due to any such decree will correspond to the gravity of the censure.

A number of the decrees of the Holy Office are in the form of responses to the question "whether such and such a doctrine can be safely taught." Examples of such are decrees about ontologism,[18] about the liceity of craniotomy,[19] about the human knowledge of Christ,[20] about the Johannine comma,[21] and about "millenarism."[22] Franz Hürth, a moral theologian who was for many years a consultor to the Holy Office, explained that such decrees express *the present judgment* of the magisterium that an opinion presents a danger to the faith, and should not be taught or put into practice.[23] A highly respected Roman theologian who became a cardinal, Louis Billot, made the following observation about decrees which declared that certain opinions could not be safely taught: "What is not safe now, given the present state of the question, can subsequently become safe, when new reasons come to light."[24]

The Holy Office confirmed the soundness of Billot's observation in a declaration which it made in 1927 about its own previous decree concerning the authenticity of 1 John 5:7 (the "Johannine comma").[25] In 1897 the Holy Office had said that the authenticity of this verse could not be safely denied or put in doubt. In 1927, when textual criticism had shown that this verse was not authentic, the Holy Office said of its own previous decree: "It by no means intended to prevent Catholic writers from studying the question more fully, nor, when they had weighed the various arguments more accurately with the seriousness and moderation that the gravity of the matter required, from favoring a judgment contrary to the authenticity of this verse, provided they professed their readiness to abide by the judgment of the church."[26] It would seem reasonable to conclude that what the Holy Office said about its decree on the "Johannine comma" could be applied to any of its decrees which responded to the question whether a particular opinion could be safely held or taught.

In the opinion of Cardinal Van Rossum, who early in this century was prefect of the Congregation for the Propagation of the Faith, it is the very nature of decisions of the Roman congregations that they are concerned rather with prudence and pastoral responsibility than with theoretical questions of truth. In the introduction to his work on the sacrament of holy orders, he said that in solving the difficult question of the essence of the priesthood, he would never refer to any decision of the Roman congregations, because, in his opinion, their decisions in the matter are necessarily governed by the principle of "sacramental tutiorism," and are therefore not concerned with the question of truth.[27] A judgment based on the principle of "tutiorism" would decide whether an opinion was not only "safe," but even the "safer" among alternatives, and, as the cardinal observed, this is not the same as judging whether it is true.

The Decree "Lamentabili"[28]

In 1907 the Holy Office issued a decree listing sixty-five propositions, followed by a "censure" in the form of the statement: "His Holiness has approved and confirmed the decree of the most eminent fathers, and has ordered that each and every one of the propositions listed above be held by all as condemned and forbidden."[29] Denzinger-Schönmetzer gives to this list the title: "Errors of Modernists," but the decree does not use this term, nor does it name the writers in whose works the condemned propositions could be found. However, the introductory note in DS names several of them, including Alfred Loisy and George Tyrrell.

In an essay which he published in 1966 on the problem which the history of dogma poses to Catholic theology, Joseph

Ratzinger discussed the significance of some of the propositions which were condemned in the decree *Lamentabili*.[30] In the context, he offered some reflections concerning the evaluation and interpretation of this decree, which, given the present role of their author, seem important enough to warrant even a fairly lengthy quotation.

In the previous section of his essay, Ratzinger had expressed his criticism of the way in which the First Vatican Council had handled the question of the history of dogma.[31] He then began his discussion of the decree *Lamentabili* in the following way.

> The same direction was taken in the second decision which the magisterium pronounced on this question at the beginning of the twentieth century, namely in the section under the heading "Revelation and Dogma" of the decree *Lamentabili* of Pius X. Here for the first time authoritative formulation was given to an axiom long taken as self-explanatory, which in its content expressed a basic datum of Christian faith, but which in its formulation manifested an altogether unsatisfactory notion of the relationship between revelation and history: namely, the statement that the revelation which forms the object of Christian faith was completed with the apostles.[32] There follows the condemnation of the statement that dogmas are not truths fallen from heaven, but are merely the interpretation of certain religious realities, which the human mind has worked out for itself with laborious effort.[33] Now it is certainly very difficult to determine the meaning and binding force of such a condemnation. It is a fact that, by analogy with similar precedents in the history of the church, one should not give too high an evaluation to the particular condemnations expressed in the decree *Lamentabili*. The decree has its meaning as a whole, insofar as it condemns a radically evolutionistic and historicist tendency, to which the global name "Modernism" is attached. The individual propositions express this tendency to a greater or lesser degree, which does not exclude the fact that individual propositions, in themselves, can have an altogether acceptable meaning. (Knox, in his book on Christian Enthusiasm, has admirably demonstrated that there is a parallel case to this in the condemnation of Quietism.)[34]

Knox no doubt was referring to the decree of the Holy Office of 1687, which condemned sixty-eight propositions drawn from

the writings of Miguel de Molinos.[35] Evidently Ratzinger agreed
with Knox's judgment that some of those propositions, like those
of the Modernists, taken individually, could have an acceptable
meaning, even though all of them had been condemned by the
Holy Office. The distinction which Ratzinger makes between the
significance of such decrees as a whole, and the binding force of
their condemnation of particular propositions, can no doubt be
used to solve problems encountered in the interpretation of
other such decrees.

Responses of the Pontifical Biblical Commission

This commission was founded in 1902 by Pope Leo XIII for
the purpose of promoting progress in Catholic biblical studies,
and of protecting such studies from dangerous errors. It was the
second of those purposes that totally dominated the work of this
commission during the campaign against Modernism led by
Pope Pius X. In the decade from 1905 to 1915, the Pontifical
Biblical Commission issued dozens of decrees, in the form of
responses to questions concerning the authorship of certain
books of the Bible, or the interpretation of certain texts, etc.
These responses determined which opinions on such matters
Catholics must hold, and which they must reject. When a question was raised as to the binding force of these decrees for
Catholic biblical scholars, Pope Pius X replied: "All are obliged
in conscience to submit to the judgments of the Pontifical
Biblical Commission, both to those already issued and those still
to be issued, in the same way that they are bound by the decrees
on doctrinal matters issued by the Sacred Congregations and
approved by the pope."[36] In other words, Pius X made the
responses of the Biblical Commission equal in binding force to
decrees of the Holy Office.

After 1915 (the first year of the pontificate of Benedict XV),
the Biblical Commission issued only one more response pro-
hibiting certain interpretations of scriptural texts; this was in
1933.[37] Ten years later Pope Pius XII issued his encyclical *Divino
Afflante Spiritu*, which has been described as the Magna Charta
for Catholic biblical studies. Given the progress which this

encouraged, it was obvious that Catholic scholars needed to be free of the constraints imposed by the previous responses of the PBC. In 1948, in a letter addressed to Cardinal Suhard of Paris, the secretary of the PBC applied to those responses an interpretation like the one which the Holy Office had given in 1927 of its earlier decree about the "Johannine comma": that they did not block further scientific study of the questions in the light of the knowledge acquired during the intervening forty years. When a new edition of the *Enchiridion Biblicum* appeared in 1954 containing all those old responses, the secretary and sub-secretary of the PBC each published a note to explain that those responses are of historical interest, as evidence of the care which the church has always had of the purity of the word of God. "However," they said, "insofar as those decrees propose judgments that are neither mediately nor immediately concerned with matters of faith and morals, the interpreter of sacred scripture can pursue his scientific investigations with full liberty, and can accept their results, provided always that he respects the teaching authority of the church."[38] Commenting on this clarification in the *New Jerome Biblical Commentary*, R.E. Brown and T.A. Collins observe that, since then, "Rome has acted consistently in its spirit, never correcting the hundreds of Catholic scholars who have used the 'full liberty' to contradict almost *every one* of the early PBC decrees."[39]

In 1971 Paul VI reorganized the Pontifical Biblical Commission, giving it a status like that of the International Theological Commission. Thus it no longer participates in papal teaching authority, but is a body of scholars advisory to the Holy See and presided over by the Prefect of the Congregation for the Doctrine of the Faith. The most recent fruit of its work is a document entitled: "The Interpretation of the Bible in the Church,"[40] which is an eloquent witness to the progress that has been made in Catholic biblical studies since the time of Pius X.

Texts of the Ordinary Magisterium on Christ's Human Knowledge

Following the lead of St. Thomas Aquinas,[41] Catholic theologians have, at least until recently, been unanimous in teaching that even during his life on earth, Christ enjoyed the immediate "beatific" vision of God, with the consequence that his human knowledge was unlimited, since in his vision of God he knew everything that God knows. While this doctrine has never been solemnly defined as a dogma of faith, it has been authoritatively taught by the ordinary magisterium. The following are some examples of such teaching.

In 1918, the Holy Office declared that the following propositions cannot be safely taught:[42]

1. It is not certain that in the soul of Christ, during his life on earth, there was the same knowledge which is had by the blessed, i.e. those who have attained final salvation.

2. Nor can one declare certain the judgment which holds that the soul of Christ was ignorant of nothing, but from the beginning he knew in the Word all things, past, present and future, in other words, everything which God knows by the knowledge of vision.

3. The opinion of some modern writers that Christ's knowledge was limited is no less acceptable in Catholic schools than the opinion of the ancient writers that his knowledge was universal.

The traditional doctrine concerning Christ's beatific vision and unlimited human knowledge, which was here authoritatively taught by the exclusion of the opposite opinion as "unsafe," was asserted in an affirmative way by Pope Pius XII in his encyclical *Mystici Corporis Christi* of 1943. His statement is as follows:[43]

The knowledge and love of our divine redeemer, of which we were the object from the first moment of his incarnation, exceed all the human intellect can hope to grasp. For hardly was he conceived in the womb of the mother of God, when he began to enjoy the beatific vision, and in that vision all the members of his mystical body were continually and unceasingly present to him, and he embraced them with his redeeming love.

Another example of the work of a Catholic theologian in weighing and interpreting documents of the ordinary magisterium can be seen in the way that Karl Rahner handled the above texts in his article: "Dogmatic Reflections on the Knowledge and Self-Consciousness of Christ."[44] Without attempting to give anything like a full account of Rahner's theory about the knowledge of Christ, I shall focus on the references he makes in that article to the official teaching on the question.

Rahner concludes his article by "formulating a kind of thesis," of which the first premise is: "The dogmatic theologian and also the exegete are not permitted to doubt the binding, although not defined, doctrine of the church's *magisterium* which states that the human soul of Jesus enjoyed the direct vision of God during his life on earth."[45] His reference to the "doctrine of the church's magisterium" is undoubtedly to the texts which we have cited above. But those texts spoke not merely of "direct vision of God" but of the "knowledge of God which is had by the blessed," or, in the words of Pius XII, the "beatific vision." Here is Rahner's justification for substituting "direct" for "beatific."

These reflections are of a dogmatic kind. Hence we ask: for what reasons must one, together with Catholic text-book theology and the *magisterium*, ascribe to Jesus even during his life on earth the kind of direct vision of God which is the basis and center of the beatific vision of God enjoyed by the blessed in heaven? If we put the question this way, it is because we wish to indicate, even in the way we put the question, that right from the beginning one ought not to speak here of a "beatific vision." For one thing, it is far too easily taken for granted as self-evident that direct contact with God must always be beatific...Furthermore, is it certain that what is meant, in the tradition of theology, by the consciousness of Jesus is really intended to convey an idea of beatitude by direct union with God over and above this union itself? In view of the data provided by the historical sources regarding Christ's death-agony and feeling of being forsaken by God in his death on the cross, can one seriously maintain—without applying an artificial layer-psychology—that Jesus enjoyed the beatitude of the blessed, thus making of him someone who no longer really and genuinely achieves his human existence as a *"viator"*? If one may reply to these questions in the negative, then the problem occupying us at present is simply a question of determining what valid theological reasons could be brought forward to convince us that we are quite correct in attributing a direct union of his consciousness with God, a *visio immediata*, to Jesus during his earthly life, but this without qualifying or having to qualify it as "beatific."[46]

At this point Rahner has a footnote, referring to the fact that the texts which we have cited above speak of Jesus' vision of God as not merely "direct" but as "beatific" or "that enjoyed by the blessed." He says: "The '*beata*' in Denz 2289 [DS 3812] or the '*beati*' in Denz 2183 [DS 3645] may without question be understood as a specifying and not as a reduplicative qualification. For the fact that Jesus was not simply as blessed on earth as the saints in heaven cannot really be denied. To maintain this would be the same as the heretical denial of his sufferings which were not merely physiological."[47]

If I understand the sense of Rahner's distinction here, he means to say that the "direct vision of God" which Jesus had on earth is of the same fundamental nature as that enjoyed by the blessed; in fact, it is "the basis and center" of that vision; but in his case it could not have been "beatific" in the strict sense of that term, because the "beatitude" enjoyed by the blessed in heaven was incompatible with the reality of Jesus' sufferings as described in the gospels.

Another point on which Rahner gave his interpretation of the texts which we have cited above had to do with the extent of the knowledge which Jesus had during his life on earth. It will be recalled that the response given by the Holy Office in 1918 required Catholics to hold as certainly true the proposition that from the beginning of his life on earth Christ knew everything that God knows.[48] This would seem to rule out any lack of knowledge in his human soul. Rahner's interpretation, however, allows for the development from implicit to explicit knowledge during Jesus' life, which means that Jesus did not from the beginning know everything that God knows, as God knows it. Here is his comment on the text of the Holy Office.[49]

> The Church's doctrinal pronouncements command us to hold fast to the direct vision of the Logos by the human soul of Jesus. They do not, however, give us any theological instructions as to what precise concept of this vision of God we must hold. It is perfectly permissible to say that this unsystematic, global basic condition of sonship and of direct presence to the Logos includes implicit knowledge of everything connected with the mission and soteriological task of our Lord.

At this point Rahner adds a footnote, in which he refers to the second of the propositions which the 1918 decree of the Holy Office said could not be safely taught.[50] The footnote is as follows:

We are of the opinion that in this way justice is done to the explanation of Denz 2184 [DS 3646]. For one will not be able to say that this text commands us to be of the opinion that Jesus had the same kind of knowledge of everything which God knows by the *scientia visionis*. This is quite inconceivable and is already excluded by the impossibility of a *comprehensio* of God by the human soul of Christ (S. Th. III, q.10, a.1), since the comprehension and noncomprehension of God is also of significance for the kind and depth of the knowledge of the rest of the possible objects. Once the difference of kind is clear, however, it will also be clear that Denz 2184 [DS 3646] must be interpreted carefully and with reticence.[51]

In the following sentence of his text, Rahner also refers to the passage which I have quoted above from the encyclical *Mystici Corporis Christi*. He says:

In this way one will also do full justice to the marginal and incidental declarations of the church's *magisterium* which point in this direction, without having to suppose for this reason that Jesus possessed a permanent, reflex and fully-formed propositional knowledge of everything after the manner of an encyclopedia or of a huge, actually completed world-history.

At the end of the phrase "marginal and incidental declarations of the Church's *magisterium*" Rahner adds a footnote, which reads: "Cf. e.g. Denz 2289 [DS 3812]. It must always be remembered that the presence of a loved person in consciousness can be conceived in many different ways."[52]

From this remark, it is clear that Rahner is qualifying as a "marginal and incidental declaration of the *magisterium*" Pius XII's statement in *Mystici Corporis Christi* that Jesus, from the time he was conceived, began to enjoy the beatific vision, and in that vision all the members of his mystical body were continually and unceasingly present to him. His reason for describing this as "marginal and incidental" is no doubt the fact that the question of Jesus' knowledge is really peripheral to the main theme of the encyclical, and that there is no evidence that the pope intended to make a doctrinal declaration on this issue. Here, then, we have an instance of the rule that in evaluating the doctrinal significance of a statement of the magisterium it is important to see whether that statement is central or marginal to the main theme of the document.

Rahner's other remark is also worth noting: that "the presence of a loved person in consciousness can be conceived in many different ways." In other words, the "presence" of all Christ's members to him, of which the encyclical speaks, does not necessarily mean presence by explicit knowledge of each individual person.

It seems to me that there are two points especially worth noting in Rahner's treatment of the official doctrine of the church regarding Christ's human knowledge. First, he takes this doctrine seriously, and even considers himself bound to do so, even though it has never been defined. Second, when his interpretation differs in some respects from the apparent meaning of the authoritative but non-definitive teaching, he takes pains to explain in what respect his interpretation differs from the official position, and gives well reasoned arguments to justify his point of view.

The Encyclical Evangelium Vitae

On March 25, 1995, Pope John Paul II signed his long-awaited encyclical letter "On the Value and Inviolability of Human Life." It surely came as no surprise that in this letter the pope confirmed the church's traditional condemnation of all direct taking of innocent human life. However, what does call for special comment is the formula which he used in specifically condemning murder, abortion and euthanasia as grave violations of the moral law. He expressed these three condemnations in the following way:

> Therefore, by the authority which Christ conferred upon Peter and his successors, and in communion with the bishops of the Catholic Church, *I confirm that the direct and voluntary killing of an innocent human being is always gravely immoral.* This doctrine, based upon that unwritten law which man, in the light of reason,

finds in his own heart (cf. Rom 2:14-15), is reaffirmed by sacred scripture, transmitted by the tradition of the church and taught by the ordinary and universal magisterium.[53]

Therefore, by the authority which Christ conferred upon Peter and his successors, in communion with the bishops—who on various occasions have condemned abortion and who in the aforementioned consultation, albeit dispersed throughout the world, have shown unanimous agreement concerning this doctrine—*I declare that direct abortion, that is, abortion willed as an end or as a means, always constitutes a grave moral disorder*, since it is the deliberate killing of an innocent human being. This doctrine is based upon the natural law and upon the written word of God, is transmitted by the church's tradition and taught by the ordinary and universal magisterium.[54]

Taking into account these distinctions, in harmony with the magisterium of my predecessors and in communion with the bishops of the Catholic Church, *I confirm that euthanasia is a grave violation of the law of God*, since it is the deliberate and morally unacceptable killing of a human person. This doctrine is based upon the natural law and upon the written word of God, is transmitted by the church's tradition and taught by the ordinary and universal magisterium.[55]

A further point to be noted is that after the words "taught by the ordinary and universal magisterium" with which each of these formulas concludes, a footnote refers to *Lumen gentium* 25. It is obvious that the reference is to the following sentence in the conciliar document:

Although the individual bishops do not enjoy the prerogative of infallibility, they do nevertheless proclaim Christ's doctrine infallibly even when dispersed around the world, provided that while maintaining the bond of communion among themselves and with Peter's successor, and teaching authoritatively on a matter of faith or morals, they are in agreement that a particular judgment is to be held definitively.[56]

The question must surely be asked whether the judgment on murder, abortion and euthanasia expressed in this encyclical meets the conditions laid down by Vatican II for the infallible teaching of the whole episcopal college dispersed throughout the world. Several reasons would seem to favor an affirmative answer.

First, it is obvious that the morality of the taking of innocent human life is a "matter of faith or morals." While the Pope admits that there is no explicit condemnation of abortion or euthanasia in sacred scripture,[57] he declares that his teaching on these, as well as on murder, is "based upon the natural law and upon the written word of God." In each case, explicit reference is made to the fact that the pope is teaching "in communion with the bishops of the Catholic Church," and, in the case of abortion, the pope refers to the consultation which showed them unanimous in condemning it. Chapter Five of the encyclical, entitled "In Communion with All the Bishops of the World," describes the consultation which preceded the writing of this encyclical: first with the cardinals in the extraordinary consistory of April 1991, and then with all the bishops by the personal letter which John Paul II wrote to each of them during that same year. Presumably the pope had that consultation in mind when he repeatedly declared that the judgment he was expressing was "taught by the ordinary and universal magisterium."

The official "Vatican Summary" of the encyclical would also seem to favor giving an affirmative answer to our question. It says:

> The encyclical is presented with great doctrinal authority: It is not only an expression—like every other encyclical—of the ordinary magisterium of the pope, but also of the episcopal collegiality which was manifested first in the extraordinary consistory of cardinals in April 1991 and subsequently in a consultation of all the bishops of the Catholic Church, who unanimously and firmly agree with the teaching imparted in it.[58]

> Here we are speaking of doctrinal affirmations of very high magisterial authority, presented with particular solemnity by the supreme pontiff. Exercising his own magisterial authority as the successor of Peter, in communion with the bishops of the Catholic Church, he "confirms" (or also, in the case of abortion, "declares") a doctrine "based upon the natural law and upon the written word of God" "transmitted by the church's tradition and taught by the ordinary and universal magisterium." In this con-

nection, in the case of each of the three doctrinal formulations there is a significant reference in a note to the teaching of the Second Vatican Council's Dogmatic Constitution on the Church *Lumen gentium*, which in Paragraph 25 declares that the bishops "even though dispersed throughout the world, but preserving for all that among themselves and with Peter's successor the bond of communion," when "in their authoritative teaching concerning matters of faith and morals, they are in agreement that a particular teaching is to be held definitively," "proclaim infallibly the doctrine of Christ."[59]

This official explanation of the doctrinal authority of the encyclical suggests that in pronouncing the church's condemnation of murder, abortion and euthanasia, Pope John Paul II intends to invoke the infallibility which Vatican II has attributed to the ordinary universal magisterium. However, one might question this interpretation in the light of remarks which Cardinal Ratzinger is reported to have made at the press conference held on March 30 when the encyclical was released. I quote from the account given in *Origins*.[60]

Cardinal Joseph Ratzinger said that Pope John Paul II considered making an infallible declaration against abortion and euthanasia in his latest encyclical "Evangelium Vitae," but the idea was dropped because the teachings were considered "so evident" in Christian faith and tradition...Ratzinger, head of the Vatican Congregation for the Doctrine of the Faith, said the encyclical as published contains strongly worded formulas condemning abortion and euthanasia, while stopping short of the "formality of dogmatization."...Ratzinger confirmed rumors that the word "infallibly" had been considered for the formulas in earlier drafts. But experts researching the question found that in the past church pronouncements on dogma had never spoken of their own infallibility. Moreover, he said, it would have been "a little absurd" to solemnize teachings so clearly evident in scripture and tradition, which is a main point of the encyclical.

Ratzinger said a formula used in the encyclical against the murder of innocent people is the strongest in the text because the pope points out that this teaching is contained in scripture. The formulas used in the cases of abortion and euthanasia are more "toned down," the cardinal said, since the pope says these teachings are based upon but not explicitly mentioned in scripture. In any case, Ratzinger said, these are authoritative teachings. "In the face of this text, one cannot seek refuge in formalistic discussions about what, when and where, and on what authority, all this is being taught," he said.

Obviously, it is a bit risky to draw firm conclusions from a partial report of what was said at a press conference. One would want to know whether any question was asked about the significance of the repeated affirmation that what the pope was declaring was "taught by the ordinary and universal magisterium." It is clear that it was decided not to issue any solemn papal definition in this encyclical and not to make an explicit claim to be speaking infallibly. And yet, to say that it would be "'a little absurd' to solemnize teachings so clearly evident in Scripture and tradition" could be taken as practically equivalent to saying that there was no need to define doctrine which was already so obviously the traditional teaching of the Catholic Church. And this is not very different from saying that the church's judgment on murder, abortion and euthanasia was a doctrine proposed by the ordinary universal magisterium as definitively to be held.

On the other hand, the cardinal's remarks, as quoted, suggest a reluctance to go so far as to claim that the church's judgment on these three issues had been infallibly taught. If it really was the intention of the pope to invoke the teaching of Vatican II about the infallibility of a consensus of the universal episcopate in proposing a doctrine as definitively to be held, one would expect the cardinal to have said so.

The following are some other questions that have been, or could be, raised. The first is: "If the pope wanted to say something was infallible, he would have used the word."[61] In reply, I would recall the fact, previously noted, that even in their solemn dogmatic definitions, popes have not explicitly said that they were speaking infallibly.[62] One has to judge, on other grounds, whether the conditions laid down by Vatican I for *ex cathedra* statements were fulfilled.

The second is that whereas *Lumen gentium* 25 mentions, as a condition for the infallible teaching of the bishops together with the pope, that they concur in proposing a judgment "as definitively to be held," this expression was not used by the pope. It is true that he did not use this expression in *Evangelium vitae*.[63] On the other hand, the formula which he used in this encyclical in condemning murder, abortion and euthanasia would seem sufficient to remove any doubt as to whether he was expressing a judgment which he, along with the bishops, wanted all Catholics to hold definitively. It is hard to see how any other interpretation would do justice to the language which he used.

A third might be that this is an encyclical, and popes have not used encyclicals to speak with infallibility. I believe it is true that no dogma has ever been solemnly defined in a papal encyclical.[64] It is also true that, prior to *Evangelium vitae*, no pope had ever declared that in preparing an encyclical he had consulted the entire episcopal college and gained their unanimous agreement on what he was going to say, or described the key points of his encyclical as "taught by the ordinary and universal magisterium." The fact that something has not been done before does not mean that it cannot be done.

Finally, from the fact that previously the church had never spoken infallibly on a question of the moral law, one might argue that it has not done so now, or even that it cannot do so. I think it is true that previously it had not done so. As to the question whether it can do so, I would agree that the church cannot speak infallibly on every moral issue, *regardless of its connection with revelation*. As we have seen above, in order to be capable of being taught with infallibility, a moral doctrine must be either formally revealed, or so intimately connected with revealed truth as to be required for its defense or exposition.[65] It would seem to me that the teaching of the encyclical on the immorality of murder, abortion and euthanasia meets that requirement.

To sum up: there are some good reasons for thinking that in this encyclical, Pope John Paul II intended to invoke, not the infallibility which Vatican I attributed to papal definitions, but the infallibility which Vatican II attributed to the teaching of the "ordinary and universal magisterium." On the other hand, questions remain, especially in view of the fact that Cardinal Ratzinger, while insisting that the encyclical's "strongly worded formulas condemning abortion and euthanasia" were "authoritative teachings," stopped short of saying that they met the conditions for infallibility.

In view of the present uncertainty, I would recall what I have said in a previous chapter: that a doctrine is not to be understood as having been infallibly taught, unless this fact is clearly established, and such a fact can hardly be said to be "clearly established" unless there is a consensus of Catholic theologians about it.[66] It is too soon to know whether there will be the consensus that would show that it is "clearly established" that the immorality of murder, abortion and euthanasia has been infallibly taught. What this would mean is that the church had taken an irreversible stand on these issues. But that would apply only to the three propositions which the encyclical declares are taught by the ordinary universal magisterium.

In an earlier chapter, which treated the criteria by which defined dogmas can be identified in conciliar decrees, we saw how important it is, especially in dealing with documents like the "chapters" of Trent, to distinguish between the precise statements that the council intended to define and the rest of the material contained in those "chapters." While everything in the decrees is taught with conciliar authority, only the defined dogmas are taught with infallibility. If it becomes certain that the immorality of murder, abortion and euthanasia has been infallibly taught, I would insist on the necessity of distinguishing between those three statements and the rest of what is taught in *Evangelium vitae*. In his article "The Pope's 'Gospel of Life,'" Richard McCormick has stressed the important difference between moral *principles* and their application.[67] To say that the three principles affirmed in this encyclical have been infallibly taught would not mean that infallible answers had now been given to the many questions that concern their *application*. The statements which the encyclical makes concerning questions of this kind have been made with papal teaching authority, but not with the infallibility that would make them irreversible.

It is particularly significant that this applies also to what is said in the encyclical about contraception. As we have seen above, Germain Grisez and some other Catholic moralists hold that the wrongfulness of any use of artificial means of contraception has been taught infallibly by the ordinary universal magisterium.[68]

While, in *Evangelium vitae*, Pope John Paul again expressed the condemnation of contraception, there is no indication that he intended to invoke the infallibility of a consensus of the universal episcopate on that issue.[69] In my judgment, it remains what it was: an authoritative but non-infallible teaching of the ordinary papal magisterium.

11 | Evaluation and Interpretation of the Documents of Vatican II

Since the Second Vatican Council was in several respects different from all the previous ecumenical councils, one cannot simply apply to its documents the principles of evaluation and interpretation which we have discussed in earlier chapters of this book. For this reason this chapter will focus on Vatican II. It will consider three issues: 1) the factors that contributed to the uniqueness of Vatican II, 2) the criteria by which the doctrinal weight of its statements should be evaluated, and 3) principles to be followed in the interpretation of its texts.

The Uniqueness of Vatican II

The primary reason for the uniqueness of Vatican II is the direction that was given to it by John XXIII, the pope who summoned it. As we have seen above, ecumenical councils of the past had been summoned by emperors and popes to meet crises facing the church. These crises in most cases were caused by erroneous doctrines that endangered the unity and purity of the faith. Hence the major work of ecumenical councils had been to condemn such errors, and to define as dogmas the truths which had been under attack.

In the speech which he gave on the opening day of Vatican II, October 11, 1962, Pope John XXIII made it clear that he had summoned this council for a different purpose. He recognized the fact that there was "no lack of fallacious teaching, opinions, and dangerous concepts to be guarded against and dissipated."

162

But, he added, "The church has always opposed these errors. Frequently she has condemned them with the greatest severity. Nowadays, however, the spouse of Christ prefers to make use of the medicine of mercy rather than that of severity. She considers that she meets the needs of the present day by demonstrating the validity of her teaching rather than by condemnations."[1]

So this council was not to condemn the erring with sentences of *anathema*. But there was to be a further difference from previous councils: namely, in the way it would present the church's beliefs to the world. Here, Pope John insisted that "the authentic doctrine...should be studied and expounded through the methods of research and through the literary forms of modern thought. The substance of the ancient doctrine of the deposit of the faith is one thing, and the way in which it is presented is another. And it is the latter that must be taken into great consideration with patience if necessary, everything being measured in the forms and proportions of a magisterium which is predominantly pastoral in character."[2]

It was these last few words that set the tone and agenda of the council. Its exercise of teaching authority was to be predominantly pastoral in character.

But what did this mean? While most agreed that it meant there would be no *anathemas*, it soon appeared that there were very different notions of what was meant by a "pastoral magisterium." This difference of opinion became most obvious when the council came to express its mind on such questions as the sacramental nature of episcopal ordination and the collegiality of the episcopate. Those opposed to the decisions which were taken by the council on these issues belittled their significance, on the grounds that, being purely "pastoral" in character, they had no truly doctrinal value, and therefore those who disagreed were free to maintain their own opinion. Others maintained that the pastoral nature of the council's teaching did not exclude the binding quality of its authoritative decisions on questions of doctrine. It became obvious that an official stand had to be taken on this basic issue. This was done in the form of an announcement made by the secretary general of the council at the general congregation of November 16, 1964 (just a few days before the promulgation of the Dogmatic Constitution on the Church). He said:

The question has been raised what ought to be the *theological qualification* of the doctrine which is set forth in the schema *De Ecclesia* and is being voted on.

The theological commission gave the answer to this question when it evaluated the *modi* pertaining to Chapter III *De Ecclesia* in these words: "As is self-evident, a conciliar text must always be interpreted according to the general rules known by all."

On that occasion the theological commission referred to its own *Declaration* of March 6, 1964. We repeat that text here:

"In view of conciliar practice and the pastoral purpose of the present council, this sacred synod defines matters of faith or morals as binding on the church only when the synod itself openly declares so.

"Other matters which the sacred synod proposes as the doctrine of the supreme teaching authority of the church, each and every member of the faithful is obliged to accept and embrace according to the mind of the sacred synod itself, which becomes known either from the subject matter or from the language employed, according to the norms of theological interpretation."[3]

There was nothing new in the first sentence. The norm already laid down in canon law would apply: no doctrine was to be understood as infallibly defined unless the council clearly expressed its intention to define it. The second sentence was clearly aimed at those who claimed that the doctrine of a "pastoral" council would have no binding force. It reminded them that an ecumenical council had the supreme teaching authority of the church. However, the "mind of the council" with regard to the binding force of any specific element of its teaching was to be determined "according to the norms of theological interpretation." One would think that this clear announcement would have settled the issue. However, it became apparent, from the articles and commentaries that appeared after the close of Vatican II, that there was still a wide spectrum of views as to the binding character of the doctrine of this "pastoral" council. This leads to our second point.

The Evaluation of the Documents of Vatican II

Three schools of thought can be distinguished on this issue: one can label them "minimizers," "maximizers," and "moderates."

The "minimizers" were those who continued to oppose the decisions taken by the council on such issues as the sacramentality of the episcopate and the collegial nature of the church's hierarchical structure. In articles published in Italian journals,[4] G. Hering, H. Lattanzi and A. Gutierrez argued that the pastoral character of the teaching of Vatican II deprived its doctrine of the binding force which conciliar decisions would normally have. Carlo Colombo, known to have been Pope Paul's most trusted theological advisor during the council, wrote a strong letter, criticizing the editor of one of those Italian journals for printing such an article, on the grounds that it contradicted the expressed mind of the pope. In fact, in the address which he gave at the opening of the third session of the council, Paul VI had said: "It is the role of the council to settle some difficult theological controversies...to explain to the faithful of the Catholic Church, and to the brethren separated from it, the true notion of the orders of the sacred hierarchy...and to do this with its certain authority, which may not be called into doubt."[5]

Among Italian theologians one also finds a "maximizer" on this issue: Umberto Betti, who contributed an article on the theological qualification of *Lumen gentium* to a volume of studies on the council's Dogmatic Constitution on the Church.[6] In J. Ratzinger's judgment, "Betti takes a view that raises most of the council's declarations practically (though not technically) to the status of dogmas."[7] Among Betti's statements which tend to justify Ratzinger's comment are the following:

> The chapters of the constitution have the same value as the doctrinal chapters of the other ecumenical councils, in particular, the Councils of Trent and Vatican I.[8] The only difference between the doctrine of Vatican I and that of Vatican II consists in the fact that the latter is not the equivalent of a definition in the technical sense of the word; that is why its denial would not involve *ipso facto* the exclusion from ecclesial communion which is attached to the profession of heresy. But even if its infallibility, and hence its irreformability, lack explicit declaration, one must not think that on that account it does not exist.[9] These brief considerations lead to the following conclusion, which it seems cannot be evaded: the doctrine set forth in the constitution, taken *en bloc*, is irrevocable. [10]

Among the "moderates" on this issue, I would mention Joseph Ratzinger and Yves Congar, who have both expressed their opinion on this question in their contributions to the same collection of studies that contains Betti's article.

Ratzinger raised this question at the end of his article, which dealt with the sections of Chapter 3 of *Lumen gentium* that treat of the episcopate.[11] He first notes that while the teaching of the council on the sacramentality of the episcopate is the one that comes closest to being a dogmatic definition, it still falls short of what that requires. Hence there is no new dogma. On the other hand, the doctrine as a whole is the expression of the supreme magisterium of the church, and that implies a certain measure of obligation to accept it. Consideration of the nature of doctrines taught, the intensive discussion that led to the decisions, and the role of the pope in the whole conciliar process brought Ratzinger to the following conclusion:

> The conciliar text by far surpasses the ordinary declarations of papal magisterium, including the encyclicals, regarding the nature of the theological obligation which it entails. It is a document produced by the most intense work over many years, and it expresses the sense of its faith at which the whole church assembled in council has arrived. It has formulated this document as a profession of its Credo...The conclusion is that it has an importance of the first rank among modern doctrinal texts, in the sense that it is a sort of central interpretation.[12]

Yves Congar has discussed the doctrinal weight of the teaching of Vatican II in the conclusion which he wrote for the same volume of studies on the council's doctrine on the church.[13]

> The only passage of the Dogmatic Constitution on the Church that could be considered a truly dogmatic declaration is the one that concerns the sacramentality of the episcopate (LG III, n. 21): in fact, it settles a question that until now had been freely disputed by theologians. At the same time it is proposed as a teaching on the same level as the others, without the use of the emphatic, repeated and solemn formulas that normally introduce a "definition."...The manner of expressing it is not that of a dogmatic definition, but the matter is so important, the place it occupies in the doctrine of the episcopate so decisive, that one can hardly see

how on this point th² council has not issued a definitive judgment. But this is without doubt the only case of this kind. On so
many other points...one might dare to say that by a unanimous act
of the extraordinary magisterium the council has proposed the
common doctrine of the ordinary, universal magisterium. This is
not the same as a "definition," but it does suffice for the doctrine
thus proposed to be binding as teaching on which the Catholic
magisterium is in unanimous agreement.[14]

I would offer a comment on Congar's phrase: "unanimous act
of the extraordinary magisterium." He is clearly using the term
"extraordinary magisterium" here to refer to the exercise of
teaching authority by an ecumenical council. An ecumenical
council is an extraordinary event, and on many accounts its magisterium is also extraordinary. On the other hand, there are good
reasons for using the term "extraordinary magisterium" as a
technical term to refer to what the First Vatican Council called
"solemn judgments," i.e. dogmatic definitions, as contrasted
with the "ordinary" exercise of magisterium, which would
include everything except solemn definitions.[15] Using the terms
in this latter sense (which I think is preferable) one would say
that, since Vatican II nowhere expressed its intention to define a
dogma, its exercise of magisterium belongs in the category of —
"ordinary," that is to say, non-defining magisterium.

The fact that the teaching of Vatican II, while it represents the
almost unanimous consensus of the whole Catholic episcopate,
including its head the pope, still remains in the category of "ordinary magisterium" is a unique feature of this council. Joseph
Ratzinger has raised one of the questions which this suggests:
How does the conciliar exercise of ordinary magisterium compare with the one with which we are more familiar: namely, that
of the popes in their encyclicals? As we have seen above, his reply
is: "The conciliar text by far surpasses the ordinary declarations —
of papal magisterium, including the encyclicals, regarding the
nature of the theological obligation which it entails." While
Ratzinger was referring to a specific conciliar text, namely that
concerning episcopal collegiality, his judgment would seem
applicable to a number of other texts in which Vatican II has
taken a position that differs from what previous popes had

taught in their encyclicals.[16] There can be no doubt that the teaching of the council on such issues as religious liberty, the ecclesial status of other Christian churches, and the significance of non-Christian religions prevails over what had been the official position of the Catholic Church put forth by the ordinary papal magisterium prior to Vatican II.

Does Ratzinger's opinion that some texts of Vatican II surpass papal encyclicals regarding the nature of the theological obligation which they entail mean that the teaching authority of an ecumenical council is greater than that of the pope alone? The answer to this question calls for a distinction between teaching authority as such, and the various ways in which that authority can be exercised. In the light of the First Vatican Council's definition regarding papal magisterium, one must say that the pope has the same supreme teaching authority that the whole episcopal college has. Rahner explains this by saying that the pope, as head of the college, can exercise the supreme authority which resides in the whole college as its one subject. Others would distinguish between the pope and the college (with the pope as its head) as two inadequately distinct subjects of supreme authority. In either theory, one must hold that the pope's authority is equal to that of the whole episcopal college.

On the other hand, when we compare a text of Vatican II with a papal encyclical, we are comparing two examples of the exercise of magisterium, in which those possessing supreme teaching authority have chosen not to use their authority in its supreme degree, but have rather chosen to teach in a non-definitive way. In other words, we are here comparing two examples of the exercise of *ordinary* magisterium. As we have seen, it is the distinctive characteristic of ordinary magisterium that it admits of varying degrees of authoritativeness. Thus, while the pope's teaching authority as such is always supreme, one rightly attributes greater authority to some documents of his ordinary magisterium than to others. Similarly, when Ratzinger attributes greater authority to a text of Vatican II than to papal encyclicals, he is comparing, not the teaching authority of the council with that of the pope, but two examples of the exercise of ordinary magisterium. As we have seen above, he argues from the fact that the Vatican document was produced by the most intense work over many years, and that it expresses the sense of its faith at which the whole church assembled in council had arrived. One could also argue that there is less chance of error in a document produced and scrutinized over many months by several thousand bishops, with the help of theologians from all over the world, than in a document produced by the pope and his advisors alone. One's confidence in a conciliar document will thus be greater, and this gives it a stronger motive of credibility and hence more doctrinal authority. Reasons such as these are appropriate for evaluating the relative doctrinal weight of different examples of the ordinary exercise of teaching authority; they do not imply that papal teaching authority as such is inferior to conciliar authority.

The fact that the ordinary exercise of magisterium admits of varying degrees of authoritativeness means that it will be important to distinguish among the various levels of authority exercised by the Second Vatican Council. While all the conciliar documents, in a global way, have the teaching authority proper to decrees of an ecumenical council, it was clearly not the intention of the council to exercise the same degree of authority in all its documents, or in all the statements made in them.

Evaluating the Varying Levels of Authority Exercised by Vatican II

The council's intention to attribute different levels of authority to its documents is manifest in the titles which it gave to them. Two are "dogmatic constitutions,"[17] one is a "pastoral constitution,"[18] one is simply a "constitution,"[19] nine are "decrees"[20] and three are "declarations."[21] It is true that the council never explained the significance which these titles have with regard to the degree of authority exercised in the respective documents. However, one incident shows that for the members of the theological commission, the titles were not insignificant. At one point during the council, when a new revision of the schema on the church was printed for distribution to the bishops, most of the members of the commission were surprised to see that its title had been reduced from "Dogmatic Constitution on the Church" to "Constitution on the Church." At the next meeting of the commission the majority insisted that the term "Dogmatic" be restored to the title. Of course, as we have seen, this does not mean that in the two "dogmatic constitutions" some new dogmas have been defined. But it does indicate the intention of the council to exercise its teaching authority in those two documents on matters of *doctrine*, to a *degree* that justified distinguishing them by this title from the other documents. On the other hand, it would be a mistake to conclude that it was only in those two "dogmatic constitutions" that the council has spoken authoritatively on matters of doctrine. It certainly did so in a number of other documents, including the one it called a "pastoral constitution." This suggests that to evaluate the level of authority exercised by Vatican II in any instance, more important than the title of the document will be the factors that indicate the "mind of the council" with regard to the authority it intended to exercise in any particular statement. As the theological commission said in its *Declaration* on this issue, this can be known from the subject matter or from the language employed, "according to the norms of theological interpretation."

One of the "norms of theological interpretation" is that very often considerable light can be shed on the intentions of a council from the study of its *acta*. In the case of Vatican II, the interpreter has available the thirty volumes of the *Acta Synodalia Sacrosancti Concilii Oecumenici Vaticani Secundi*, in which to follow the progress of any text through the council. One factor that must be taken into account in weighing the level of authority exercised in any text is the degree to which the decision expressed in it was a major focus of discussion and deliberation during the council. This factor clearly entered into the judgment expressed by Congar concerning the authoritativeness of the decision taken by the council on the question of the sacramentality of the episcopate. As we have seen above, the "intensive discussion that led to the decisions" was likewise a key element in Ratzinger's estimate of the doctrinal weight of the conciliar decision on episcopal collegiality. Study of the *Acta Synodalia* will show that, in the course of the council, certain issues stand out as having been the object of the most intense discussion and deliberation, in not a few cases involving an intervention of the pope himself in the proceedings. It is reasonable to conclude that decisions reached by the council on issues like these will have a degree of doctrinal weight that is proportionate to the seriousness of the deliberations by which they were reached. In some instances of this kind (though by no means all) the council expressed its intention to make a particularly important doctrinal statement by introducing it with the phrase: "This sacred synod teaches."[22] Another way in which the council added a certain solemnity to some of its statements was by the use of the term: "We believe," where this was clearly an expression of Catholic belief, and not of mere opinion.[23]

The Evaluation of the Council's "Pastoral" Statements

In his recent book *Theology and Church*, Walter Kasper has observed that while everything Vatican II said was meant pastorally, "there are also pastoral statements in the narrower and more specialized sense. We find these particularly in *Gaudium et spes*, which bears the name 'Pastoral Constitution.'"[24] In what follows, it is clear that by "pastoral statements in the more specialized sense," Kasper is referring to those which deal with matters of practical morality, that is, the application of moral principles to specific situations. He notes that where practical morality is concerned, general principles are not enough. Clear directives are necessary, and such directives presuppose an evaluation of the particular situation into which the general principles have to be translated. Kasper concludes that in evaluating the binding force of this kind of conciliar teaching, the following special considerations should be kept in mind.

> In these pastoral statements a clear distinction has to be made between the different levels of a statement and their varying degrees of obligation. To be more precise, a distinction has to be made between the generally binding doctrinal foundation, the description of the situation, and the application of the general principles to the pastoral situation described. In the description of the situation, the council had to fall back on recognitions of a secular kind, for which it possessed no special ecclesiastical teaching authority. The binding nature of these situational decisions is therefore dependent on the validity of the arguments which are brought into play. Their authority is therefore essentially different and, above all, less than the authority of the doctrinal statements

themselves. This in its turn has consequences for the application of generally binding statements about faith and morals to the specific situation. The obedience required here cannot be simply the obedience of faith, in the sense of *fides divina et catholica*. And yet this does not by any means relegate such statements to the sector of what is not obligatory at all, and a matter of pure choice. Nor are they solely disciplinary. Catholics are required to enter into such statements with a religiously motivated inner assent, and to go along with them. But this assent and response includes co-responsibility, spiritually and morally. The possibility that here the individual Christian, after a mature examination of conscience, may arrive at a different judgment from that of the church's magisterium is in line with the best theological tradition.[25]

Interpretation of the Texts of Vatican II

In the same section of his book, Walter Kasper has observed that besides the usual principles for the interpretation of conciliar texts, given the unique features of Vatican II "there are also a number of particular principles for the hermeneutics of this council's doctrinal statements." He suggests four such principles.

1. The texts of Vatican II must be understood as a whole; it will not do to stress certain statements in isolation.

2. The letter and the spirit of the council must be understood as a unity. Every individual statement can only be understood in the light of the spirit of the whole. The spirit of the whole, and hence the meaning of an individual text, can only be discovered by pursuing the textual history in detail, and from this extracting the council's intention. This intention was the renewal of *the whole* tradition, and that means the renewal, for our time, of the whole of what is Catholic.

3. Vatican II must be understood in the light of the wider tradition of the church. It belongs within the tradition of all previous councils, and it is this tradition which it wished to renew. The council must therefore be interpreted in the context of this tradition, particularly the trinitarian and christological confessions of the ancient church.

4. The continuity of what is Catholic is understood by the last council as a unity between tradition and a living, relevant interpretation in the light of the current situation. This principle was

already at work in previous councils (even if only implicitly), when these councils lent tradition a precise, articulated form, in the light of some specific error. But what then took place in particular cases, was thought about explicitly by the last council, and was given a universal reference: for the council talks about a relation to the 'signs of the time.'[26]

Hermann Pottmeyer, another prominent German Catholic theologian, has written a very perceptive article about the special problems involved in the interpretation of the documents of Vatican II.[27] Surveying the previous twenty years of interpretation of the council, he finds that two interpretive approaches are in conflict: one looks exclusively to the new beginnings promoted by the majority, the other looks exclusively to statements that reflect pre-conciliar theology. The two approaches share the same method of selective interpretation. They fail to recognize the transitional nature of the council, which strove to achieve renewal of the church while remaining faithful to its tradition.

As Pottmeyer sees it, what gives rise to selective interpretation is the fact that the council did not achieve a synthesis of the two factors, but rather used the method of juxtaposition. Alongside a doctrine couched in preconciliar language is set a doctrine that formulates some aspect of the renewal sought by the majority. While such juxtaposition represents a compromise, Pottmeyer insists that this was necessary for the achieving of consensus, and in any case the council probably could not have succeeded in going beyond juxtaposition to a new synthesis.

Some have criticized the council's method of juxtaposition for what they judge to be internal contradiction, but Pottmeyer replies that this reproach can be leveled not so much at the council itself as at the post-conciliar use of selective interpretation that seizes upon one thesis without attending to the complementary thesis.

Pottmeyer calls for the abandonment of selective interpretation, and the application of a hermeneutic that reflects fidelity to the council, its intention, its procedure, and its transitional character. Such a hermeneutic pays careful attention to the history of the texts, in both the pre-conciliar and the conciliar phase.[28]

An appropriate hermeneutic requires, therefore, that the texts be interpreted in the light of the evolution both of the council and its texts, and of the tendency manifested therein. When dealing with the juxtaposition of two theses, we must take into account the council's will to continuity as well as its will to move in a new direction.

"Progressive" interpretations have occasionally forgotten that the council retracted nothing in the dogmas of Trent and Vatican I. It did indeed relativize these dogmas in the sense that it no longer regarded their formulations as the absolutely final stage of development in the understanding of the faith, but instead located them within the whole tradition of faith. "Conservative" interpretations have occasionally forgotten that despite their will to continuity the council fathers attached differing values to the theses in question. The theses defended by the minority do not represent the will of the council to the same degree as the theses that passed by an overwhelming majority.[29]

Pottmeyer then calls attention to a danger that in his view "progressive" interpretations of the council have not always avoided: of a hermeneutical misunderstanding that attempts to separate the "spirit" of the council from its letter, and then leaves the letter behind. He insists that this does not represent fidelity to the council. The "spirit" of the council makes itself known from the direction given in the texts; on the other hand, it is only in this "spirit" that the texts are properly understood.[30]

The final paragraph of Pottmeyer's article seems a fitting conclusion to this chapter.

In fact, the reception of Vatican II is not yet complete. All attempts to break off the process of reception—whether through overly restrictive legislation or through a "progressive" interpretation—are incompatible with a professed fidelity to the council. A new phase in the process of reception is certainly due, one that will end the conflict of selective interpretations and explain the letter of the conciliar text in accordance with the "spirit" of the council, aided by a hermeneutic that does justice to the character of Vatican II as a transitional council.[31]

12 ‖ Cooperation in a Charitable Duty

A reader who has persevered through eleven chapters of this book may be willing to grant that the work of theologians in weighing and interpreting documents of the magisterium is important for orthodoxy, but still want to know what, if anything, it has to do with orthopraxy. I cannot think of any better answer to that question than the one which John Henry Newman gave in his *Letter Addressed to His Grace the Duke of Norfolk on Occasion of Mr. Gladstone's Recent Expostulation*, where he described the interpretation of dogmatic statements as a "charitable duty" in which it is a "special work" of the church's theologians to cooperate.[1] I shall therefore conclude this book with Newman's explanation of what he meant by that "charitable duty."

I must first briefly describe the historical situation which led up to the writing of that celebrated letter. The major factor in the situation was the definition of papal infallibility by the First Vatican Council. In a previous chapter we have seen that after this dogma had been defined, Newman wrote, referring to those who had most zealously promoted the definition: "They hoped to get a decree that would cover the Syllabus, and they *have not* got it."[2] There is no doubt that one of those to whom Newman was referring was Henry Edward Manning, archbishop of Westminster since 1865, and leading figure in the English Catholic hierarchy. In 1867, after Pope Pius IX had announced his intention to convoke Vatican I, Manning took a vow to do all he could to bring about the definition of papal infallibility at the council.[3] One of Newman's strongest reasons for opposing the definition was his ⇥

175

concern that Manning and his associates might succeed in getting the council to issue a decree that would confirm their idea of the extremely broad range of papal pronouncements (including the *Syllabus of Errors*) that should be recognized as infallible. This explains the satisfaction with which Newman could say, when he saw the decree, "They *have not* got it."

Newman was confident that the dogma as defined by the council was moderate in its formulation, putting the kind of strict limits on the exercise and subject matter of papal infallibility which he himself had been describing in his private notes.[4] However, it soon became evident that Manning had not abandoned his own ideas as to the extent of the exercise of papal infallibility. On October 13, 1870 the archbishop published a pastoral letter, setting forth his authoritative interpretation of the Vatican dogma. The passage in it that most disturbed Newman was the following:

> In like manner all censures, whether for heresy or with a note less than heresy, are doctrinal definitions in faith and morals, and are included in the words *in doctrina de fide vel moribus definienda*. In a word, the whole *magisterium* or doctrinal authority of the Pontiff as the supreme Doctor of all Christians, is included in this definition of his infallibility. And also all legislative or judicial acts, so far as they are inseparably connected with his doctrinal authority; as, for instance, all judgments, sentences, and decisions, which contain the motives of such acts as derived from faith and morals. Under this will come laws of discipline, canonisation of Saints, approbation of religious Orders, of devotions, and the like; all of which intrinsically contain the truths and principles of faith, morals, and piety.[5]

About a month after this pastoral appeared, Newman received a letter from a prominent member of Manning's diocese, Lady Simeon, who spoke of her distress after reading her archbishop's pastoral letter. Newman's reply contained the following scathing remarks on that subject:

> The Archbishop only does what he has done all along—he ever has exaggerated things, and ever has acted towards individuals in a way which they felt to be unfeeling...And now, as I think most cruelly, he is fearfully exaggerating what has been done at the Council. The Pope is not infallible in such things as you instance. I enclose a let-

ter of our own Bishop, which I think will show you this...Therefore, I say confidently, you may dismiss all such exaggerations from your mind, though it is a cruel penance to know that the Bishop where you are, puts them forth. It is an enormous tyranny.[6]

A few months later Newman received a letter from a convert clergyman, William Maskell, urging him to speak out publicly against Manning's extreme interpretation of the Vatican dogma. In his reply, declining this suggestion, Newman said:

I have full confidence that such extravagances as mark some Pastorals is but for the moment—things will in time gradually set-tle down and find their level...We cannot force things. The Council cannot force things—the voice of the Schola Theologorum, of the whole Church diffusive, will in time make itself heard, and Catholic instincts and ideas will assimilate and harmonize into the credenda of Christendom, and the living tra-dition of the faithful, what at present many would impose upon us and many are startled at, as a momentous addition to the faith.[7]

As one sees in this passage of his letter, Newman looked to what he called the "voice of the Schola Theologorum" as a mod-erating influence that would eventually prevail against the "extravagances of some Pastorals." While Newman claimed that he himself was not a theologian, he had very high regard for the role which he understood theologians to play in the life of the church. Here are two of the many passages of his correspon-dence in which he describes that role.

How can we interpret the decisions of that Council, how the Pope's decisions in any age, except by the Schola Theologorum, the great Catholic school of divines dispersed all over the earth?[8]

All these questions are questions for the theological school—and theologians will as time goes on, settle the force of the wording of the dogma, just as the courts of law solve the meaning and bear-ing of Acts of Parliament.[9]

Confident that Catholic theologians would eventually "settle the force of the wording of the dogma," Newman remained firm in his resolve not to enter into controversy with the archbishop of Westminster. For four years after the council he busied himself with other projects, confining to his private correspondence any expressions of disagreement with Manning's interpretation of the dogma. However, in November 1874 a challenge presented itself that he felt he could not ignore, in the form of a pamphlet by the prime minister, William Gladstone, entitled: "The Vatican Decrees in Their Bearing on Civil Allegiance. A Political Expostulation." Gladstone's thesis that the Vatican decrees excluded the civil allegiance and personal freedom of Catholics was based in large part on the fact that he accepted Archbishop Manning's extreme interpretation of the Vatican definition of papal infallibility. Newman saw a golden opportunity presented him not only to defend his fellow Catholics against Gladstone's charges, but to put forth and to justify a moderate interpretation of the Vatican dogma, thus effectively refuting Manning's view without mentioning his name. As Newman put it: "We can speak against Gladstone, while it would not be decent to speak against Manning."[10]

As he began his reply to Gladstone, Newman had reason for added confidence that his interpretation of the Vatican dogma was sound, because he had obtained a copy of a book written by Bishop Joseph Fessler, who had been the general secretary of the Vatican Council.[11] Fessler wrote his book to refute an attack on the Vatican dogma by an "Old Catholic" named Schulte. In his work, which received the full approval of Pope Pius IX, the former secretary of Vatican I had set forth a very moderate interpretation of the nature and limits of papal infallibility.

Having provided this brief account of the historical background of Newman's "Letter to the Duke of Norfolk," I shall now let Newman explain, in his own inimitable style, what he meant by describing the work of theologians in interpreting dogmatic statements as "cooperation in a charitable duty."

Now I am to speak of the Vatican definition, by which the doctrine of the Pope's infallibility has become *de fide*, that is, a truth necessary to be believed, as being included in the original divine revelation, for those terms, revelation, *depositum fidei*, dogma, and *de fide*, are correlatives; and I begin with a remark which suggests the drift of all I have to say about it. It is this:—that so difficult a virtue is faith, even with the special grace of God, in proportion as the reason is exercised, so difficult is it to assent inwardly to propositions, verified to us neither by reason nor experience, but depending for their reception on the word of the Church as God's oracle, that she has ever shown the utmost care to contract, as far as possible, the range of truths and the sense of propositions, of which she demands this absolute reception. "The Church," says Pallavicini, "as far as may be, has ever abstained from imposing upon the minds of men that commandment, the most arduous of the Christian Law—viz., to believe obscure matters without doubting." To cooperate in this charitable duty has been one special work of her theologians, and rules are laid down by herself, by tradition, and by custom, to assist them in the task. She only speaks when it is necessary to speak; but hardly has she spoken out magisterially some great general principle, when she sets her theologians to work to explain her meaning in the concrete, by strict interpretation of its wording, by the illustration of its circumstances, and by the recognition of exceptions, in order to make it as tolerable as possible, and the least of a temptation, to self-willed, independent, or wrongly educated minds. A few years ago it was the fashion among us to call writers, who conformed to this rule of the Church, by the name of "Minimizers;" that day of tyrannous *ipse-dixits*, I trust, is over; Bishop Fessler, a man of high authority, for he was Secretary General of the Vatican Council, and of higher authority still in his work, for it has the approbation of the Sovereign Pontiff, clearly proves to us that a moderation of doctrine, dictated by charity, is not inconsistent with soundness in the faith.[12]

The infallibility, whether of the Church or of the Pope, acts principally or solely in two channels, in direct statements of truth, and in the condemnation of error. The former takes the shape of doctrinal definitions, the latter stigmatizes propositions as heretical, next to heresy, erroneous, and the like. In each case the Church, as guided by her Divine Master, has made provision for weighing as lightly as possible on the faith and conscience of her children.[13]

To be a true Catholic a man must have a generous loyalty towards ecclesiastical authority, and accept what is taught him with what is called the *pietas fidei*, and only such a tone of mind has a claim, and it certainly has a claim, to be met and handled with a wise and gentle *minimism*. Still the fact remains, that there has been of late years a fierce and intolerant temper abroad, which scorns and virtually tramples on the little ones of Christ.[14]

The vehemence of this last remark shows how strongly Newman felt that people who were engaged in the interpretation of dogmatic statements for the faithful had to be concerned with charity as well as with truth. I conclude that while Newman did not use these terms, he surely would have agreed that the interpretation of dogma calls not only for orthodoxy but for orthopraxy as well.

Afterword

Infallible teaching on the ordination of women?

In his apostolic letter *Ordinatio sacerdotalis*, issued on May 30, 1994, Pope John Paul II declared that the church has no authority whatsoever to confer priestly ordination on women, and that this judgment is to be held definitively by all the church's faithful. When I was writing the second chapter of this book, and describing the various levels of authority that have been exercised in documents of the magisterium, I said that I thought that this statement excluding the ordination of women to the priesthood would have to be put at the top of any scale measuring the degree of authority that has been exercised by popes in their ordinary magisterium.[1] At that time I considered this judgment expressed by Pope John Paul II, despite the very strong language he used, to fall into the category of ordinary papal teaching. Obviously that meant that I did not think it had been infallibly defined by the pope. In an article which I wrote for *The Tablet* soon after the publication of *Ordinatio sacerdotalis*, I further said that it seemed to me at least doubtful that the judgment expressed in this papal letter had been infallibly taught by the ordinary universal magisterium.[2]

On November 18, 1995, when the present book was already well on its way to publication, the Congregation for the Doctrine of the Faith issued a statement declaring two things: that the doctrine excluding the ordination of women to the priesthood pertains to the deposit of faith; and that it has been infallibly taught by the ordinary and universal magisterium. To say that something "pertains to the deposit of faith" means that it is a truth

181

revealed to us by God. Leaving it to scripture scholars to discuss the grounds on which this doctrine is said to be "founded on the written Word of God," I shall comment on the Congregation's statement that it has been infallibly taught.

While Catholic theologians have commonly taught that there are some articles of faith which have never been solemnly defined, but have nonetheless been infallibly taught by the "ordinary and universal magisterium," the recent declaration of the CDF marks the first time, to my knowledge, that an authoritative document of the Holy See has specifically declared that a particular doctrine has been infallibly taught in this way.

Canon 749 of the Code of Canon Law declares that no doctrine is understood to have been defined infallibly unless this fact is clearly established. As I have explained earlier in this book, there are sound theological reasons for applying this same rule to the claim that a doctrine has been infallibly taught by the ordinary universal magisterium.[3] Hence I take the CDF's statement to mean that it is a clearly established fact that the world-wide Catholic episcopate is in agreement with Pope John Paul II in teaching that the exclusion of women from ordination to the priesthood is a divinely revealed doctrine that must be held definitively by all the faithful. I think it is a fair question to ask how they know that this is a clearly established fact. One thing, at least, is certain: the statement of the CDF to this effect is not infallible, because, even published with papal approval, it remains a statement of the Congregation, to which the pope cannot communicate his prerogative of infallibility.

When a doctrine has been infallibly defined, or when it is absolutely certain that it has been infallibly taught, it is irreversible. Further development can clarify the meaning of such a doctrine, and can lead to its being better expressed, but cannot reverse it. On the other hand, the history of Catholic doctrine provides some examples of propositions which, up to a certain point in time, seemed to be the unanimous teaching of the whole episcopate, and yet, as a result of a further development of doctrine, are no longer the teaching of the church. To give an example: the bishops gathered at the Council of Florence in 1442 no doubt expressed the common teaching of the whole episcopate at that time when they said that all pagans and Jews would certainly go to hell if they did not become Catholics before they died.[4] This is certainly not the doctrine of the modern Catholic Church. Other examples of doctrines that had a long tradition but were subsequently reversed concerned the morality of owning slaves and exploiting their labor, and the obligation requiring rulers of Catholic nations to prevent the propagation of Protestantism in their territories.

Such examples suggest that appeal to a long-standing tradition of the past might not suffice as proof that a doctrine has been taught infallibly by the ordinary and universal magisterium. What has to be clearly established is that the tradition has remained constant, and that even today the universal body of Catholic bishops are teaching the same doctrine as definitively to be held. How can this be demonstrated? In his encyclical *Evangelium vitae* Pope John Paul indicated one way this can be done: namely, by consulting all the bishops. When he declared that the doctrine condemning direct abortion was "taught by the ordinary and universal magisterium," he said that he was teaching this "in communion with the bishops—who on various occasions have condemned abortion and who in the aforementioned consultation, albeit dispersed throughout the world, have shown unanimous agreement concerning this doctrine."[5] Another criterion was suggested by Pope Pius IX, who said that the response of faith must be given to "those things which are handed on by the ordinary magisterium of the whole church dispersed throughout the world as divinely revealed, and therefore are held by the universal and constant consensus of Catholic theologians to pertain to the faith."[6] A third criterion is proposed in can. 750 of the Code of Canon Law, which says that when a doctrine is proposed as divinely revealed by the ordinary and universal magisterium, this is "manifested by the common adherence of Christ's faithful." Official documents, then, have proposed three ways of establishing that a doctrine is taught by the ordinary and universal magisterium: consultation of all the bishops, the universal and constant consensus of Catholic theologians, and the common adherence of the faithful. The CDF has not invoked any of these criteria in support of its assertion that the doctrine excluding women from the priesthood has been set forth infallibly by the ordinary and universal magisterium.

The changes in church doctrine that have actually taken place in the course of history show that a tradition could hold firm until advances in human knowledge or culture obliged the church to look at the question in a new light. Through honest re-examination of its tradition in this new light, the church has sometimes come to see that the reasons for holding to its previous position were not decisive after all. There is no denying the fact that many of the reasons given in the past to justify the exclusion of women from the priesthood are such as one would be embarrassed to offer today. No doubt, better reasons than those have been presented in the recent documents of the Holy — See. The question that remains in my mind is whether it is a clearly established fact that the bishops of the Catholic Church are as convinced by those reasons as Pope John Paul II evidently is, and that, in exercising their proper role as judges and teachers of the faith, they have been unanimous in teaching that the exclusion of women from ordination to the priesthood is a divinely revealed truth to which all Catholics are obliged to give a definitive assent of faith. Unless this is manifestly the case, I do not see how it can be certain that this doctrine has been taught infallibly by the ordinary and universal magisterium.

Notes

1. Weighing and Interpreting Documents of the Magisterium

1. *Quodl.* 3, q.4, a.1 (9 - Marietti 47).

2. LG 25 a.

3. Barcelona/Freiburg/Rome/New York: Herder, 1991. Hünermann provides a German translation of the documents.

4. Denzinger-Schönmetzer, Herder, 1967, p. 7.

5. "Membership of the Church according to the Teaching of Pius XII's Encyclical 'Mystici Corporis Christi,'" in *Th. Inv.* II:2.

6. Yves Congar, "Du bon usage de 'Denzinger,'" in *Situations et tâches présentes de la théologie* (Paris: Cerf, 1967) 111-133.

7. Fifth revised and enlarged edition, Bangalore: Theological Publications in India, 1991. Hereafter the abbreviation ND will be used in referring to this work.

8. *Decrees of the Ecumenical Councils,* ed. Norman P. Tanner, S.J., 2 vols., London: Sheed & Ward/ Washington: Georgetown University Press, 1990.

9. Vatican City, 1990; edition by St. Paul Books and Media, p. 13, n. 17.

10. Ibid. p. 17, n. 24.

11. Avery Dulles, "The Church, Sacrament and Ground of Faith," in R. Latourelle and G. O'Collins, eds., *Problems and Perspectives of Fundamental Theology* (New York/Ramsey: Paulist, 1982) 272.

12. David Tracy, *The Analogical Imagination, Christian Theology and the Culture of Pluralism.* New York: Crossroad, 1981, p. 66.

13. *Dei Verbum,* 8.

14. *Method in Theology,* New York: Herder and Herder, 1972, 125-145.

15. Karl Rahner, "The Development of Dogma," *Th. Inv.* I:76.

16. "A Theology We Can Live With," *Th. Inv.* XXI:107-08.

17. Edward Schillebeeckx, "The Magisterium and Ideology," *Journal of Ecumenical Studies* 19 (1982) 13.

18. Avery Dulles, "The Church: Sacrament and Ground of Faith," in R. Latourelle and G. O'Collins, eds. *Problems and Perspectives of Fundamental Theology.* New York/Ramsey: Paulist, 1982, p. 272.

2. Evaluating the Level of Authority Exercised in Documents of the Magisterium

1. *Catechism of the Catholic Church,* Chicago: Loyola University Press, 1994, p. 5.

2. "The Catechism of the Catholic Church and the Optimism of the Redeemed," *Communio* 20/3 (1993) 479.

3. This new formula was originally published in *L'Osservatore Romano* for February 25, 1989, p. 6. It was subsequently published in *Acta Apostolicae Sedis* 81 (1989) 104-06. Canon 833 obliges various persons to make such a profession of faith.

4. DS 3011, ND 121.

5. Canon 749.3.

6. LG 25 b.

7. DS 3011, ND 121.

8. DS 3074, ND 839.

9. LG 25 b.

10. The Congregation for the Doctrine of the Faith has declared: "According to Catholic doctrine, the infallibility of the Church's magisterium extends not only to the deposit of faith but also to those matters without which that deposit cannot be rightly preserved and expounded." (Declaration *Mysterium Ecclesiae* 3, AAS 65, [1973] 401.)

11. *Instruction* n. 16.

12. Peter Chirico disagrees, however, arguing that in his risen humanity Christ is the fullness of revelation, and that there can be no natural law that is not exemplified by that humanity. See his note: "Revelation and Natural Law," TS 52 (1991) 539-40.

13. See my article: "The Secondary Object of Infallibility," *Theological Studies* 54 (1993) 536-50.

14. See F. Marin-Sola, *La Evolucion homogenia del Dogma catolico,* Valencia, 1923, and Charles Journet, *The Church of the Word Incarnate* vol. 1, *The Apostolic Hierarchy* trans. A.H.C. Downes, (London/New York: Sheed & Ward, 1955) 342-46. In his article "Faits dogmatiques et foi ecclésiastique" in *Sainte Eglise* (Unam Sanctam 41), (Paris: Cerf, 1963, 357-73) Yves Congar expressed his approval of this opinion in the

form in which it was presented by M. L. Guérard de Lauriers in his *Dimensions de la foi* (Paris: Cerf, 1952) vol. 2, 299-301.

15. Many, but not all such theologians, described the proper response to infallible teaching about matter only "connected with revelation" as an act of "ecclesiastical faith." By this they meant faith that is based not on the authority of God revealing, but on the infallible authority of the church defining. Congar names fourteen who did so ("Faits dogmatiques," 359).

16. "The Catechism ... the redeemed," p. 477.

17. LG 25 a.

18. Declaration on Religious Freedom *Dignitatis humanae*, 14.

19. *Instruction*, n. 16.

20. See the Declaration of the Theological Commission, which was the subject of a formal announcement made by the Secretary General to the assembled bishops on Nov. 16, 1964. This Declaration is printed with the documents of the Council, immediately following the text of *Lumen gentium*.

21. *Instruction*, n. 18.

22. Can. 753.

23. *Instruction*, n. 24.

24. Nos. 23-24.

25. AAS 42 (1950) 568.

26. *Origins* 24/4 (June 9, 1994) 51.

27. *L'Osservatore Romano* (English edition) (19 June 1994), 7.

28. LG 25 a; Can. 752.

29. The new version of the documents of Vatican II given in the Tanner edition of the decrees of the ecumenical councils is mistaken, I believe, in translating *obsequium* by "assent." See Tanner, II:869.

30. *Instruction*, no. 24.

31. Ibid.

32. *Instruction*, no. 29.

33. *Origins* (July 5, 1990), 119.

34. Ibid.

3. What Is a Dogma of Faith?

1. DS 3011; ND 121.

2. DS 2880.

3. See Walter Kasper, *Dogma unter dem Wort Gottes* (Mainz: Matthias-Grünewald, 1965), p. 36.

4. 1 Cor 12:3.

5. Rom 10:9.

6. 1 Cor 12:3.

7. *The Ascent of Mount Carmel* 2:22,3 in K. Kavanaugh and O. Rodriguez, trans., *The Collected Works of St. John of the Cross*. Washington, DC: Institute of Carmelite Studies, rev. ed., 1991, 230.

8. See *The Apostolic Tradition* of Hippolytus, xxi, 12, ed. G. Dix and H. Chadwick, London: Alban Press, 1992, p. 36-37.

9. *Dei Verbum* 8.

10. *Dei Verbum*, 10. That the Latin word *authentice* is correctly translated by "authoritatively" is clear from the phrase: "whose authority is exercised in the name of Jesus Christ."

11. LG 25 a.

12. George Lindbeck, *The Nature of Doctrine: Religion and Theology in a Post-liberal Age*, Philadelphia: Fortress Press, 1984.

13. *Declaration in defence of the Catholic doctrine on the Church against certain errors of the present day*, Vatican City, 1973, chap. 5, p. 12-14.

14. "Mysterium Ecclesiae," in *Th. Inv.* XVII:149.

15. Ibid., 151.

16. Ibid., 148-49.

17. *Th. Inv.* V:42-66.

18. "Actus credentis non terminatur ad enuntiabile sed ad rem." *Sum. th.* 2a 2ae, q.1, a.2, ad 2.

19. *Dogma unter dem Wort Gottes*, Mainz: Grünewald, 1965. Italian tr. *Il Dogma sotto la Parola di Dio*, Brescia: Queriniana, 1968, p. 145 ff.

20. Karl Rahner and Karl Lehmann, *Kerygma and Dogma*, New York: Herder & Herder, 1969, p. 98.

21. Karl Rahner, "Yesterday's History of Dogma and Theology for Tomorrow," in *Th. Inv.* 18:11-12. The reference is to Pius XII's encyclical *Humani generis* where he said: "As regards .. what is called polygenism, the sons of the Church do not at all have the same freedom. For the faithful cannot lend support to a theory which involves either the existence on this earth, after Adam, of true men who would not originate from him, as the ancestor of all, by natural generation, or that 'Adam' stands for a plurality of ancestors. For, it is not at all apparent how such a view can be reconciled with the data which the sources of revealed truth and the documents of the Church propose concerning original sin, namely, that it originates from a sin truly committed by one Adam, is transmitted to all through generation and is in each proper to him (cf. Rom 5:12-19)." (AAS 42 [1950] 576 - DS 3897/ND 420).

4. Identifying Defined Dogmas in Conciliar Decrees: Criteria

1. DS 1501; ND 210.
2. *Dei Verbum* 8.
3. *Dei Verbum* 9.
4. *Dei Verbum* 8.
5. See above, p. 16-17, and also my note: "The 'Secondary Object' of Infallibility," *TS* 54 (1993) 536-550.
6. DS 2803, 3903, 3073; ND 709, 715, 839.
7. DS 3011; ND 121.
8. Can. 749.3
9. The "twelve anathemas" are given in DS 252-63 and ND 606.
10. See Hermann Josef Sieben, *Die Konzilsidee der alten Kirche*, Paderborn: F. Schöningh, 1979, pp. 171ff.
11. 2a 2ae, q.1, a.10: "sententialiter determinare quae sunt fidei, ut ab omnibus inconcussa fide teneantur." It should be noted that in the medieval period, *sententialiter determinare* must be translated by a very strong expression such as "to settle decisively."
12. DS 3075; ND 840.
13. DS 3074; ND 839.
14. Can. 751.
15. DS 3045; ND 140.
16. Session 5, DS 1510-16; ND 507-13.
17. Session 7, DS 1600-30; ND 1311-23, 1420-36.
18. DS 1613; ND 1323.
19. DS 1627; ND 1433.
20. DS 1659; ND 1534.
21. DS 1708; ND 1648.
22. DS 1772; ND 1715.
23. DS 1806; ND 1813.
24. DS 1811; ND 1818.
25. DS 1652; ND 1527.
26. DS 902; ND 405.
27. Albert Lang, "Die Bedeutungswandel der Begriffe 'fides' und 'haeresis' und die dogmatische Wertung der Konzilsentscheidungen von Vienne und Trient," *Münch. Th. Zeit.* 4 (1953) 139.
28. DS 906.
29. DS 1302; ND 324.

5. *Identifying Defined Dogmas in Conciliar Decrees:*
Application of Criteria

1. DS 125-26; ND 7-8; T 5.
2. DS 150-51; ND 12-13; T 24,31.
3. T 28.
4. DS 250-63; ND 604-06; T 40-61.
5. DS 300-303; ND 613-16; T 83-87.
6. DS 265; T 65.
7. T 41.
8. DS 290-95; ND 609-612.
9. DS 302; ND 615.
10. DS 421-38; ND 620-23; T 114-122.
11. DS 550-59; ND 635-37; T 124-30.
12. See his letters in DS 487-88.
13. DS 544-45.
14. DS 548.
15. DS 553-59; ND 635-67; T 128-30.
16. DS 552.
17. DS 563.
18. DS 600-609; ND 1251-52; T 133-38.
19. DS 650-664; ND 1253; T 160-186,
20. Mansi 17:490; PL 161:285.
21. DS 657; T 175.
22. DS 800-819; ND 19-21; T 230-33.
23. DS 800-802; ND 19-21; T 230-31.
24. T 233.
25. DS 790-97.
26. DS 802; ND 21; T 230.
27. *Salvation Outside the Church? Tracing the History of the Catholic Response*, New York/Mahwah: Paulist Press, 1992.
28. DS 800; ND 19.
29. Can. 749,3.
30. *Opusculum XIX, De articulis fidei et sacramentis ecclesiae* in *Opera Omnia*, ed. Parma, 17:300-306.
31. Letter to Cardinal Willebrands, 5 October 1974, AAS 66 (1974) 620.
32. DS 850; ND 321; T 314.
33. DS 851-61; ND 22-29.
34. DS 3067; ND 833.
35. ND p. 16.
36. DS 900-904; ND 405; T 361.

37. See above, p. 52-53.

38. T 409; not given in DS; partial citation in ND 806.

39. Joseph Gill, "The Fifth Session of the Council of Constance," *Heythrop Journal* 5 (1964) 131-143.

40. Cf. 2 Cor 13:10.

41. "Hermeneutics and History. The Problem of *Haec sancta*" in T.A. Sandquist and M.R. Powicke (eds.) *Essays in Medieval History Presented to B. Wilkinson*, Toronto: Univ. of Toronto Press, 1969, 354-70, at 363.

42. *Bischofliches Konzil oder Kirchenparlament. Ein Beitrag zur Ekklesiologie der Konzilien von Konstanz und Basel*, Basel & Stuttgart: Verlag Helbing & Lichtenhan, 1965.

43. Such as A. Riedlinger, "Hermeneutische Überlegungen zur den Konstanzer Dekreten," in *Das Konzil von Konstanz*, ed. A. Franzen and W. Müller, Freiburg i B., 1964, 214-238, and A. Franzen, "The Council of Constance: Present State of the Problem," in *Historical Problems of Church Renewal*, N.Y.: Paulist, 1965, 29-68.

44. DS 1251.

45. T 438-49.

46. The complete text is in Tanner, 523-28.

47. DS 1300-08; T 526-28.

48. DS 1300-01; ND 322-24.

49. *I Believe in the Holy Spirit*, New York: The Seabury Press, 1983, vol. 3, p. 131.

50. Ibid., p. 187.

51. See above, p. 53-54.

52. DS 1303; ND 1508.

53. DS 1304-06; ND 2308-09.

54. DS 856-58; ND 26.

55. See *Catechism of the Catholic Church*, n. 1261, for the modern Catholic approach to this question.

56. DS 1307; ND 809.

57. DS 3059; ND 825.

58. DS 1308; ND 809.

59. *I Believe*, vol. 3, p. 187.

60. DS 1310-28; T 534-50.

61. DS 1330-53; T 567-82.

62. *I Believe in the Holy Spirit*, vol. 3, p. 189, note 23. On the work of St. Thomas to which he refers, see above, note 28.

63. "Le décret du Concile de Florence 'pour les Arméniens.' Sa valeur dogmatique," *Bull. Lit. Eccl.* 20 (1919) 81-95, 150-62, 195-215.

64. Ibid., p. 214. See also the remark in ND, the note preceding 1305: "This document is neither an infallible definition, nor a docu-

ment of faith. It is a clear exposition of the sacramental theology commonly held at that time in the Latin Church."

65. Joseph Gill, *The Council of Florence*, Cambridge: University Press, 1959, p. 325.

66. *I Believe*, p. 132, note 15.

67. DS 1326; ND 1705.

68. DS 3859; ND 1737.

69. DS 1351; ND 810; T 578.

70. See my book *Salvation Outside the Church?* pp. 66-69.

71. DS 1440-41; ND 410; T 605.

6. Identifying Defined Dogmas in Papal Documents

1. DS 3074; ND 839.

2. As we have seen above, *The Catechism of the Catholic Church*, no. 88, says that the church can define as dogmas calling for the assent of faith not only revealed truths but also truths having a necessary connection with them. It is hoped that this controverted opinion will not be retained in the definitive Latin edition of the Catechism.

3. DS 2001-06; ND 1989.

4. DS 2012.

5. *Origins of Papal Infallibility, 1150-1350*, Leiden: Brill, 1972, p. 269.

6. *Sum. th.* 2a 2ae, q.1, a.10.

7. See my book *Magisterium*, pp. 92-93. The reference to "consulting the cardinals" reflects the important role which they played in papal government at that period, and shows that Terreni was referring to solemn papal pronouncements which would not be made without such consultation.

8. Paul C. Empie, T. Austin Murphy and Joseph A. Burgess, eds., *Teaching Authority and Infallibility in the Church*, Minneapolis: Augsburg, 1978, pp. 49-51.

9. "Welche bisherigen päpstlichen Lehrentscheidungen sind 'ex cathedra'? Historische und theologische Überlegungen," in W. Löser, K. Lehmann, M. Lutz-Bachmann, eds., *Dogmengeschichte und katholische Theologie*, Würzburg: Echter, 1985, pp. 404-22.

10. The noted Roman canonist Felix Cappello wrote concerning *Apostolicae curae*: "It is an example of an infallible judgment proclaimed *ex cathedra*, so that no doubt can be had about the nullity of Anglican ordinations." (*De Sacra Ordinatione*, Rome, 1935, p. 234.) The moralist A. Vermeersch expressed his view on *Casti connubii* in the title of his

article: "Definitio infallibilis in Enciclica *Casti connubii*," in *Divus Thomas* (Piacenza) 35 (1931) 402-11. Recently Ermenegildo Lio has published a very large volume: *Humanae Vitae e Infallibilità. Paolo VI, il Concilio e Giovanni Paolo II*, Vatican City: Libreria Ed. Vaticana, 1986, whose thesis is that the moral evil of artificial contraception has been defined both in *Casti connubii* and in *Humanae vitae*. I have not seen any review of his book that expresses agreement with this thesis.

11. *Teaching Authority and Infallibility*, p. 50.

12. DS 1451-91.

13. DS 1492.

14. 1st edition, Rome, 1898, 657-59; 2nd ed. 1903, 658-60.

15. Vol. 7, 1927, 1703 f.

16. *Die Konzilsidee der Alten Kirche*, Paderborn, 1979.

17. DS 290-95; ND 609-12.

18. DS 542-45.

19. DS 1000-02; ND 2305-07.

20. DS 2001-06; ND 1989.

21. DS 2601-04; 2615, 2659, 2693.

22. DS 2803; ND 709.

23. DS 3903; ND 1715.

24. DS 875; ND 804.

25. DS 802; ND 21.

26. *Contra errores Graecorum* 2:32, ed. Parma 15:257.

27. "Whosoever, knowing that the Catholic Church was made necessary by God through Jesus Christ, would refuse to enter her or to remain in her, could not be saved" (LG 14).

28. "The Bull *Unam sanctam* of Boniface VIII," in *Papal Primacy and the Universal Church* (Lutherans and Catholics in Dialogue V), Minneapolis: Augsburg, 1974, 105-119.

29. DS 3074; ND 839.

30. *Das neue Volk Gottes. Entwürfe zur Ekklesiologie*, Düsseldorf: Patmos-Verlag, 1969, p. 144 (my translation).

31. LG 25 c.

32. B.C. Butler, "Authority in the Church," *The Tablet* 231 (1977) p. 479; also in "The Limits of Infallibility," *The Tablet* 225 (1971) p. 400.

33. DS 2001-06; ND 1989.

34. DS 2601-04, 2615, 2659, 2693.

35. These five are: *Exsurge Domine* of Leo X (DS 1451-92); *Caelestis Pastor* of Innocent XI (DS 2201-69); *Cum alias* of Innocent XII (DS 2351-74); *Unigenitus* of Clement XI (DS 2400-2502); and *Quanta cura* of Pius IX (DS 2890-96).

36. DS 680-86.

37. DS 851-61; ND 22-29.
38. DS 1862-70; ND 30-38.
39. DS 1863; ND 31.
40. DS 1864; ND 32.
41. DS 3537; ND 143.
42. AAS 59 (1967) 1058.
43. AAS 60 (1968) 433-445; ND 39.
44. AAS 81 (1989) 104-06. We have presented the contents of this new formula above in Chapter 2. The list of those required to make a profession of faith is given in can. 833 of the 1983 Code.
45. The imposition of the "Oath of Fidelity" amounts to a new law, not contained in the 1983 Code of Canon Law. Since the CDF is not a legislative body, this new law became obligatory when Pope John Paul II approved the texts of the Profession of Faith and Oath of Fidelity along with the norms pertaining to them, and ordered that all this be promulgated in the *Acta Apostolicae Sedis*. See *Rescriptum ex audientia*, AAS 81 (1989) 1169.

7. Undefined Dogmas

1. *Unitatis redintegratio* 11.
2. Rom 10:9.
3. *Adversus haereses III, 4, 1-2.*
4. *Adv. Haer. III, 3, 1.*
5. DS 1-76.
6. *Contra Epist. Parmen.* 3,4,2.
7. *De Baptismo* 7, 53, 102; *CSEL* 51:373.
8. DS 25-30.
9. As we have seen above, the Decree for the Armenians of the Council of Florence was based on an *opusculum* of St. Thomas entitled "On the Articles of Faith and the Sacraments of the Church" (*Opera*, ed. Parma, 16:115-122). The first part of this work is an exposition of the doctrines contained in the creed.
10. DS 222-230; ND 501, 1901-06.
11. DS 370-397; ND 504-05, 1915-1920.
12. DS 503; ND 703.
13. DS 525-32; ND 308-16.
14. DS 621-33.
15. See my *Magisterium*, p. 85.
16. *Magisterium*, p. 91.
17. *Quodl.* 9, q.8, a.1 (16 - Marietti 194).

18. *De Ecclesia militar*e, III:14; in *De Controversiis* II, ed. Giuliani, p. 98.

19. DS 1510; ND 507.

20. DS 1514; ND 511.

21. DS 1520; ND 1924.

22. DS 1635; ND 1512.

23. DS 1637; ND 1514.

24. DS 1740; ND 1546.

25. DS 2875-80.

26. DS 2879. I have used the English translation given by John P. Boyle in his article: "The Ordinary Magisterium: Towards a History of the Concept," *Heythrop Journal* 20 (1979) 380-98; 21 (1980) 14-29. The translation is on p. 397.

27. See preceding note.

28. *Die Theologie der Vorzeit*, Münster: Theissing, 1853, 2nd. ed. 1867, pp. 47-52.

29. In the paragraph following the one we have quoted above, he used the term *praefata Ecclesiae dogmata* where it clearly includes both defined and undefined dogmas (DS 2880).

30. DS 3011; ND 121.

31. Mansi, 51:35 A.

32. Mansi 51:322.

33. LG 25 b (my translation).

34. For the history of the text on this point, see Roger Aubert, *Vatican I* (Histoire des Conciles Oecuméniques, vol. 12, Paris: Éd. de l'Orante, 1964) p. 211, 225-26, and also Umberto Betti, *La Costituzione Dommatica "Pastor Aeternus" del Concilio Vaticano I* (Roma: Pontificio Ateneo "Antonianum", 1961) pp. 175, 389-404.

35. *Acta Synodalia Conc. Vat. II*, III/1, 251.

36. Mansi 50:70; 53:170, 175.

37. Mansi 53:212, 297.

38. DS 1513; ND 510.

39. DS 3897; ND 420.

40. "The Sin of Adam," in *Th. Inv.* XI:247-262, at 252.

41. "Contraception and the Infallibility of the Ordinary Magisterium," *TS* 39 (1978) 258-312.

42. Ibid., p. 277.

43. Ibid.

44. Ibid., p. 278.

45. Ibid. p. 273.

46. "Response to Francis Sullivan's Reply," *TS* 55 (1994) 737.

47. Canon 749.3.

48. "Infallibility and Specific Moral Norms: A Review Discussion," *The Thomist* 49 (1985) 248-87; reprinted in *Dissent in the Church* (Readings in Moral Theology, 6), ed. C.E. Curran and R.A. McCormick (New York: Paulist, 1988) 58-96; p. 80 of this edition.

49. DS 3011; ND 141.

50. Can. 750.

51. Can. 751.

52. See above, p. 43.

8. The Interpretation of Doctrinal Texts

1. "Theology and the Magisterium," in *Problems and Perspectives of Fundamental Theology*, ed. R. Latourelle and G. O'Collins, New York: Paulist Press, 1982, 340-56 at 351.

2. Ibid.

3. DS 3008; ND 118.

4. DS 3886; ND 859. The reference to Pius IX is to his letter: *Inter gravissimas* of October 28, 1870; *Acta Pii IX* pars I, vol. 5:260.

5. In H. Vorgrimler, ed., *Commentary on the Documents of Vatican II*, vol. 3 (New York: Herder & Herder, 1969) 197.

6. *Mysterium Ecclesiae*, 5; see above, p. 34.

7. DS 802, 1351; ND 21, 810.

8. I have traced the history of this development in my book *Salvation Outside the Church?* New York/Mahwah: Paulist Press, 1992.

9. AAS 42 (1950) 569; DS 3881-83.

10. Paul VI, *Mysterium fidei*, September 3, 1965, AAS 57 (1965) 758.

11. *Unitatis redintegratio*, 17.

12. *Gaudium et spes*, 62. Here the council was echoing a statement made by Pope John XXIII in his opening address to the council on October 11, 1962; see W.A. Abbott, *The Documents of Vatican II*, p. 715.

13. *The Survival of Dogma*, Garden City, N.Y.: Doubleday Image Books, 1973, p. 197.

14. We have quoted the relevant passage of *Mysterium Ecclesiae* above, pp. 34-35.

15. *Origins* 20 (May 17, 1990) 3-14.

16. Section B II 2; *Origins*, pp. 6-7.

17. Section C III; *Origins* pp. 12-13.

18. Section C III, 1, *Origins*, p. 12.

19. Section C III, 3, *Origins* p. 12.

20. Section C III, 3, *Origins* pp. 12-13.

21. "Heresies in the Church Today?" in *Th. Inv.* XII:131-32.

22. "Theology and 'he Church's Teaching Authority After the Council," *Th. Inv.* IX, 94-95.

23 Ibid., p. 95.

9. Some Examples of Interpretation

1. DS 1642; ND 1519.

2. DS 1652; ND 1527.

3. *Th. Inv.* IV:287-311.

4. "The Presence," p. 297.

5. "The Presence," pp. 200-301.

6. "The Presence," pp. 302-03.

7. J. Ratzinger "Das Problem des Transubstantiation," *Theol. Quartal.* 147 (1967) 129-76 at 150.

8. *The Final Report,* London: CTS/SPCK, 1982. The original statement: "Eucharistic Doctrine" was completed at Windsor in 1971; the subsequent "Elucidation" was done at Salisbury in 1979.

9. "Eucharistic Doctrine," 6, *Final Report,* p. 14.

10. Ibid., 9, p. 15.

11. Ibid., 10, pp. 15-16.

12. "Eucharistic Doctrine, Elucidation" 6, *The Final Report,* pp. 20-21.

13. *Response to the Final Report of the Anglican-Roman Catholic International Commission,* London: Catholic Truth Society, 1985, no. 15, p. 7.

14. *Origins* 21/28 (19 December, 1991), pp. 441-47.

15. *Origins,* p. 43.

16. DS 1661; ND 1536.

17. DS 1647; not given in ND.

18. Melchior Cano, *De Locis Theologicis* V, 5, p.166, cited by Maurice Bévenot, "A Problem at Trent and 'Humanae vitae,'" *Heythrop Journal* 10 (1969) 135-45, at 139.

19. Canon 916.

20. DS 1609; ND 1319

21. "The Sacramental Character at the Council of Trent (17 January– 3 March, 1547)," in *Hermeneutics of the Councils and Other Studies,* Leuven: University Press, 1985, pp. 214-246.

22. Ibid., p. 246.

23. DS 1807; ND 1814.

24. "Ehescheidung im Falle von Ehebruch," *Scholastik* 27 (1952) 526-56; "Ehescheidung bei Ehebruch," *Scholastik* 29 (1954) 537-560; 30

(1955) 33-49. These were reprinted in his volume: *Hermeneutics of the Councils and Other Studies*, pp. 126-197.

25. "The Authority of Councils," in John Todd (ed.) *Problems of Authority*, Baltimore: The Helicon Press, 1962, pp. 43-78. at 75-76.

26. *Faithful Dissent*, Kansas City: Sheed & Ward, 1986, p. 270.

27. *Faithful Dissent*, pp. 268-69.

28. *Faithful Dissent*, p. 272.

29. DS 1510-16; ND 507-13.

30. *Gregorianum* 52 (1971) 595-635.

31. Ibid., pp. 623-24.

32. Ibid., p. 628.

33. Ibid., p. 629.

34. DS 1511; ND 508.

35. "Il decreto," p. 634.

36. Ibid., p. 635.

37. DS 30; ND 5.

38. DS 150; ND 12.

39. DS 291; ND 609.

40. DS 422; ND 620/2.

41. DS 503; ND 703.

42. DS 1880; ND 707.

43. LG 57.

44. *Biblical Exegesis and Church Doctrine*, New York/Mahwah: Paulist Press, 1985, p. 35.

45. R.E. Brown, K.P. Donfried, J.A. Fitzmyer, J. Reumann, eds., *Mary in the New Testament*. Philadelphia: Fortress; New York: Paulist, 1978, pp. 291-92.

46. *Biblical Exegesis*, p. 37.

47. DS 44; not given in ND.

48. *De virginibus velandis* 6, PL 2:898.

49. *Comm. in Matt.* 10:17; PG 13:877.

50. *De perpetua virginitate b. Mariae adversus Helvidium*, PL 23:193-216; Eng. tr., J.N. Hritzu, *Fathers of the Church* 53:3-43.

51. *Homilia de sancta generatione Christi* 5, PG 31:1468.

52. The canon quoted above (p. 137) from the Lateran council of 649 has often been taken to affirm *virginitas in partu*, but Michael Hurley has shown that in the context of the Christological issue with which that council was dealing, it is better understood to refer to the belief that it was because Mary conceived Jesus "without seed" that she brought him forth "without corruption," that is, free of the stain of original sin. See his article: "*Born Incorruptibly*: The Third Canon of the Lateran Council (A.D 649)," *Heythrop Journal* 2 (1961) 216-36.

53. *"Virginitas in part z,* A contribution to the problem of the development of dogma and of tradition," *Th. Inv.* IV:134-62, at 162.

54. "Letter on the 'Virgin Birth'," *Communio* 15/2 (1988) 262-266 at 265.

10. Documents of the Ordinary Magisterium

1. DS 2901-80.
2. DS 2915.
3. DS 2955.
4. DS 2980.

5. On February 6, 1869, the Jesuit journal *La Civiltà Cattolica* published an article which described French Catholics as desiring the solemn proclamation of the doctrines of the Syllabus by the future council, and also as hoping that it would define papal infallibility by acclamation.

6. Letter of November 1, 1870 to Lady Simeon, in C.S. Dessain et al., eds., *The Letters and Diaries of John Henry Newman,* XXV:224.

7. The full title is: *Letter Addressed to His Grace the Duke of Norfolk on the Occasion of Mr. Gladstone's Recent Expostulation,* London: B.M. Pickering, 1875.

8. Ibid., p. 79.
9. Ibid., pp. 81-82.
10. Ibid., pp. 83-84.
11. See above, p. 20.
12. DS 2880.
13. DS 3045.
14. DS 2166.
15. DS 2171.
16. DS 2575.
17. DS 2763.
18. Ds 2841-47.
19. DS 3258.
20. DS 3645-47;
21. DS 3681-82.
22. DS 3839.

23. "De valore formulae magisterii 'Tuto doceri non potest,'" *Divinitas* 5 (1961) 838-48.

24. *De Ecclesia Christi, Rome,* 1921, p. 432.
25. DS 3681.
26. DS 3682.

27. G. M. Van Rossum, *De essentia sacramenti ordinis*, Rome, 1914, p. 8, cited by Piet Fransen in *Hermeneutics of the Councils and Other Studies*, p. 282.

28. DS 3401-66.

29. DS 3466.

30. *Das Problem der Dogmengeschichte in der Sicht der katholischen Theologie*, Köln und Opladen: Westdeutscher Verlag, 1966.

31. DS 3020.

32. DS 3421.

33. DS 3422.

34. *Das Problem*, p. 10.

35. DS 2201-69.

36. Letter issued *motu proprio*, 18 November 1907, DS 3503.

37. DS 3750-51.

38. A. Miller, *Benediktinische Monatsschrift* 31 (1955) 49-50; A. Kleinhans, *Antonianum* 30 (1955) 64-66.

39. *NJBC* 72:25; p. 1171.

40. *Origins* 23/29 (January 6, 1994) 497-524.

41. *S. Th.* III, qq. 9-11.

42. DS 3645-47.

43. *Mystici Corporis Christi*, n. 75; DS 3812; Claudia Carlen, *The Papal Encyclicals 1939-1958*, p. 52.

44. *Th. Inv.* V:193-215.

45. Ibid., p. 215.

46. Ibid., p 203.

47. Ibid., p. 203, note 10.

48. DS 3646.

49. Ibid., p. 213.

50. See above, p. 150.

51. Ibid., p. 213, note 12.

52. Ibid., p. 214, note 13.

53. No. 57, p. 100-102 in the Vatican English edition.

54. No. 62, p. 112.

55. No. 65, p. 119.

56. LG 25 b (my translation).

57. No. 44, pp. 77-78.

58. *Origins* 14/42 (April 6, 1995) 728.

59. Ibid., 729.

60. *Origins* 14/43 (April 13, 1995), 734.

61. Bishop Anthony Bosco of Greensburg, Pennsylvania, is quoted as having made this remark, in the *Pittsburgh Post-Gazette*, March 30, p. A-5.

62. See above, p. 82.

63. He did use it in his apostolic letter on the ordination of women, where he said that his judgment that the church has no authority to ordain women to the priesthood "must be held definitively by all the Church's faithful." However, in that case he was not invoking the infallible teaching of the universal magisterium, nor, as we have been informed by Cardinal Ratzinger, was he invoking papal infallibility. See my article, "New Claims for the Pope," *The Tablet* 248/8028 (June 18, 1994) 767-69.

64. As we have seen above, p. 83, some Catholic theologians have claimed that in *Casti connubii* Pius XI defined the church's doctrine on contraception, but there is no consensus about this.

65. See above, p. 16.

66. See above, pp. 106-107.

67. *America*. April 29, 1995, 10-17.

68. Above, p. 105. Other Catholic moralists who agree with Grisez on this are Joseph Boyle, John Finnis and William E. May; see their article: "'Every Marital Act Ought to be Open to New Life': Towards a Clearer Understanding," *The Thomist* 52 (1988) 365-426, at 417, where they say: "It is beyond reasonable doubt that the Church's teaching that contraception is always wrong has been infallibly proposed by the ordinary magisterium. This teaching ought to be accepted by every Catholic as a matter of faith."

69. *Evangelium vitae* 13, pp. 23-24.

11. Evaluation and Interpretation of the Documents of Vatican II

1. Walter M. Abbott, *The Documents of Vatican II*, p. 716.

2. Ibid., p. 715. The English version of Pope John's opening speech published by Abbott is an accurate translation of the original Italian text, which was published in *L'Osservatore Romano*, Oct. 12, 1962, p. 3, and in *La Civiltà Cattolica* n. 2697 (Nov. 3, 1962) 209-17, here 214. However, the same issue of *L'Osservatore Romano*, pp. 1-2, gives the official Latin text of the Pope's address, which has an expanded version of the sentence that begins with the words: "The substance." This could be translated: "For the deposit of faith, or the truths which are contained in our venerable doctrine, are one thing, and the way they are expressed is another, with, however, the same sense and same meaning" (p. 2, col. 5).

3. In the editions of the documents of Vatican II, this is found immediately following the text of *Lumen gentium*. In the Abbott edition it is on pp. 97-98.

4. *Palestro del Clero* 44 (1965) 577-92; *Divinitas* 9 (1965) 393-414, 421-46.

5. *AAS* 56 (1964) 809.

6. "Qualification théologique de la Constitution," in G. Barauna, ed., *L'Eglise de Vatican II*, (Unam Sanctam 51b) Paris: Cerf, 1967, vol. 2, pp. 211-218.

7. *Commentary on the Documents of Vatican II*, New York: Herder & Herder, 1967, I:299.

8. "Qualification théologique," p. 214.

9. Ibid., p. 217.

10. Ibid., p. 218.

11. "La collégialité épiscopale, développement théologique," in Barauna, vol. 3, pp. 763-90.

12. Ibid., pp. 789-90.

13. "En guise de conclusion," vol. 3, pp. 1365-73.

14. Ibid., pp. 1366-67.

15. See DS 3011; ND 121.

16. J. Robert Dionne has made a thorough study of five doctrines which had been taught in papal encyclicals, on which Vatican II has taken quite a different stand. See his book: *The Papacy and the Church. A Study of Praxis and Reception in Ecumenical Perspective*, New York: Philosophical Library, 1987.

17. "On the Church" and "On Divine Revelation."

18. "On the Church in the Modern World."

19. "On the Sacred Liturgy."

20. "On the Instruments of Social Communication," "On Ecumenism," "On Eastern Catholic Churches," "On the Bishops' Pastoral Office in the Church," "On Priestly Formation," "On the Appropriate Renewal of Religious Life," "On the Apostolate of the Laity," "On the Ministry and Life of Priests," and "On the Church's Missionary Activity."

21. "On Christian Education," "On the Relationship of the Church to Non-Christian Religions," and "On Religious Freedom."

22. Examples of this are the following: "Basing itself upon sacred scripture and tradition, it [this sacred synod] teaches that the church now sojourning on earth as an exile, is necessary for salvation"(LG 14). "Therefore this sacred synod teaches that by divine institution bishops have succeeded to the place of the apostles as shepherds of the church" (LG 20). "This sacred synod teaches that by episcopal consecration is conferred the fullness of the sacrament of orders" (LG 21).

23. Two examples of this are found in the Decree on Ecumenism: "It was to the apostolic college alone, of which Peter is the head, that we

believe our Lord entrusted all the blessings of the New Covenant..." (UR 3 d), and "This unity, we believe, dwells in the Catholic Church as something she can never lose..." (UR 4 c).

24. Walter Kasper, *Theology and Church*, New York: Crossroad, 1989, p. 173.

25. Ibid., p. 174-75. Since writing these lines, Walter Kasper has become Bishop of the diocese of Rottenburg-Stuttgart. An instance of the application of the principle he expressed here can be seen in the joint pastoral letter which he, along with Archbishop Oskar Saier and Bishop Karl Lehmann, published on the pastoral care of divorced and remarried Catholics. See *Origins* 23/38 (March 10, 1994) 670-73.

26. Ibid., pp. 172-73.

27. "A New Phase in the Reception of Vatican II: Twenty Years of Interpretation of the Council," in G. Alberigo, J-P. Jossua and J.A. Komonchak, eds., *The Reception of Vatican II*, Washington: The Catholic University of America Press, 1987, pp. 27-43.

28. An extremely valuable instrument for following the history of the Dogmatic Constitution *Lumen gentium* from the first draft to its final text is provided by the volume *Constitutionis Dogmaticae "Lumen gentium" Synopsis Historica* edited by G. Alberigo and F. Magistratti, Bologna: Ist. Sc. Relig., 1975.

29. Ibid., p. 40.

30. Ibid., p. 42.

31. Ibid., p. 43.

12. Cooperation in a Charitable Duty

1. London: B. M. Pickering, 1875, p. 111.

2. Above, p. 142.

3. E.C. Purcell, *Life of Cardinal Manning: Archbishop of Westminster*, New York/London: Macmillan, 1896, 2:420.

4. See J. Derek Holmes, *The Theological Papers of John Henry Newman on Biblical Inspiration and on Infallibility*, Oxford: Clarendon Press, 1979, p. 99-160, and also F. A. Sullivan, "Newman on Infallibility," in Ian Ker and Alan G. Hill, eds., *Newman after a Hundred Years*, Oxford: Clarendon Press, 1990, 419-446.

5. *The Vatican Council and its Definitions: A Pastoral Letter to the Clergy*, London, 1870, pp. 89-90.

6. *The Letters and Diaries of John Henry Newman*, ed. Charles S. Dessain *et al.*, vol. 1-31, Oxford and London, 1961-84; 24:230.

7. *Letters and Diaries* 25:284.

8. Letter of October 20, 1869 to Mrs. Helbert, *Letters and Diaries* 24:355.

9. Letter of December 10, 1871 to Sir William Henry Cope, *Letters and Diaries* 25:447.

10. *Letters and Diaries* 27:123.

11. Newman first obtained the French edition of this work: *La Vraie et la Fausse Infaillibilité des Papes*, ed. E. Cosquin, Paris, 1873. He subsequently commissioned his friend Ambrose St. John to prepare an English translation from the original German; this was published as *The True and the False Infallibility of the Popes: A Controversial Reply to Dr. Schulte* (London, 1875).

12. *A Letter Addressed to his Grace*, 111-12.

13. Ibid., 120.

14 Ibid., 125.

Afterword

1. See above, pp. 22-23

2. *The Tablet*, 18 June 1964, p. 769.

3. See above, pp. 106-107.

4. DS 1351.

5. *Evangelium vitae* no. 62; *Origins* p. 711.

6. DS 2879.

Index